IMPROVING LEARNING

NEW PERSPECTIVES

Edited by Paul Ramsden

KOGAN
PAGE

First published in Great Britain 1988
by Kogan Page Ltd, 120 Pentonville Road, London N1 9JN

Printed and bound in Great Britain by
Billing & Sons Ltd, Worcester

British Library Cataloguing in Publication Data
Improving learning: new perspectives.
  1. Learning by students
  I. Ramsden, Paul
  370.15'23

  ISBN 1-85091-381-1

First published in the United States of America 1988
by Nichols Publishing Company, PO Box 96, New York NY 10024

Library of Congress Cataloging in Publication Data

Improving learning.

  Bibliography: p.
  1. Learning. 2. Teaching. 3. Science – Study and teaching
(Secondary) – Case studies. 4. College teaching – Case studies.
I. Ramsden, Paul.
LB1060.I47 1988   370.15'23   88-7237
ISBN 0-89397-309-2

Contents

Preface

This book presents a distinctive view of how learning in educational institutions can be improved, a view that rests on a shared belief in the primacy of a certain sort of learning. These writers contend that the dominant focus of learning in college and school should be on changing students' conceptions of aspects of the world around them. The way in which students think about particular subject content is the core of education. No one denies that the acquisition of facts and skills and the capacity to reason quantitatively is important. We simply assert that changes in conceptions should take priority.

Conceptual change learning is high-quality education. Learning that embraces changes in conceptions implies a confident grasp of ideas, breadth of comprehension and secure knowledge of facts and procedures. It means understanding the significance and persuasiveness of concepts in science and arts. There is ample evidence that children and older students, despite having experienced formal education and having acquired large bodies of factual knowledge, have often not changed their conceptions. They do not think about the subjects they have 'learned' in the way that subject experts do. They cannot use the main ideas in these subjects to explain disarmingly simple real-world phenomena. These same students often display a tendency to see education as a burden to be carried rather than a rigorous, challenging and exciting experience that enables them to inquire into and control their world.

The solution lies in a recognition that teaching and curricula should take much more careful account of what students *already know* about two things: the subject matter itself and the educational conditions in which they learn that subject matter. In our view it does not make much educational sense to talk about improving learning processes or teaching methods separately from improving students' understanding of subject content. Nor does it make sense to ignore the fact that students often interpret what teachers want quite differently from teachers. The substance of teaching and curriculum design is the learner's ideas. A sympathetic grasp of the differences between the learner's understanding of content and the expert's understanding of it is central to good teaching.

Our argument is that teachers and educational researchers should each try to learn more about what students understand, and then apply what they learn from students to making teaching better. This is the fundamental principle of the science of education that we advocate. The heart of this discipline is the cooperative development of knowledge about how different types of subject content are learned and taught. This way of looking at teaching and learning has potentially revolutionary implications for teacher education at all levels.

Most of the articles that follow have been specially prepared for this volume and appear here for the first time. The contributors represent an unusually broad range of subject areas and countries. All these writers are immersed in the real world of classrooms and lecture halls – as teachers, researchers, and teacher-researchers. Among the contributors are medical doctors, engineers, chemists, professors of education and secondary school science teachers. They work in the diverse educational systems of Australia, Sweden, Britain and the USA. This breadth and depth of experience adds cogency to the argument of the book.

In order to produce a book of acceptable dimensions, it has been found necessary to restrict the articles to a relatively small number and to curtail the length of many of the chapters. This is a delicate task for an editor and reflects his personal preferences as well as the availability of articles. An attempt has been made to bring unity to the book, to reduce repetition, and to avoid a succession of editorial footnotes by cross-referencing the chapters and, in some cases, by substantially rearranging the text. Differences in international nomenclature have, however, been retained.

In the selection of representative articles an emphasis has been placed on two areas in which sound research traditions are developing: learning and teaching science in the later stages of primary education and in secondary schools, and learning processes in post-compulsory education. The strong accent on science, technology and medicine indicates merely that it is these domains which have received the bulk of research attention in this field, rather than that the humanities and social sciences are valued less highly by the editor or his contributors, or that the view of learning here represented is any less applicable to other subjects.

Some of the ideas in this book are perhaps difficult to grasp. No doubt some will feel that this reduces its practical usefulness. The authors and I have tried to make the arguments as intelligible as possible. But relevance to teaching and simplicity of content are not the same thing. There are inevitably some parts that are harder than others. They are no less relevant for that. Pretending that the steps needed to improve learning and teaching are more elementary than they really are does not seem to make anyone's task simpler in the long run.

To get the best from the book it will sometimes be necessary to learn some new subject matter, because the book is about learning subject content, and more often than not the educational principles can only be described in relation to that content. The level of difficulty of the chapters varies. For example, while nearly everyone will be able to understand the physical concepts in Roth and Anderson's chapter (such as the role of light in enabling us to see things), non-chemists (and even some chemists) may have trouble with the 'mole concept' in Chapter 5. A second source of difficulty may be the method of looking at learning adopted in several chapters called 'phenomenography'. Most readers will probably not have met this way of examining problems in teaching and learning before. Chapter 2 is strongly recommended as an introduction to it.

There will be much in this book to capture the interest of everyone with a concern in education, whether as a teacher, student, or parent. Each article can be read with both a specific and a general purpose in mind. While each contribution usually focuses on teaching and learning in a particular subject area or stage of education, it will be found to yield insights into problems of how to improve students' understanding in many others. Readers should not, however, expect to unearth ready-made solutions to teaching problems. Instead, they will encounter practical suggestions and theoretical ideas that they must actively reinterpret in the context of their own classes and subjects. This process reflects both the view of learning and the vision of professional teaching we seek to advance. If the book encourages teachers to begin to change their way of thinking about learning and teaching, it will have achieved its end.

Acknowledgements

I am indebted to more people than I can remember in the production of this book. Several authors have laboured long and hard with me in the rewriting of chapters and I am sincerely thankful to them for their willingness to help without any prospect of reward and, at one stage, without even the hope of publication. The subject expertise of a number of these people has been invaluable. My special gratitude goes to John Bowden and Leo West for their constant support and realistic advice, and to Ference Marton, who immediately endorsed my hesitant suggestion for the book, however impractical it may have seemed at the time, one quiet Spring evening in Melbourne.

Paul Ramsden
Melbourne, February 1988

Part 1
Rationale

Chapter 1
Studying Learning: Improving Teaching

Paul Ramsden
University of Melbourne, Australia

But this is that which will indeed dignify and exalt knowledge, if contemplation and action may be more nearly and straightly conjoined and united together than they have been.

(*Francis Bacon, The Advancement of Learning*)

A view of learning

This is a book about teaching and learning in schools, universities and colleges. It aims to be a practical book, but its suggestions are based on theory. It is concerned with presenting an argument for how education can be enhanced. It is about how we may develop professionalism in teaching by sharpening our insights into learning.

Throughout the book the authors argue that teaching should be directed towards helping students to understand phenomena and ideas in the way that scientists or historians or other subject experts understand them. This requires learners to change their ways of seeing, experiencing and conceiving aspects of the real world around them. Teaching is an activity that assumes an understanding of learning. To teach in a way that encourages changes in conceptions, instructors must recognize how students already think about phenomena – they must make themselves aware of, and use, the conceptions students already have. Teachers should, in fact, become scholars of their own students' learning, and an important implication of this argument is that teaching and research in education are two sides of the same coin.

I hope the significance of this reasoning will gradually unfold as you read the book. In one sense we are saying nothing new. Like so many greater thinkers before us, we believe that teaching, even when it is carried out by conscientious and caring teachers, often overestimates the relevance of transmitting information and procedures to students, and underestimates the importance of helping students to change their ways of thinking and understanding. In order to remedy this situation, teachers themselves must change *their* conceptions.

Why learning needs to be improved

At the nucleus of any curriculum should be an understanding of ideas and processes. In science, for example, we should aim to teach students something about the body of concepts that has enabled us to interpret and control the physical and biological worlds: at the same time, we want students to grasp the nature of the scientific process which generates that understanding. How successful have we been in achieving these goals?

During the last ten years or so, a huge body of data has been collected about what students in schools and colleges know and do not know. It is a depressing litany. The message of scores of studies of student learning is unambiguous: many students are highly adept at very complex skills in science, humanities, and mathematics; they can also reproduce large amounts of factual information on demand; they have appropriated enormous quantities of detailed knowledge; they pass examinations successfully. But they are unable to show that they *understand* what they have learned. They harbour profound misconceptions about mathematical, physical and social phenomena. They have hazy notions of the accepted forms of expression in the subjects they have studied.

It is not possible to present anything resembling a review of these findings here; instead, let me take just two or three examples from the research. The best-known studies are in science and mathematics learning. According to Lochhead (1985), for example, 80–90% of US college students don't really understand ninth-grade algebra, despite being able to manipulate the symbols and meet standard behavioural objectives. So, if college students are asked to express the equation $A = 7S$ in an English sentence, nearly three-quarters will interpret it incorrectly (ie backwards). There is quite compelling evidence that students who are accomplished at substituting numbers into complex memorized physics formulae, and computing the answer correctly, cannot answer simple questions about the implications of fundamental principles in electricity and mechanics (see Chapter 3). McDermott (1984) found that even students who did well in course examinations were often incapable of demonstrating a qualitative understanding of acceleration as the ratio $\Delta v / \Delta t$ when they were asked to apply the concept to a real example of motion. The belief that 'motion implies a force' among college students (contrary to the fundamental precepts of Newtonian mechanics) has also been widely reported (see Chapters 3 and 4). A most disturbing educational phenomenon is the fact that trainee teachers seem to have a similar range of misconceptions about the physical world (see, eg Sjøberg and Lie, 1981, quoted in McDermott, 1984).

While such worrying examples of gaps in conceptual understanding may be most evident in physics and mathematics, there are also numerous instances of gross misconceptions in humanities and social science subjects, even though these areas have been less closely researched. Halldén (1986) and Hounsell (1984), for example, identify highly resistant misunderstandings by school and university students concerning what the subject of history is *about*, and corresponding weaknesses in their written work. Some successful university economics students have been found to have a belief that price is determined by the production costs of a common commodity rather than the relation between demand and supply for it – the exact opposite of the (counterintuitive) understanding required in basic economics (Dahlgren, 1984).

These examples could be proliferated and provided at all levels of education and in nearly every subject. The students who have been the subjects of these investigations have sometimes successfully negotiated even graduate-level courses. Some now teach other students. They have shown themselves perfectly able, within the confines of certain classroom exercises and tests, to perform adequately or better. But they have not acquired an understanding of physical principles, of ways of thinking mathematically, of ways of seeing as an artist sees, or writing as a historian writes. When faced with apparently simple questions that go to the heart of their knowledge, they are lost. Something is seriously wrong here. But what?

What needs improving?

In an important sense these learners have not learned at all. In the view of the authors represented in this book, if learning in an educational setting means anything, it means a movement towards being able to solve unfamiliar problems, towards recognizing the power and elegance of concepts in a subject area, and towards being able to apply what one has learned in class to problems outside class. It means a realization that 'academic' learning is useful for interpreting the world we live in. It means having changed one's understanding.

From our point of view, the underlying reasons for students' failure to learn effectively can probably be found in the ways that teachers and other educators currently think about teaching and assessment. We are not interested in blaming teachers or students, however; we simply want to find answers to the puzzle.

In the early 1980s a research team based at Lancaster University in the north of England carried out a careful study of elementary-school children's learning experiences (Bennett, Desforges, Cockburn and Wilkinson, 1984). This investigation is of interest here: it is one of the few studies of classroom learning that has focused on the quality of student learning rather than on the quantity of learning outcomes or the quality of social life in a classroom. On p 175 we encounter one of many interactions between teachers and children reported in the book:

Fiona: Miss, I can't work out the fourth and fifth. 2 54 : 3 51.

Teacher: Well, you ought to be able to, oughtn't you? And your pencil's thick and black for a start . . . You've forgotten how to do this? You'd better practice at home this weekend. How many twos in five?

F: Two.

T: Where does the two go?

F: In there.

T: Write it down at the top. How many left over? $2\overline{)54}$ with 2 above

F: One.

T: Now what do we say? How many twos in . . . ?

F: Four.

T: In what? How many twos in . . . ?

F: One.

T: No.

F: Five.

T: How many twos in . . . ?

F: Four.

T: But that isn't four. What number is that? $2\overline{)5^14}$ with 2 above

F: One.

T: But you can't say how many twos in one, can you? Because there aren't any, and that's your number. How many twos in . . . ?

F: Fourteen.

T: Yes, now come on. You were busy talking and you're stopping other people from working as well . . . Right, now come on. Do this one $(3\overline{)51}$.

(Bennett, Desforges, Cockburn and Wilkinson, 1984)

   The authors argue that it is evident that Fiona does not know the rules for 'carrying' in division sums. We can probably go further and say she does not have an appropriate conception of part–whole relations – the meaning of the transformation of units into tens from which derive the 'carrying' rules – in counting by tens. But the teacher did not attempt to find out why Fiona was doing the division wrong. She concentrated on gaining the correct response by repetitive questioning ('How many twos in . . . ?').

This example illustrates one of the recurring points in the study by Bennett and his colleagues. Teachers often did not discover the sources of children's mathematical errors. To do this would have required a diagnostic stance, focused on eliciting the typical process or strategy a child used. Instead, teachers reacted to the *product* of a child's performance, often providing direct instruction to remedy the mistake, but ignoring the misconception underlying the errors. Such instruction frequently did not work because it failed to address the proper origin of the error. Rather than seeing the mistakes as data to be used as evidence of a pupil's conception (or misconception), teachers were apt to see them simply as mistakes that needed to be put right.

The effect of this approach to teaching is revealing. The child's misunderstanding would not only be perpetuated, but children would often move on to more complicated problems without understanding simpler ones. So, they stored up obstacles to learning mathematics. Moreover, the pupils 'learned', with great success, many strategies unrelated to mathematics in order to provide their teachers with what they predicted the teachers would reward (the correct answers). These included guessing and conferring with other pupils, so that the teacher could be supplied with correct answers even though the child did not understand the process of reaching them.

It is easier for a researcher, who is removed from the immediate demands of classroom management, to adopt a diagnostic stance than it is for a teacher – at least at the same time as he or she is teaching. But perhaps we can glimpse in Bennett's findings a clarification of the problem of why so many students fail to understand what they have 'learned' in school. It seems that in our teaching methods we often encourage rather than discourage superficial approaches to learning, and at the same time we allow students to avoid changing their conceptions of phenomena related to the world around them.

Learning in its natural setting

What can teachers do to improve learning? The contributors to this volume believe that nothing less than a change in our outlook on teaching, learning and educational research is needed. The process of change has already begun, in recent cognitive psychology and in the study of students' misconceptions in science. In this chapter I refer to a group of studies that is perhaps less well known. The pioneering work of several authors represented in this book has led to descriptions of learning in the real-life setting of classrooms, lecture halls, and assessments. These studies have looked at learning not from the perspective of the psychologist or the teacher but from the student's point of view. Like the investigations of students' understanding of concepts in science, they have focused not on general mechanisms of learning but on the learning of specific subject matter. In short, they have looked at the *content* of learning in its natural *context*.

Perhaps the first writer to carry out an extensive study of this kind was William Perry (whose work is represented in Chapter 7). Perry discovered that the learning difficulties experienced by new college students were not rooted in their lack of motivation, their study skills, or their ability: they sprang from their view of knowledge itself. For many years, intelligent students had succeeded in an orderly educational world where the material to be learned was conveniently packaged as pieces of information to be remembered and reproduced. They came to believe that knowledge consisted of factual statements. Alternative perspectives were introduced by teachers as distractions or tricks; there was always an absolute truth to be discovered behind the dissimulation. Learning was the same thing as adding facts and procedures to one's repertoire. Perry describes the gradual change in these students' conceptions from an absolutistic and reified view of knowledge and learning to a relativistic one where knowledge is dynamic and uncertain and the truth remains provisional.

Perry's work helps us to realize that the educational process may actually create misconceptions of what learning is about. Similarly, misunderstandings of subject phenomena may be a *result* of studying academic subjects in educational settings. A related conclusion could be drawn from another series of investigations that began in Sweden in the early 1970s and has since influenced researchers all over the world, particularly in Britain and Australia. These studies have looked at learning in situations that either resemble normal classrooms or private study, or *are* the everyday, real situations in which ordinary students learn. Thus the results generally have immediate relevance to practice. The main findings have been extensively reported elsewhere (Marton *et al.*, 1984) and only some of the chief conclusions are described here.

Ference Marton and his colleagues originally studied what university students learned from reading an academic text. The text was about reform in higher education. The researchers carefully analysed what students said when they were asked to describe what they had been reading. They found evidence of *qualitative* differences in the outcome of students' reading. The differences were not about how much the students could remember, but about the meaning the author had tried to convey. Some students fully understood the argument being advanced and could relate it to the evidence used to support it; others partly understood the author's message; others could only mention some of the remembered details.

These researchers found that different *approaches* to learning used by different groups of students led to the different *outcomes*. If someone concentrated on memorizing facts and treated the task of reading the article as an external imposition (a 'surface' approach), they would end up with a poor understanding and knowledge of detail. But, if they intended to understand and thus interacted vigorously with the content of the article (a 'deep' approach), they stood a better chance of getting the author's message and being able to remember the supporting facts. The connection between process and outcome was not just empirical; there was a certain logical inevitability about it. If students did not try to discover the author's message, they could not help but miss it (Marton and Säljö, 1984). The *content* and the *process* of learning (the 'what' and the 'how' of learning) formed part of a unified whole.

The original ideas of this particular experiment have since been extended and generalized to students' work on a range of tasks – such as writing assignments in humanities and problem-solving in science – within everyday educational settings. The defining features of the different approaches are summarized in Table 1.

Table 1. *Different approaches to learning*

Deep approach

Intention to understand
  Focus on 'what is signified' (eg the author's argument)
  Relate and distinguish new ideas and previous knowledge
  Relate concepts to everyday experience
  Relate and distinguish evidence and argument
  Organize and structure content
  Internal emphasis: 'A window through which aspects of reality
  become visible, and more intelligible' (Entwistle and Marton, 1984)

Surface approach

Intention to complete task requirements
  Focus on the 'signs' (eg the text itself)
  Focus on discrete elements
  Memorize information and procedures for assessments
  Unreflectively associate concepts and facts
  Fail to distinguish principles from evidence, new information
  from old
  Treat task as an external imposition
  External emphasis: Demands of assessments, knowledge cut off
  from everyday reality

One important characteristic of this way of looking at learning is that the approach and outcome being described are seen from the student's perspective rather than from an external point of view. The results are not statements about the contents of memory but are descriptions of how the learner interprets a phenomenon. The explanation is not given in terms of a pre-existing cognitive theory, nor is there an attempt to infer from the performance of the student the processes that have been used. Nor is the explanation given by referring to differences in outcome in terms of individual differences in personality or ability. Instead, the focus is on the student's subjective description – the student's externalization – of his or her *relation* to the task.

An approach to learning or a conception of a particular phenomenon is not something that is 'inside' a student but something 'between' the student and the task or concept. It has both personal and situational elements but cannot be meaningfully reduced to the sum of both sets. In the next chapter we will see how students' conceptions of phenomena have also been found to vary between contexts, and indeed how even experts' conceptions have varied between historical periods in the development of disciplines (see also Chapters 5 and 11). The major implications of this research for how we should study learning – the focus on realistic tasks as experienced by students rather than as interpreted from previous theoretical frameworks, and the provision of a rigorous qualitative methodology to enable students' experiences to be explored systematically – are also taken up in Chapter 2.

Deep approaches exemplify the type of learning that employers and teachers expect students to demonstrate. Only through using these approaches can students gain mastery of concepts and a firm hold on detailed factual knowledge in a given subject area. Such approaches embody the imaginative and adaptive skills and wide sphere of interests that are increasingly demanded in the world of work. In acute contrast, surface approaches epitomize low-quality learning, are geared to short-term requirements, and focus on the need faithfully to reproduce fragments of information presented in class or textbooks. Like Fiona's attempts at division sums, surface approaches are concerned with 'getting the right answer' to the exclusion of knowing how to get it and of what it means when it has been obtained.

These superficial relations with subject content lead inexorably to poor long-term recall of detail and, even more seriously, to misunderstanding of fundamental principles and concepts. Still worse, the habitual use of surface approaches may leave our students with the idea that 'learning' belongs exclusively to an artificial realm of pleasing teachers and passing examinations. Instead of being a window through which the real world can be seen more clearly, learning becomes nothing more than the tedious recapitulation of other people's ideas, the substitution of numbers into formulae, or the retelling of facts (Entwistle and Marton, 1984).

We can now, perhaps, see our way more clearly to implications for teaching. The different approaches provide part of the solution to the enigma of how qualitative differences in understanding come about. An approach to learning, far from being an individual characteristic of a learner, is a response to the teaching environment in which the student learns. It is the student's subjective perception of the requirements of teachers – the *context of learning* – that is the driving force behind much of their learning. Most students try to deliver what they predict their teachers will reward, as Bennett's study, referred to above, illustrated. Unfortunately, what the students perceive teachers will reward may lead these students to adopt the opposite approaches to those that will enable qualitative changes in understanding to occur.

Improving teaching

Our argument, based on the distinctive view of learning I have outlined, is that teachers must learn about what students 'know' and apply what they discover to improving their teaching. The study of learning is a means of providing teachers with information about how they can help students develop different ways of thinking about subject matter. The inherent educational optimism of this perspective means that amendments to teaching will focus on what can be *changed* in the learner's understanding of the world.

If learning is about changing one's conceptions, then teaching is about discovering students' conceptions and helping them to change their conceptions. The teacher's task entails learning about two related aspects of student's 'knowledge'. The first aspect concerns developing an intimate acquaintance with students' current conceptions and models of the concepts and phenomena in a subject area. The second aspect concerns the students' perceptions of the educational setting in which the learning takes place.

Learning about students' models of subject matter
I have already said that an implication of our view of learning for teaching is that instructors must learn to see teaching as a process aimed at changing student conceptions. But saying this does not go quite far enough. I do not mean that teachers should *tell* students the concepts of 'electrical circuit' or 'opportunity cost', or whatever. This would be no more than transmitting another sort of authoritative information for students to regurgitate. Changing students' conceptions demands more than the transfer of concepts from teacher to student. You cannot, in the normal sense of the word, 'tell' anybody what an electrical circuit or the civil constitution of the church during the French Revolution *mean*.

This suggests that teaching methods that enable students to work on discrepancies in a supportive environment – one that permits incorrect thoughts to be retraced and remedied – are likely to be appropriate. Simply telling students the 'right' conception cannot work, because change involves an active working upon and interaction between the old way of thinking and the new; there is a real sense in which new conceptions grow from older ones. Change in conceptions requires teachers to arrange situations where students must confront the discrepancies between their present way of thinking about the subject matter and the new way desired by the teacher, and where students can come to realize the personal value of the new way. This realization may take a very long time to mature. Time for contemplation, reflection, working things out, and discussion with others learning the same subject matter is thus not a luxury, but a necessity.

Students rarely have *no* knowledge about a topic, or *no* strategy when they tackle a problem. There is almost always some understanding, however limited. Another ramification of our view of learning is that much greater acknowledgement must be given to the understandings and models that students construct for themselves during the learning process (see Pines and West, 1986). From an instructional point of view, it may be more useful to know about an inappropriate model that a student has assembled of a phenomenon than to be aware of the 'missing' knowledge or skill that results from his or her application of that inappropriate model.

In the following chapters we will see several examples of how effective teaching for conceptual change makes use of these principles. The logic of the argument that instructors must learn more about students' thinking may already be plain. If teachers do not know what the students already know, how can they arrange appropriate encounters? If they do not make use of what students already know, are they not discarding a most useful resource? And if they do not use diagnostic procedures to monitor student learning, how will they find out what students know?

A fine example of what it means to use students' conceptions is provided in Svensson and Högfors' study of first-year college students' descriptions of forces acting on moving bodies (Chapter 8). It is apparent that the ability to repeat the words of Newton's first law, or to solve a 'problem' of the form: 'Given velocity **X** at time $t1$ and velocity **Y** at time $t2$, calculate the acceleration' tells us precisely nothing about students' understanding. Understanding is revealed when students are required to recognize the law of inertia's pertinence and usefulness to everyday phenomena. The lack of understanding shown in the 'wrong' answers to the questions described by Svensson and Högfors is a highly fertile teaching resource. These different students did not just get the question wrong: they got it wrong in different ways and, moreover, it is easy to see how they would need different sorts of intervention to change their conceptions. We can easily imagine how the much younger students in Bennett's study could have been asked similarly searching questions by their teachers which would have probed to the heart of their understanding of elementary number phenomena, and how they might have been helped to confront their misconceptions in class (cf Neuman, 1987).

A related aspect of students' conceptions of subject matter concerns their knowledge of the *methods* that disciplines characteristically use to study the phenomena in their domains. Borrowing a term from Schwab (1962), I shall call this the syntactic structure of conceptions in order to distinguish it from the substantive structure, which constitutes the body of concepts in the subject area to which I have been referring above.

Teachers have a responsibility to learn about, and change, their students' conceptions of a subject's syntactic as well as substantive structure. Many problems in learning derive from sincerely held misconceptions about what subject experts (usually represented by teachers) do and how they think. An extreme version of this type of misconception is the view that a subject consists of a large amount of factual knowledge that has to be remembered, and that subject experts are experts because they know a lot of facts – a view that comes close to the absolutism of Perry's students or the naive view of learning as amassing quantities of knowledge.

Such would seem to have been the conception of social science held by some students in Marton's study of text processing (Marton and Säljö, 1984). The students failed to understand the main point of the text for a startlingly simple reason – they were not looking for it. For these students, texts were a flat landscape of facts to be remembered, rather than an area dotted with salient features representing principles or arguments around which stretched plains of evidence. It is easy for teachers, especially subject experts, to fail to realize that students are not understanding because they are not 'seeing' the structure of subordinate examples and superordinate principles.

Halldén's study (1986) provides an example of differing conceptions of the syntactic structure of the discipline of history. Halldén shows how high-school students' common-sense beliefs about 'what counts as historical explanation' may conflict with their teachers'. Students typically interpreted their teacher's questions and statements within a framework remote from that within which expert historians explain phenomena. The students worked with a framework of explanations in terms of individual motives. Because they failed to understand what the information presented in lessons was supposed to explain, they *could not learn* what the teachers were trying to teach.

Complementary evidence is available which supports the need for teaching to address students' understanding of ways of thinking and reporting in science and in the humanities. In this book, for example, White and Roth will show how misconceptions of the nature of scientific knowledge and its causal models often go hand in hand with students' failure to understand important concepts. Students' understanding of the methods of a discipline and their understanding of its concepts are intimately related, and must be accorded equal import in teaching. The same message emerges in each example given above: it is necessary for teachers to explore students' conceptions and to devise ways in which changes towards the desired conceptions can occur. The cardinal rule is that teachers must *listen* to what students are saying, and *then* act appropriately.

Learning about students' perceptions of the educational context

We have known for many years that a great deal of student 'learning' is not immediately about physics or English or biology, but about what will please teachers and gain high grades. The teacher has to predict how students will respond to his or her requirements, and to adopt teaching and assessment strategies that will make the desired responses more likely to occur. The desired responses will represent an intention to understand and provide evidence of changes in conceptions. The goal, easily stated but difficult to achieve, is to make the pleasing of teachers and the demonstrating of understanding as closely overlapping as possible.

One of the lessons this book attempts to teach is that the question of which conditions will most encourage effective learning cannot be answered without considering our students' interpretations of the circumstances in which they learn. To improve learning, we should certainly change the conditions under which people learn, rather than try to change the people themselves; but changing the conditions is only half the battle. One side of this view of learning is that what a student does should be understood in the context of the task: the other side is that the effect of the conditions has to be understood in terms of the perception of the individual learner.

Our view, then, goes one important step further than the argument that situational constraints and opportunities are *the* dominant forces in influencing learning. It would be a mistake to suppose we can wave a magic wand composed of innovative teaching methods or new technologies and expect students to change with alacrity. In fact, it is often logically impossible to produce deterministic predictions about the effects of educational situations on people (Marton, 1986, p 213). Students often react to educational situations differently from the ways teachers or experimenters predict. This is because they react to the requirements *they* perceive, not always the ones we define.

This position has a very important consequence for activities aimed at improving teaching and learning. It means that we can never discover technical solutions that will necessarily solve problems in learning, whether the proposed solutions focus on altering the teaching methods or the attitudes and skills of the learners. It places an extraordinarily high premium on the professional skills of the teacher. Ference Marton and I take up this issue at greater length in Chapter 14.

What aspects of students' perceptions of the educational context do teachers need to learn about? An impressive body of evidence has been collected in the last decade, mainly concerning students in post-compulsory education, to justify the assertion that students' perceptions of assessment and teaching profoundly affect their approaches to learning and the quality of what they learn. The evidence is often negative; pleasing teachers, gaining high grades and understanding do not necessarily overlap.

Perhaps the most significant single influence on students' learning is their perception of assessment. It is in the assessment process that the greatest opportunity arises for student's perceptions of the educational context and their understanding of concepts to diverge. We now know that assessments may encourage passive, reproductive forms of learning while simultaneously hiding the inadequate understanding to which such forms of learning inevitably lead (see, eg Entwistle and Ramsden, 1983).

Findings of this sort are not so surprising. Implicit in much of our current assessment theory and practice is a view of learners as absorbers of quantities of provided wisdom. Many items on standard achievement tests assess students' abilities to recall and apply facts and routines presented during instruction. Some university assessments require only the memorization of detail: they seek evidence that students have become saturated with factual data presented in class or in textbooks and are able to reproduce these on command. Other examination items, although supposed to assess higher-level learning outcomes such as 'comprehension' and 'application', often require little more than the ability to recall a formula and to make appropriate substitutions to arrive at a correct answer (Masters, 1987, Masters and Hill, in press).

The implications of our view of learning for assessment are of course very different. Far from being a receptive process through which new facts and skills are added to a student's repertoire in much the same way as bricks might progressively be added to a wall, learning from our point of view is centrally about qualitative changes in how people interpret subject content. When student achievement is *de facto* measured in terms of reproducing facts or implementing memorized procedures and formulae, an operational definition of what it means to be highly competent in a subject area is consequently provided. This definition is readily learned by students, and leads them to adopt strategies at variance with teachers' aims.

One answer to the problem lies therefore in refining assessment to provide data not only about students' abilities to reproduce information, but also about qualitative differences in their levels of understanding of key concepts. In so far as assessment is in the teacher's control, he or she must strive to ensure that this most visible feature of the learning context provides a clear message about what sort of changes are demanded. It would be a mistake to cast assessment in the role of arch-villain. On the contrary, assessment is a window through which teachers can study their students' learning. Through this window, both instructor and student may see what progress has been made in learning a subject and what specific aspects of the content are partially understood or misunderstood. The sort of assessment that reveals differing conceptions of phenomena related to Newton's first law, as in the example given above, provides a good model for other topics and subjects.

I have dwelt a little on assessment because of its importance in the context of learning. But I must emphasize that a finely tuned awareness of the uncertainty and slowness of the learning process, which the teacher who takes time to study student learning will develop, includes more than this. Research tells us much that the sensitive teacher will find in practice about the effects of intrinsic interest in learning tasks, the time to contemplate and discuss central issues and the freedom to make mistakes, on students' intentions to understand and the quality of their understanding. Perhaps the most immediate need in many science courses is a drastic reduction in 'coverage'. If we want students to know more, we will probably have to tell them less. If teaching does not encourage students' curiosity and does not allow for these processes, we should not be shocked if students display a desperate desire to memorize authoritative statements, nor if they develop a view of science or literature as an inexplicable mystery irrelevant to everyday concerns.

A relational view of teaching and learning

In this chapter I have tried to show that the serious deficiencies in student learning identified in recent research are capable of being remedied through a change in our view of learning and teaching. While there are differences in emphasis, the 'new perspectives' represented in this book share a common view of educational research and development that I call *relational*. This relational view of learning and teaching has several aspects, each of which will be apparent in one or more of the following chapters, and it is appropriate to summarize these features here.

1. Learning is about changes in conceptions
The first aspect concerns a certain view of learning itself that I have already described, a view that is restated in many different ways in the remainder of the book. A relational view concerns *changes in people's conceptions of aspects of reality*. Being able to repeat facts and plug numbers into formulae to get the right answers is handy, even essential. But it is not what education is fundamentally about, and a view of learning in educational institutions in these terms is dangerously misleading.

The kind of learning we discuss in this volume is not *about* adding more and more facts and procedures to one's store of knowledge in much the same way as water might be poured from one vessel to another. It is not the simple, additive, incremental process that some everyday conceptions of knowledge and much of educational measurement theory and practice may suggest (Masters, 1987). Diagnosis of what students do not know is not a matter of finding that the water has not reached a certain point on the scale and deciding to add a little more.

The learning we are concerned with is about the quality of a person's understanding, not the quantity of information he or she can reproduce on demand. It is about the kinds of changes that the recent research described above suggests we have so signally failed to encourage in so many of our students.

Our way of thinking about learning as a qualitative change in a person's way of conceptualizing something has a long history in educational theory, and is quite fundamental to the practice of western science (see, eg, Kuhn, 1962). The opposite notion – that the acquisition of facts and skills alone is 'what really matters' – is, nevertheless, tenacious. The quantitative view of learning has exercised a remarkable fascination in educational thinking over the years. Its genesis is in common-sense conceptions of learning: it is not a product of educational systems, even though they may reinforce it. We cannot enter here into the reasons for its endurance; others (see, eg Best, 1985; Dahlgren, 1984) have offered explanations in philosophical and political terms.

2. Learning always has a content as well as a process

The second characteristic of a relational view is its concern with the process (or 'how') of learning and the outcome (or 'what' of learning) as a unified whole. Learners always learn something. Does that sound obvious? Many attempts have been made to identify fundamental processes of 'good learning' that apply to *all* subject matter. But if learning is about changes in conceptualizations, then it makes little sense to separate these two logically associated elements in the ways we think about improving education. Changing conceptions entails a certain sort of thinking process that typically involves finding connections between new and previous knowledge, explaining theoretical ideas in terms of common sense, facing up to discrepancies, taking time to think, etc. The logical trap avoided by a relational view of education is the conviction that we can teach students these skills as entities separate from subject matter or teaching context.

3. Improving learning is about relations between learners and subject matter, not teaching methods and student characteristics

The next key feature of this view of learning is that it focuses on *relations* between students, what they are required to learn, and what teachers do. So it is not primarily concerned, unlike most views deriving from psychology, with the things that go on inside students' heads or with the discovery of individual differences in learning ability or style. It is of course concerned with exploring students' conceptions of subject matter and how these can be changed. A conception always has two parts to it: the idea being conceptualized and the person doing the conceptualizing; and a relational view embraces both these parts.

A relational perspective is not about psychological characteristics; neither is it about teaching methods. It is not concerned with comparing the general effectiveness of instructional methods separately from the subject matter they are intended to convey, nor yet with the structure of disciplines separately from how they are actually learned. These elements are subordinated to a focus on an autonomous domain of knowledge concerning the teaching and learning of subject content. A relational view is by nature an educational view.

4. Improving learning is about understanding the student's perspective

A relational view focuses, from the point of view of the student, on the relation between a student and what the student learns. It explores the *student's* perspective on learning. In doing so it helps to explain some of the 'odd' findings in educational research. Sometimes research findings are repeated so many times in so many situations that they provide overwhelming support for a general hypothesis. But often, very often in education, the results are equivocal or contradictory.

This is not because people are varied and quirky, although of course they are, but because their thoughts and actions are profoundly contextual. They make decisions about what they will do in different circumstances, and the circumstances influence their decisions. Such decisions are often based on information that the teacher or researcher does not have access to, so they may appear inconsistent and their consequences may seem irrational. Students' perceptions may be quite different from the researcher's. A whole class of things (such as phenomena relating Newton's first law to projectile motion) may seem the same to a teacher or researcher, but quite different to a student. So his or her performance on different tasks related to the first law may vary, not because of a weakness in teaching or experimental design, but because of hidden imperatives that derive from his or her perceptions and experiences.

A relational perspective does not search for elegant general laws of learning, but for guiding hypotheses about typical conceptions and approaches that will help teachers to convey particular subject matter in certain educational circumstances. These predictions have to be critically interpreted by teachers; they can never be set down as a set of teacher-proof rules. The reason is that the connection between a student and learning is *systematic*, not *concrete* (cf Luria, 1966). In other words, there are many different pathways between where a student is now and where you desire him to be. Adding a link or removing another does not *necessarily* guarantee or prevent learning. All this makes a relational view an intellectually challenging way of looking at learning, but one which is potentially more relevant in the classroom.

5. Educational research and teaching are more closely related than people sometimes believe

The final characteristic to be mentioned – one that is implicit in what has already been said – is the distinctive tendency of a relational view to reduce the distance between professional educational research and the profession of teaching. The results of research using this perspective are about the material that teachers work with – the ideas of their students. There is an affinity between the diagnostic process by which a teacher seeks to assess a child's understanding in his classroom interactions and the rigorous isolation of differing conceptions of phenomena which the researcher undertakes. More will be said in the final chapter about the implications of this aspect of a relational view for teacher education and cooperative research.

The structure of the book

The book is organized in four parts. Chapter 2 forms a complement to the present chapter and completes Part 1: it examines some of the issues that arise in trying to study the educational process in a way that does justice to a view of learning as changes in conceptions. Säljö pays particular attention to the methods of 'phenomenography' which he pioneered with Ference Marton at Gothenburg in the 1970s, and his chapter is essential reading if you are unfamiliar with this particular method of studying learning.

Parts 2 and 3 constitute the heart of the book. Here, different ways in which practice has been informed by systematic inquiries into student learning are described. Part 2 focuses on learning science at middle- and high-school level. Chapter 3 provides an overview of recent advances in the area of science learning from the perspective of learning as constructing understanding. Chapter 4 describes an approach to science education, based on extensive interview studies of learners' reasoning about force and motion, that enables 11-year-olds to learn the principles of Newtonian mechanics and to grasp something of what it means to 'think like a scientist'.

Chapter 5 presents the findings of an investigation of a crucial aspect of the secondary chemistry curriculum: students' understanding and misunderstanding of the concept of amount of substance and its unit (mole). Important implications for future chemistry curricula are drawn out. Part 2 concludes with an extended chapter of central relevance to the book's argument. Chapter 6 describes in some detail the differences between teaching that successfully encourages conceptual change learning and teaching that promotes a view of science as acquiring and memorizing facts. The need for *teachers* to change *their* conceptions of teaching is emphasized: this, one of the persistent themes of the book, is treated in detail in the final two chapters.

Part 3 shifts the focus to higher education. Chapter 7 brings to life the findings of William Perry's analysis of how college students develop more complex conceptions of the nature and purpose of academic subject matter during their studies. This development reflects the major distinction which recurs again and again in the book. Chapter 8 returns us to the issue of how to improve students' understanding of physics concepts, this time at college level; several teaching strategies designed to encourage conceptual change learning, based on knowledge of students' conceptions, are outlined.

Chapters 9 and 10 examine aspects of medical education. Whenever a teaching 'expert' recommends attention to students' understanding rather than to memorizing, you can be sure someone will say that some subjects require the student to rote-learn large quantities of factual material. Anatomy is often thought to be the apotheosis of such subjects. Chapter 9 shows us how wrong this view is: it reports methods of teaching and assessment, derived from recent research findings, that encourage students to use approaches to learning leading to an understanding of anatomical principles. Chapter 10 considers clinical teaching. It describes a study of clinical students' learning strategies which has directly influenced its author's own teaching. Recommendations for the design of computer-assisted learning programs in higher education that take account of the view of learning adopted in the book are examined in Chapter 11. Chapter 12 discusses aspects of a computer-based adventure game intended to help students reflect on the context and content of learning in college.

Part 4 is an attempt to integrate the previous chapters in differing ways. Chapter 13 explains how teachers can be encouraged to teach for conceptual change by providing in-service education focused on students' misconceptions of phenomena. It also considers changes in the context of teaching that will reward a concern on the teacher's part with changing students' conceptions. The final chapter summarizes what has gone before and, we hope, does more than that. It points up the argument, presented in different forms throughout the book, for changing teaching practices in a way that is informed by an understanding of how and what students learn. It makes explicit recommendations for promoting changes in learners' conceptions. And it sets the scene the future work on how specific subject matter is learned and taught: the work which, we believe, is the cornerstone of an authentic science of education.

References

Bennett, N, Desforges, C, Cockburn, A and Wilkinson, B (1984). *The Quality of Pupil Learning Experiences*. Hillsdale, New Jersey: Lawrence Erlbaum.

Best, D (1985). Primary and secondary qualities: Waiting for an educational Godot. *Oxford Review of Education*, **11**, 73–84.

Dahlgren, L O (1984). Outcomes of learning. In: F Marton *et al.* (eds), *The Experience of Learning*. Edinburgh: Scottish Academic Press.

Entwistle, N J and Ramsden, P (1983). *Understanding Student Learning*. London: Croom Helm.

Entwistle, N J and Marton, F (1984). Changing conceptions of learning and research. In: F Marton *et al.* (eds), *The Experience of Learning*. Edinburgh: Scottish Academic Press.

Halldén, O (1986) Learning history. *Oxford Review of Education*, **12**, 53–66.

Hounsell, D J (1984). Learning and essay-writing. In: F Marton *et al.* (eds), *The Experience of Learning*. Edinburgh: Scottish Academic Press.

Kuhn, T S (1962). *The Structure of Scientific Revolutions*. Chicago: University of Chicago Press.

Lochhead, J (1985). New horizons in educational development. In: E W Gordon (ed), *Review of Research in Education 12*. Washington, DC: AERA.

Luria, A P (1966). *Higher Cortical Functions in Man*. New York: Basic Books.

Marton, F (1986). Some reflections on the improvement of learning. In: J A Bowden (ed), *Student Learning: Research into Practice*. Melbourne: Centre for the Study of Higher Education.

Marton, F, Hounsell, D J and Entwistle, N J (eds) (1984). *The Experience of Learning*. Edinburgh: Scottish Academic Press.

Marton, F and Säljö, R (1984). Approaches to learning. In F Marton *et al.*

(eds), *The Experience of Learning*. Edinburgh: Scottish Academic Press.

Masters, G N (1987). New views of student learning: Implications for educational measurement. Research Working Paper 87.11, Centre for the Study of Higher Education, University of Melbourne.

Masters, G N and Hill, P (in press). Assessing student achievement in the senior secondary school. *Australian Journal of Education*.

McDermott, L C (1984). Research on conceptual understanding in mechanics. *Physics Today*, **37**, 24–32.

Neuman, D (1987). *The Origin of Arithmetic Skills: A Phenomenographic Approach*. Gothenburg: Acta Universitatis Gothoburgensis.

Pines, A L and West, L H T (1986). Conceptual understanding and science learning: An interpretation of research within a sources-of-knowledge framework. *Science Education*, **70**, 583–604.

Schwab, J J (1962). The concept of the structure of a discipline. *Educational Record*, **43**, 197–205.

Sjøberg, S and Lie, S (1981). Technical Report 81–11, University of Oslo.

Chapter 2

Learning in Educational Settings: Methods of Inquiry

Roger Säljö
University of Linköping, Sweden

Introduction

Practically all authors of introductory textbooks in the fields of education and psychology point to the centrality of the phenomenon of learning. Statements such as 'virtually everything the mature human organism does, or is capable of doing, can be viewed as a result of learning' (Horton and Turnhage, 1976, p 3), and that 'at most times during their lives people are engaged in some learning activity or other' (Borger and Seaborne, 1982, p 9), serve to signal to the prospective student the significance of the topic of learning. This appreciation of the importance of the phenomenon of learning is by no means limited to the opinions of textbook writers and researchers in the area, but is underpinned by similar attitudes in everyday thinking and lay epistemologies. Learning, by being associated with concepts such as change, development and growth, has positive connotations even to the extent that official government agencies point to the necessity of entire nations becoming 'learning societies' (UNESCO, 1972) when attempting to cope with a challenging future.

Attempts to improve human learning thus seem to be highly worthwhile enterprises, gaining support from many sources. But what precisely does it mean to improve human learning? At one level, the answer might seem obvious. The improvement of learning must imply that people will be able to acquire knowledge and information more efficiently, and that they should remember and be able to use what they learn in everyday settings. At this level of precision the problem appears fairly straightforward. The solutions to problems of teaching and learning would seem to reside in the development of new and more efficient methods of transferring knowledge and information.

There are obvious complications to this way of conceiving problems of teaching and learning. We have already been introduced to some of these in Chapter 1. Even a superficial analysis of the concept of learning itself reveals that there are many different kinds of learning activities. As human beings we are involved in such diverse learning projects as acquiring basic social and communicative skills (eg a first language), manual and physical skills (swimming, riding a bicycle, typing), and intellectual or academic skills of various kinds (mathematics, history, computer programming), to mention just a few of the possible variants of learning that people engage in. Do all these instances constitute examples of one common and indivisible phenomenon? Can we have – or expect to have – a single theory of learning that will cover all these (and many other) processes?

On this issue, researchers disagree. Some would argue that such a theory could be achieved provided we succeed in gaining more knowledge about the significant determinants of 'good learning'. Once we have these insights, the methods of teaching and learning could be matched to the intellectual resources of various groups of students in an optimal way.

Other researchers – including those contributing to the present volume – would argue that there is something fundamentally wrong in the assumption 'that phenomena of learning consititute a homogeneous set of phenomena and/or that the eventual differences are not important in describing what is general and common' (Svensson, 1979, p 1). The notorious difficulties in achieving a satisfactory definition of the concept of learning so often pointed out in the literature (see, for example, Bower and Hilgard, 1981; West and Foster, 1976) may arise because there is *no* innermost, common denominator to 'learning'. It is quite conceivable, as Neisser (1982) put it in his discussion of cognitive psychology, 'that "learning" in general does not exist' (p 12), except as a very abstract linguistic category that cannot guide our efforts in empirical research aimed at understanding and improving education.

The point of our argument so far is thus that it is misleading to assume that by referring to an activity as learning, one has delimited the phenomenon in a precise way. Learning is an aspect of life and all situations provide potential learning experiences. On the other hand, many situations that are set up for the specific purpose of teaching and learning do not result in learning. An illustration of the second half of this paradox is given in an important ethnographic study of life in classrooms carried out by Phillip Jackson in the 1960s. Even though classrooms are commonly conceived as places where teachers teach and pupils learn, it is evident from Jackson's study that this account of what goes on is highly abstract and tells us very little about what people actually do. On closer scrutiny, learning in a strict sense is not a prominent activity for pupils, whereas waiting is. Similarly, teaching in the sense of instructing pupils on specific topics to be learned is not necessarily the most dominant activity of the teacher. Keeping the children busy with various tasks may be more important, since this maintains order in the classroom. To understand a particular type of learning, for example the kind taking place in educational institutions, we have to turn our eyes to the classroom and the educational system to scrutinize the activities that go on and that constitute elements of the specifically human activity of studying.

What comes first: theory or method?

'Studying' is an activity that takes place in man-made institutions that now have a long history. In our view it is an important epistemological premiss for the arduous task of understanding teaching and learning that these phenomena exist 'out there' in the classroom environment prior to any sophisticated theorizing about them. To influence the way people go about teaching and learning, we must gain access to such phenomena and analyse, in detail, representative instances of people engaged in such activities. Conceived in this way, the research task has an anthropological flavour to it and involves as central ingredients the problems of bringing conceptual clarity to a complex and diverse reality.

The problem of providing conceptual frameworks that are sensitive to the complexities of learning in everyday studying indicates the need for a broad repertoire of methods. A genuinely scientific attitude presupposes that the methods used for doing empirical research are subordinated to the research problem and the current status of knowledge existing within an area. As understood in this volume, the issue of deepening our understanding about the phenomena of learning in the context of everyday studying entails rigorous description of the activities of teaching and learning in educational settings. We aim to discover what is common and what varies in such settings. Only in this way can we begin to obtain an understanding of learning as an *educational* phenomenon.

The necessity of generating categories of description that provide an accurate basis for theorizing and intervention is largely underestimated in the behavioural sciences. Research mostly follows the hypothetico-deductive paradigm and the *independent variables*, such as intelligence, motivation, social class or any other of the factors that are used in research on learning, and the *outcome variables* (grades, test results, level of interest, etc) are borrowed from existing theories, or perhaps sometimes even taken from everyday assumptions about how such factors relate. The tacit assumption of this strategy is that educational phenomena constitute instances of phenomena that exist in many other social contexts also. The implicit argument seems to be that since intelligence, social class, and so on, are important determinants of people's success in other areas, they should be central also in the area of education. Our point is not that such relationships do not exist and are not vital to an understanding of education. Rather, our assumption is that the choice of 'variables' (descriptive categories and explanatory concepts) to be used should be related to the type of *knowledge interest* a given study represents.

Knowledge interest *vis-à-vis* education of various groups in a society may differ. Politicians, administrators, parents and teachers, to mention some of the groups with a potential interest in teaching and learning, all view education from their own, only partially overlapping, perspectives. Interactions in the classroom and the activities of learning may quite legitimately not be in focus for the politician who has to decide on funding or the administrative structure of certain parts of the educational system in a community or country. Similarly, for the teacher of physics or modern languages, immediate interest in improving the quality of teaching may be related to having gained knowledge about the specific problems that exist in those areas of instruction. This is, we would argue, a legitimate knowledge interest that can be developed through research.

The knowledge interest determines the *level of description* that is chosen in a specific case. In comparison with traditional research into learning, a characteristic feature of the studies to be reported here is that there is a simultaneous concern for *how* students learn, as well as *what* they learn. The 'how' of learning concerns the general strategies of studying that students use, all the way from their overt behaviour such as when and for how long they study, if they use underlinings or summaries, etc, to the covert activities such as their approaches to learning, ie their way of thinking while learning, their attempts to relate what they read/hear to what they already know etc. The 'what' of learning, perhaps even more in focus in this book, concerns the central issue of how students interpret and comprehend what they encounter in teaching and learning.

To sum up, the focus on trying to understand human learning in educational settings requires a detailed analysis of the activities that people engage in in such situations. There is thus an emphasis on the activity of generating concepts that accurately reflect what goes on as well as on verifying (see Glaser and Strauss, 1967) and refining these concepts across teaching and learning settings.

Qualitative and quantitative methods

In many discussions in the behavioural sciences over the past few decades, the relative advantages and disadvantages of qualitative and quantitative methods have provoked heated debate. This is not the place to repeat the arguments presented in these discussions. However, in the research to be reported in the following chapters it is a basic tenet that there is no necessary conflict between qualitative and quantitative approaches for generating and analysing data. Indeed, it is highly questionable whether it is meaningful at all to argue about method without simultaneously considering the research problem one is facing and the knowledge interest being pursued. Given the conception of learning outlined above and in the previous chapter, it is evident that the family of methods conventionally referred to as qualitative is of primary importance. A thorough understanding of what learning means in concrete terms in various settings presupposes a detailed analysis of how students deal with the tasks they are presented with in schools and with their reactions to, and perspectives on, what goes on. In saying this we are trying to establish another fundamental assumption behind the research into everyday human learning that is focused on by the authors of this book. Access to *the learner's perspective* on the activities of teaching and learning is essential for understanding educational phenomena – and for improving education.

Studying the world as perceived

In order to understand the activities that count as learning in educational settings, it is not sufficient to have a firm knowledge of the assumed objective characteristics of the situations in which learning takes place. We also need access to the learner's perspective on what he or she is trying to accomplish. Differently expressed, and following the terminology suggested by Marton (1981), our object of inquiry is within a *second-order perspective* and concerns how the world is construed by the actors. The underlying rationale behind this type of research is that people act on their interpretation of the situations they find themselves in rather than on the objective, matter-of-fact characteristics of situations (if, indeed, such characteristics could be established). A corollary of this assumption is that changing social settings – such as schools and universities – with the aim of improving learning, means not only modifying the objective situation, but also people's perceptions of the activities they are involved in (Ramsden, 1984).

The phenomenographic approach

Marton (1981) coined the term 'phenomenography' to refer to research that systematically focuses on the second-order perspective. Phenomenography as outlined below should be viewed as one attempt to deal explicitly with the problem of analysing the meaning that people ascribe to the world and to the concepts and 'texts' they encounter in educational settings. At the level of research methods, phenomenography has obvious similarities with the early work of Jean Piaget (see Piaget, 1973), although the epistemological assumptions differ in important respects. The similarities can be found in the orientation towards understanding and describing how people (not necessarily children, although it was in that particular context that the Piagetian approach grew) construe significant phenomena in the world.

What are the methodological assumptions of a phenomenographic approach? Consider the following excerpts taken from Piaget's studies (1927–73) of children's understanding of the concept of 'life'. Here the two interviewees, Gries and Kaen, are questioned about their conceptions of what constitute the defining characteristics of living things:

Gries: You know what it is to be alive?
Yes, to be able to move.

Is the lake alive?
Not always.

Why not?
Sometimes there are waves and sometimes there aren't.

Is a cloud alive?
Yes, it moves as if it were walking . . .

Is a bicycle alive?
Yes, it goes . . .

Kaen: Is a stream alive?
Yes, it goes.

Is the lake alive?
Yes, it is always moving a bit.

Is a cloud alive?
Yes, you can see it moving . . .

Grass?
Yes, it can grow.

(Piaget, 1973, p 229)

Piaget's interpretation of this particular mode of construing 'life' is that children at this stage of development seem to assume that living things are characterized by the fact that they can move. In other words, there is a systematic quality to children's answers: they seem to judge whether an object is alive or not through the specific quality of movement. This particular conception of life – according to Piaget – has developed from a more indiscriminate conception of life (where a wide class of objects are assumed to be alive) and it will eventually be replaced by a conception where only animals and plants are construed as being instances where the concept of 'life' applies.

The notion of *conceptions of reality* used throughout this volume should thus be interpreted as pointing to a particular level of description that, within a certain epistemological perspective on humanity, is understood as an autonomous and legitimate topic of research. Simply put, it is the 'what' of thinking, the *meaning* people see in and ascribe to what they perceive. In the Piagetian context, the differing conceptions of the world are construed as results of the age and/or developmental level of the person responding. In the phenomenographic approach, assumptions concerning the possible source of variations in conceptions held by people are postponed and considered as an issue for the theoretical framework utilized in a specific research project. In this sense phenomenography is a methodological approach that is compatible with a relatively broad set of theoretical perspectives that focus on people's conceptions of reality.

The basic point of departure is the adoption of an epistemological perspective in terms of which the world is considered as inherently multifaceted and open to variations in interpretation (Rommetveit, 1988). The essential reason for paying an interest in people's conceptions of the world is a commitment to an epistemological position where the existence of a 'real' reality, common to all and available through 'unbiased' observation of the world, is not recognized. There is always a filter through which the world is seen if it is to be meaningful. The interest in this filter – the conceptions of reality that we have acquired as participants in human communication – is what characterizes phenomenography as a scientific undertaking.

A corollary of this position is that differences in conceptions of reality are not just characteristic of variations in intellectual maturity. In complex societies, varying conceptions of reality are typical of, for instance, the differences between a common-sense conception of a phenomenon on the one hand and the conception used within a scientific framework for understanding the very same phenomenon on the other. An illuminating example of this has been given by Dahlgren (1978, 1984) with respect to people's conceptions of 'price'. To arrive at an understanding of how people construe the origin of prices Dahlgren put the seemingly trivial question: 'Why does a bun cost about one [Swedish] crown?' (1984, p 30). Applying a phenomenographic approach to the analysis of data, the variation in the answers could be reduced to two main conceptions of price:

A: The price is dependent on the relationship between the supply of and demand for buns.

B: The price is equal to the (true) value of the bun.

(Dahlgren, 1984, p 30)

The B-conception typically implies that price can be explained by adding together the costs of production (ingredients, labour, distribution, etc) and the assumed level of profit. This seems to be the natural common-sense understanding of price that most of the students interviewed by Dahlgren used spontaneously. In the particular context of economic theorizing, this conception, for a variety of reasons, does not provide the most interesting starting point for explaining how prices are established in a market economy. Instead of explaining the price by looking at the bun as a concrete object, adding the values of constituents, the preferred mode of thinking is systems-orientated and the price is considered to be the point where sellers and buyers meet on the market where the bargaining takes place.

This example is a tangible illustration of the fact that in a complex society there is a rich variety of conceptions of reality providing varieties of explanatory frameworks that are used for different purposes. To adopt the language suggested by Berger and Luckmann (1967), societies contain differing 'provinces of meaning' and science can be considered as one (or many) such province(s) where specific ways of construing reality are adopted for the purpose of developing theoretical accounts of nature and society. To be more precise with respect to the kind of learning to be attended to in the following chapters, it can be understood as the acquisition of conceptions of reality that stem from this specific province of meaning and that differ from those employed in everyday thinking.

Generating and analysing data

Although methodological openness is a prime virtue in research, it is evident that in studies within a second-order perspective, methods such as *participant observation in naturalistic settings, interviews* and use of *written documents* produced by students play a prominent role. Although such methods have appeared at a relatively late stage in the study of learning and instruction, they are the natural approaches to generating data in areas such as anthropology, certain branches of sociology and ethnography. The problems of analysis of data of this nature are different from those that apply to data that are already precategorized according to some criterion by the researcher.

When using questionnaires, the response alternatives are decided on by the researcher and the acceptable variation in answers has been limited in advance. It is important to note that this procedure in no way implies the absence of problems of interpretation similar to those that arise in the analyses of interviews or of written material. With respect to the answers to a questionnaire, there are strong assumptions that people reponding with the same alternative really mean the same thing. In many cases, it can be argued that even a simple 'yes' or 'no' in a questionnaire can hide a considerable variation with respect to what is meant. Focusing for the moment on interviews, it is evident that the analysis of such data is less algorithmic than is the case with more structured methods of analysis. To establish the conceptions of reality that people express *vis-à-vis* phenomena that interest us, a typical mode of procedure is either to ask people direct questions or to have them solve or explain a problem of some kind.

To give an illustration of the first type of approach, consider the following examples from a study of teacher students' conceptions of evolution, natural selection and the relationships between the environment and the characteristics of living organisms (excerpts taken from Pedersen, 1985, my translation). The participants were asked to reason about evolution in a variety of aspects. The quotations presented below, taken from discussions with Calle and Frida, are comments on how human characteristics could change in the future and they were given when reacting to a drawing showing a human being with a changed physical appearance that was supposed to be able to tolerate new environmental conditions caused by pollution and other changes in the ecological balance.

Interviewer: What is the role of the environment do you think in that adaptation?

Calle: Well, in time you first have the changes in the environment and then the human adaptation to the environment.

Interviewer: And this adaptation . . . how does it come about?

Calle: Well, it can be like this that when humans experience the environmental change, then well, to be able to survive something develops . . . or it must depend on how they live in this here environment.

Interviewer: Is it the environment that starts this adaptation of the species?

Calle: Yes, I think it is . . . it is the change in the environment that starts a process of adaptation of the species.

Interviewer: And this process of adaptation of the species, what could that be . . . what does it mean?

Calle: Well, it could be . . . that humans in some way live in this new environment, that their way of living in some way can affect their hereditary factors or genes and so on, and that the hereditary factors change and that then, when new individuals are born then they get another appearance eventually . . . gradually a different kind of individual appears.

Interviewer: How does such an adaptation come about?

Frida: In man?

Interviewer: Just as an example . . . or you could take some other plant or animal species and talk about it.

Frida: This must have been going on for an awfully long time, but that one thing at a time has . . . 'cause there could have been some defect in man from the beginning and which turns out to be just in this climate then . . . as you say about animals then that's a mutation . . . successful mutation which makes that animal get on better than the others and survive and have offspring that have this disposition and then, maybe one of those offspring gets another mutation which also turns out to fit the present conditions.

Interviewer: So the cause of this change of humans is mutation, then; where does that come from . . . ?

Frida: Well that must be a random . . . if nature is to have its way then I think it is through mistakes that there is this kind of . . .

Interviewer: And those mistakes are in . . . ?

Frida: Mutations.

Interviewer: What does the environment do , then?

Frida: What the environment does? . . . Well, it does nothing . . . it is what it is . . . I think.

(Pedersen, 1985)

Considering these excerpts from the point of view of the research approach described more fully in the previous chapter, the focus on the *what* of thinking implies a description of human cognition in terms of its content. The basic philosophy is that without *someone to do the thinking* and *something to think about*, there is no human cognitive activity. At first glance, these excerpts may seem diffuse and open to many interpretations. One of the prerequisites for analysing data is that the researcher is acquainted with the subject matter in question. In the above case, familiarity with concepts such as mutation, adaptation, genes, is necessary to make sense of the excerpts. The process of analysis as a practical activity, then, presupposes that the analyst reads and rereads the transcripts several times. The purpose of this careful reading is to generate categories describing the conceptions of evolution that seem to underlie the statements made by the respondent. Questions that the analyst asks himself or herself during this phase of reading are: How does the respondent construe the phenomenon? What concepts does he or she use to explain it? What types of similarities with other phenomena are introduced?, etc.

In these two excerpts it is, we argue, possible to discern two differing conceptions of evolution. Calle accounts for evolutionary change by assuming that acquired characteristics can be inherited through changes in the genetic material. He claims that 'you first have the changes in the environment and then the human adaptation to the environment', and that the 'way of living [of humans] in some way can affect their hereditary factors or genes'. The modifications of the latter are thus assumed to take place as a result of the conditions of life that people live in. Frida, on the other hand, does not allow for the possibility of acquired characteristics having any effects on the genes. She seems to assume that evolution is a process where the plants and animals that survive have, by chance, a characteristic that adds to their ability to cope with the environmental conditions. The role of the environment is thus, in a sense, reversed in comparison to the explanation given by Calle. While Calle assumes that the genetic material changes as a result of the conditions of life, Frida states that the environment 'does nothing . . . it is what it is' and that evolutionary changes are the results of random factors that have provided certain species with suitable characteristics for specific environmental conditions.

It is worth remarking, in passing, that in this particular context the two conceptions of evolution have a close similarity with the historically well-known difference between a Lamarckian explanation of evolution (adhered to by Calle) and a (neo-) Darwinian (adopted by Frida). In other words we have here a fascinating observation of one of the students presenting a conception of evolution that was previously accepted in the scientific world as the correct version. And, judging from the results of several studies (eg Brumby, 1984; Halldén, 1987; Pedersen, 1985) this mode of understanding evolution is part of common sense and seems resistant to change (for some examples of common-sense conceptions in other areas of science, see West's chapter in this volume). Even after exposure to explicit instruction, many students keep to the Lamarckian version and assume that acquired characteristics can be inherited.

This historical dimension can provide important clues to understanding learning difficulties. Quite often one finds that the conceptions of reality represented among groups of people have appeared in the history of science as the dominant form of reasoning. Through studying conceptual change in history there is a possibility of understanding why certain ways of construing reality are difficult for students to adopt. The historical dimension can also be valuable in pointing out the time and effort it took for experts to change from one conception to another, and this may serve as a reminder for teachers of the difficulties involved in accepting certain forms of thought.

The status of conceptions and the use of research

Assuming that one accepts the difference between these ways of talking about price and evolution as indicating different conceptions of a pheno-menon, several questions can be raised with respect to the methodological assumptions and the validity and reliability of this approach. The concrete praxis of phenomenography implies that the variation in forms of talking about phenomena is reduced to a limited set of categories (usually between three and five) that depicts significant differences in ways of construing this phenomenon. The assumption is that conceptions of reality can be expressed in a large number of linguistic forms without necessarily changing the basic way in which the phenomenon is construed. Again, this is parallel to the assumptions held by Piaget and many other approaches to the analysis of this type of data.

Questions that are immediately evident when approaching this kind of qualitative analysis concern the status of the conceptions of phenomena that people express. How do we know that the interviewees would not have said something different had we asked the question in a different way, using a different strategy and other examples? The answer to this question is that one has to accept human thinking as contextually deter-mined. All human thought takes place in a communicative setting and is in part determined by specific circumstances in terms of situation and expectations. This is the case irrespective of the method we use for generating data, although the problems may be more readily perceived in the case of interviews and other qualitative approaches to data collection. Against the background of this epistemological perspective, there are two assumptions within the phenomenographic approach that should be added.

The first assumption is that conceptions of reality are not considered as residing within individuals. In other words, people do not *have* specific conceptions of phenomena in the world around them in the sense that behavioural scientists have had a tendency to ascribe intellectual capaci-ties or developmental stages to individuals. People may – and do – have a tendency to use particular conceptions of reality in a number of settings or in relation to a number of problems, but they cannot always be assumed to adopt that particular perspective on reality. This is illustrated in a study by Johansson (1981; Johansson, Marton and Svensson, 1985; see also the chapter by Svensson and Högfors in this volume) of university students' conceptions of the physical entities force and motion.

In this investigation, students of mechanics were given a set of tasks that involved accounting for the forces affecting moving objects and changes in their motion. The objects used were a car, a bicycle, an ice-hockey puck, a rail coach, etc. The differences that were found in students' conceptions of forces in motion could be described in terms of a dichotomy. When asked a question of the following kind: 'A car is driven at a high constant speed straight forward on a highway. What forces act on the car?', the essential variation in explanatory frameworks concerned a focus on explaining constant speed on the one hand, or acceleration and/or deceleration on the other. The concept of force, and changes in force, was used either to explain why objects move or, in the case of acceleration or deceleration, why the velocity changes. In the second case, a Newtonian conception, movement at constant velocity is the starting point and the concept of force is used to account for *changes in velocity*, while in the first case it is the *motion* itself that is being explained by referring to forces that affect the objects. It seems as if students using the non-Newtonian conception start from the common-sense notion that rest is the natural state of objects and it is the motion that has to be explained. This conception reflects an Aristotelian understanding of motion where force is a quality that is assumed to be inherent in the object. Deceleration of an ice-hockey puck, to take an example, takes place because the force put into it by the stick is reduced as it moves on the ice. The Newtonian conception, on the other hand, understands constant velocity as the natural state of objects where forces are in equilibrium and, hence, it is the change in velocity which has to be explained by referring to a change in the forces acting upon the object.

What Johansson showed is that when presented with a set of similar problems the students oscillated between an Aristotelian and a Newtonian conception, sometimes using the concept of force to explain motion, and sometimes changes in velocity. For instance, it was more common to use an Aristotelian mode of thinking in the context of movement of bicycles than in movement of cars (Johansson, 1981, p 143). Perhaps, Johansson argues, the experience of the physical effort it takes to keep a bicycle at a constant velocity makes it difficult to explain constant velocity by referring to an equilibrium of forces. It is easier to assume that the forward motion has to be explained and to do this one refers to the forces put into the movement through the rider.

In a similar vein, in the studies by Dahlgren (1978, 1984) referred to above there was a clear tendency for people to explain prices of commodities differently depending on the type of object that was mentioned in the question. For instance, when asking why jewels are expensive, even small children tended to use the concepts of supply and demand, saying that there was a shortage of jewels which made them expensive. Using the bun in the question, even some of the university students of economics failed to use this explanatory framework. Instead they used the everyday type of explanation where price was seen as a sum of the various costs of production.

In traditional perspectives on learning, the observation that people change their ways of thinking in various contexts might be understood as a complication, perhaps even as a threat to a genuinely scientific understanding of human thinking. Rogoff (1984) expresses this view when she points out that context has been treated as a 'nuisance variable' in research into cognition. In the perspective outlined in this chapter and the previous one, it is accepted that context is integral to our way of making sense of reality. Situational variation in how people construe meaning is the natural point of departure. How, then, the reader might well ask, is generalizable knowledge – knowledge that teachers can rely on if they want to learn from this research – possible?

To answer this question, a second important assumption of the phenomenographic approach has to be introduced. A corollary of what has been said above is that conceptions are conceived as *relational* phenomena rather than as inherent qualities in the mind of the thinker or in the objects/ phenomena themselves. Conceptions are abstractions from reality (as are all linguistic expressions) and these abstractions can be, and are, made in different ways in various 'provinces of meaning'. In accordance with this reasoning, the categories of description constitute the most significant outcome of research. In other words, the findings presented above, with respect to how people reason about evolution and motion, constitute the *results* of the research endeavour. They form the outcome of a systematic attempt to account for the various ways in which people perceive these particular phenomena. We have here an instance of a conceptual generalizability where the variation in conceptions arrived at applies to a very wide class of learning situations. If our research has managed to discern the conceptions of the phenomenon being investigated, we have – metaphorically speaking – a map of a territory in terms of which we can interpret how people conceive of reality.

So what is the use of this insight in other people's conceptions of reality? The answer is related to the particular knowledge interest that is prominent in educational contexts. Teaching and learning are communicative activities and they involve attempts to change people's conceptions of reality in order to adopt the particular forms of thought characteristic of specialized linguistic and cognitive communicative communities such as the ones represented by physicists, geographers, historians, etc. The use of insights from phenomenographic research provides intellectual tools that can be used when planning teaching (how is this phenomenon construed in everyday thinking?; what are the fundamental differences – if any – between the explanations and concepts used in everyday life and in the specific discipline with respect to phenomenon X?), when communicating with students as a framework for understanding what is being understood or misunderstood, and when evaluating the success of teaching.

The description of conceptions of phenomena can be seen as a metalanguage usable in the context of understanding the process of learning and in terms of which difficulties in understanding can be made explicit and reflected upon. This may sound a somewhat abstract enterprise. In fact, the attitude of consciously reflecting on how our interlocutors construe the world is not unnatural in certain settings such as when talking with young children in everyday conversations or when a lawyer explains to a client the specifics of a complex legal situation – to mention just two examples. In the work of Perry (Perry, 1970, and Chapter 7 in this book), it was precisely an interest in how students subjectively construe phenomena such as knowledge and learning that generated a picture of a variation that, in turn, played a significant role in the students' study activities and in their understanding of what the teachers were trying to put across.

The research process and the reliability of findings
Phenomenography is a form of 'rigorous qualitative analysis' (Entwistle, 1984). As described here, the research process has as an essential ingredient – the aim of generating a picture of the variation in human conceptions of phenomena in the world. The outcome of this endeavour results in a description of categories depicting conceptions of reality. A distinguishing feature of the research process is thus that the categories 'are systematically worked out in relation to the data during the course of research' (Glaser and Strauss, 1967, p 6). This type of work takes place in what Reichenbach (1938) refers to as the *context of discovery*, where the critical issue is one of providing concepts in terms of which the phenomena observed can be accounted for. It is thus not possible to prove that the categories are the best possible ones. The categories are the constructions of the researcher and there is always a possibility that another researcher would have arrived at a different categorization. In fact, to be logical, it follows from a constructivist conception of reality that the possibility of interpreting reality differently applies to the activity of describing conceptions of reality itself. So how is it possible to argue for the validity and reliability of the categories of description?

There are several different problems involved in these issues. One problem has to do with whether it is possible to delimit categories and to communicate their meanings. To deal with this particular aspect, a procedure of writing *judgement instructions* to be used by a co-judge can be used. These instructions then specify at a general level the differences between categories and provide examples of statements that should be considered as instances of conception A or B. The co-judging can then be understood as a process of testing if it is possible to communicate the findings to another person in a sufficiently explicit way that this person would classify the statements made by interviewees in the same way as the researcher has done. It is important to note that co-judging is a check of the communicability of categories and thus gives the researcher information that someone else can see the same differences in the material as he or she has done.

The process of writing judgement instructions serves as a mode of clarifying the essential differences between categories and the relationship between statements made by the participants and the category system. In most cases, the interjudge reliability is between 80 and 90%. Low interjudge agreement signals that there have been problems in communicating the meaning of the categories in a sufficiently explicit form so that the co-judge has been in a position to see what they mean in relation to the data. This can then be remedied by reformulating the instructions and repeating the judging with another co-judge. Reaching perfect agreement between judges is in most cases very difficult. The data do not always allow for a definite decision on people's conceptions of a phenomenon. A statement can be genuinely ambiguous in the sense that is is not possible to decide what is meant. This is not merely a technical problem in coding but reflects a concrete reality in which linguistic statements can be difficult to interpret.

While it is not possible to prove in a strict sense that the category system is the most appropriate one on the same set of data from which it derives, there are additional modes of dealing with the problem of validity. One of these modes of scrutinizing validity is through comparisons with other studies. Such cross-study comparison can be used to test the applicability of particular categories. The accumulation of knowledge thus takes place by examining results arrived at by different researchers and by scrutinizing the applicability of categories across investigations adopting a similar perspective.

Another source of verification of the appropriateness of a set of categories is the internal logic of the categories themselves. The examples of people's conceptions of price, evolution and force illustrate that differing conceptions of reality relate to each other in specific ways. There may be an internal structure to a category system in the sense that what separates conceptions of a phenomenon is what is assumed to be in need of being explained. In the case of force, the most significant difference lies in whether it is assumed that it is motion or rest that is the most suitable point of departure for an explanation of what one observes. Focusing on rest as the 'natural' state of an object implies a particular conception of force, while focusing on motion implies a different (and Newtonian) conception. In a similar way, looking at the bun and its constitutents when explaining the price implies one conception of price, while looking at the economic system in which the bun is being sold implies a different conception.

A further aspect of the internal structure of categories that depict different conceptions of a phenomenon is that learning can be described as the change from one conception within this structure to a different one. A good illustration of this is given in the chapter by White and Horwitz where students are provided with a set of computer-based learning experiences in order to help them change from an Aristotelian conception of force to a Newtonian one. In this sense, learning occurs when an individual changes his or her conception of a phenomenon. This change takes place within the structure depicted by the category system (provided, of course, that the category system has been derived from a broad enough body of data).

Concluding comments

A common feature of the contributions that make up this collection is an interest in learning of the kind that implies changes in our conceptions of reality. The problems dealt with concern how people acquire (or fail to acquire) modes of conceiving reality that are characteristic of scientific disciplines. A basic assumption that makes such an endeavour meaningful is that detailed knowledge of people's conceptions of reality forms an important basis for improving communication in education and for understanding the difficulties that students experience. Although the theoretical schools represented by the chapters in the remainder of this book differ, a common denominator is an interest in *meaning* – in 'ways of worldmaking' to borrow an expression from the philosopher Nelson Goodman (1978). In this chapter, we have attempted to give a general introduction to methodological issues prominent in such research and to present in more detail one attempt to deal systematically with the problem of analysing meaning – phenomenography. This approach has not been the explicit point of departure for all the research to be reported in the book. It has also not been possible to specify in detail at an algorithmic level exactly how a phenomenographic method can be applied. To some extent, the use of such an approach has to be adapted to the context in which it is being employed and the particular types of problems that are being pursued. An important strategy for learning about qualitative analysis is therefore by analogy with other studies carried out on a broad set of problems. In the present volume, the chapter by Lybeck provides the most thorough example of the phenomenographic perspective, but all the chapters enable us to see how the analysis of meaning can enhance research on student learning and contribute to the development of better teaching.

Acknowledgements
The research reported here has been financed by the Swedish Council for Research in the Humanities and Social Sciences.

References

Berger, P, and Luckmann, T (1967). *The Social Construction of Reality*. New York: Doubleday.

Borger, R, and Seaborne, A E M *The Psychology of Learning* (second edn) (1982). Harmondsworth, Middlesex: Penguin.

Bower, G, and Hilgard, E (1981). *Theories of Learning*. Englewood Cliffs, New Jersey: Prentice Hall.

Brumby, M (1984). Misconceptions about the concept of natural selection by medical biology students. *Science Education*, **68**, 493–503.

Dahlgren, L O (1978). Effects of university education on the conception of reality. Reports from the Department of Education, University of Göteborg, No 65. Dahlgren, L O (1984). Outcomes of learning. In: F Marton *et al.*

(eds), *The Experience of Learning*. Edinburgh: Scottish Academic Press.

Entwistle, N (1984). Contrasting perspectives on learning. In F Marton *et al.* (eds), *The Experience of Learning*. Edinburgh: Scottish Academic Press.

Glaser, B G, and Strauss, A L (1967). *The Discovery of Grounded Theory*. New York: Aldine.

Goodman, N (1978). *Ways of Worldmaking*. Indianapolis: Hackette Publishing.

Halldén, O (1987). The evolution of the species: Pupil perspective and school perspective. Paper presented at the Second EARLI Conference, Tübingen.

Horton, D and Turnhage, T (1976). *Human Learning*. Englewood Cliffs, New Jersey: Prentice Hall.

Jackson, B (1964). *Streaming: An Education System in Miniature*. London: Routledge and Kegan Paul.

Johansson, B (1981). Forces in motion. Technological students' conceptions of some basic phenomena in mechanics. Reports from the Department of Education, University of Göteborg, No 14.

Johansson, B, Marton, F and Svensson, L (1985). An approach to describing learning as change between qualitatively different conceptions. In: A L Pines and L H T West (eds), *Cognitive Structure and Conceptual Change*. New York: Academic Press.

Marton, F (1981). Phenomenography – Describing conceptions of the world around us. *Instructional Science*, **10**, 177–200.

Neisser, U (1982). Memory: What are the important questions? In: U Neisser (ed), *Memory Observed*. San Francisco: Freeman.

Pedersen, S (1985). Inheritance and adaptation. In: L O Dahlgren and R Säljö (eds), *Didactics at the University*. Stockholm: NBUC.

Perry, WG (1970). *Forms of Intellectual and Ethical Development in the College Years: A Scheme*. New York: Holt, Rinehart and Winston.

Piaget, J (1973). *The Child's Conception of the World*. St Albans: Paladin. (Original work published in 1926.)

Ramsden, P (1984). The context of learning. In: F Marton *et al.* (eds), *The Experience of Learning*. Edinburgh: Scottish Academic Press.

Reichenbach, H (1938). *Experience and Prediction*. Chicago: University of Chicago Press.

Rogoff, B (1984). Thinking and learning in social context. In: B Rogoff and J Lave (eds), *Everyday Cognition: Its Development in Social Context*. Cambridge, Massachusetts: Harvard University Press.

Rommetveit, R (1988). On literacy and the myth of literal meaning. In: R Säljö (ed), *The Written World*. Berlin, Heidelberg and New York: Springer-Verlag.

Svensson, L (1979). The context-dependent meaning of learning. Reports from the Institute of Education, University of Göteborg, No 2.

UNESCO (1972). *Learning To Be*. Paris: Unesco.

West, C and Foster, S (1976). *The Psychology of Human Learning and Instruction in Education*. Belmont: Jones Publications.

Part 2
Research into Practice: School Science Learning

Chapter 3

Implications of Recent Research for Improving Secondary School Science Learning

Leo West
Monash University, Australia

We stand at an important crossroads if we wish to take advantage of recent advances to improve learning in secondary schools.

In the last decade or so, a new movement in research in learning (mainly but not exclusively in science) has developed, and with that movement two important new conceptualizations (at least, for many of us on both sides of the research–teacher interface) of learning and research have emerged. In this chapter I trace the emergence of these two new (related) concepts and their implications for improving learning by reference to a case study of action research (or innovative teaching if one views it from a different perspective) in a secondary school. The final conclusions, however, are not confined either to secondary schools or to the learning of science.

A new field of research

Starting sometime in the 1970s, a new group of researchers began to investigate what students know before, during and after teaching, about some aspect of science (and, sometimes, other disciplines). 'Can this be new?', one might ask; 'Isn't that what tests have always done?' What *was* new was that researchers began to listen to what students said, using unusual ways of eliciting student talk about their knowledge.

The eliciting procedures included interviews about concepts, objects, instances, events, tasks, etc, all within the domain of a student's interests. For example, Osborne and Freyberg (1985) used cards with a person riding a bicycle (an instance) and asked: 'Is there a force on the bike?'; Nussbaum (1979) asked young students to explain how Columbus could sail around the world (an event); White and Gunstone (1980) asked science graduates to explain why electrical wires have a plastic coating (an object); Lybeck and his colleagues (see Chapter 5) used an apparently simple chemistry question: 'Which group of cylinders contains 1 mol of each element?' (a problem). All these researchers recorded the students' responses in detail, prompting the students to explain fully what they said. Champagne *et al.*(1980) introduced a techinque they called DOE (demonstrate, observe, explain) in which students were asked to write down their prediction of something that was about to be demonstrated, then to write down their observation and their explanation. Novak and Gowin (1984) and also Champagne *et al.* (1981) instructed students to construct concept maps about some area of their knowledge.

The data in all these investigations were student discourse. Unlike conventional research these data were not transformed into scores or test results. The use of student discourse as the data was an important development. As was suggested in Chapter 1, students can be very good at answering test questions, and at being able to say the right words in response to questions, but when their knowledge is explored by in-depth questioning they often reveal conceptions that are at variance with their test answers or their first responses to questions. Ultimately, of course, the student discourse data have to be transformed in some way.

The transformation of the data has mainly been of three types. The simplest was to point to serious gaps in learning, either quoting specific examples of student discourse or classifying the responses into categories and providing counts or percentages of the incidences of these categories. An extension of this approach was to infer from the responses the existence of a small number of internally consistent sets of ideas or conceptions. These have been called 'alternative frameworks' or 'alternative conceptions'. The term 'misconceptions' has been generally avoided, partly because misconceptions are, after all, conceptions and their 'mis-' derives externally because some expert group favours a particular conception (is a Marxist conceptualization of wealth always a misconception?), and partly because the term 'mis-' has a negative connotation which some researchers, at least, would prefer to avoid. A third type of transformation was quite different. Some researchers produced structures of student knowledge, semantic networks, cognitive structure, concept maps, call them what you will. These were attempts to capture what students knew, the nature of the relationships that students perceived between the components of what they knew, and the overall structuring they provided for a larger set of things they knew. In the next sections I provide a limited number of examples of each of these kinds of transformations.

Serious gaps in learning – some examples
Science graduates who were undertaking a Diploma in Education were interviewed by White and Gunstone (1980) about simple physics concepts. The following are some of the examples quoted by the interviewers.

Conductors

Conductors help electric current keep going.

AC,DC

Perhaps DC and AC have something to to do with the way a battery is connected. I think we have DC in houses.

Plastic insulation on wires

The coating on the wire is an insulator. This insulating coating keeps electrons within their pathway, on wires preventing any loss of electricity.

The plastic coating on wires has a resistance. Perhaps resistance could be reduced by devising good outer coatings.

For readers not familiar with physics, these statements are outrageously incorrect, especially when made by science graduates. They could be compared to a statement like: 'Margaret Thatcher is the President of the United States.'

West, Fensham and Garrard (1985) interviewed freshmen chemistry students after they had completed a section on phase changes and phase diagrams. The interviews used, as stimuli, real-world applications of the content taught. The following extract is from an interview about pressure cookers. The interviewee was an excellent student who had demonstrated mastery of the topic, and in particular that the boiling point is not fixed but changes with pressure (indeed, the student had calculated the boiling point of water at a pressure for which the answer was *not* 100 degrees Celsius).

I: What's the advantage of a pressure cooker?

S: Cooks things faster.

I: Why do they cook things faster?

S: I suppose the increase in pressure.

I: Anything else?

S: I don't know.

I: Let's take a different tack. If you are cooking in an oven, how can you cook faster?

S: Turn up the temperature.

I: What is the limit on temperature?

S: About 500 degrees.

I: What if you are cooking in a saucepan on top of the stove?

53

S: Depends on what you are cooking.

I: Say you are cooking peas or beans in water, what is the temperature limit?

S: 100 degrees.

I: Let's get back to the pressure cooker, what do you think is happening inside the pressure cooker?

S: It's exceeding that limit.

I: How come?

S: Increasing the pressure. I don't know what you do on the phase diagram. Just must be. I don't know.

I: So you are saying increasing the pressure increases . . . what else?

S: Must increase. No, it can't increase the temperature . . . water boils at 100 . . . or can it . . . I don't know.

(West, Fensham and Garrard, 1985)

This is an amazing contradiction. Here is a student who, having stated that the boiling point is not fixed but changes, is unable to draw what is – to the student at that point in the interview – the obvious conclusion because of a belief that 'water boils at 100 degrees' (a fixed boiling point).

Gunstone and White (1981) used the DOE technique with a group of physics students. One of the demonstrations was a pulley with a bucket of sand and a weight at rest at equal heights. These were shifted so that the bucket was higher and held in that position. Students were asked to write down their predictions of what would happen when the system was released. When they had done this, the system was released, and the students were asked to write down their observations and explain any variations between their expectations and their observation. As part of the analysis of the students' responses, Gunstone and White reported the following expectations:

System will remain stationary 54%
System will return to original position 35%
Bucket will fall 9%
Block will fall 2%

The first answer is correct and its understanding is fundamental at the level of physics studied by these students.

Findings such as these, which are common, have a 'shock' value. We frequently encounter students who have studied a subject at a high level, and have been successful in the conventional ways, but who display naive and often contradictory conceptions when their knowledge is explored in depth. These errors are so serious that we are forced to ask: 'What is going on in science education?'

Alternative frameworks – some examples

Nussbaum (1979) transformed the data from interviews (reproduced in Figure 1) with elementary-school children about their knowledge of earth as a cosmic body into six categories or alternative frameworks.

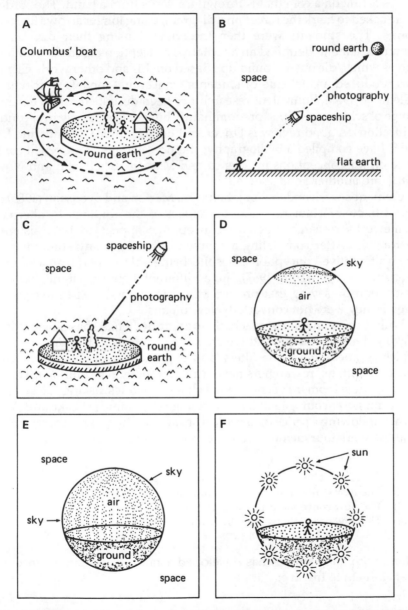

Figure 1. *Children's alternative conceptions of the earth (redrawn from Nussbaum, 1979)*

The conceptions shown in Figure 1 are not individual errors – they are six internally consistent sets of conceptions about the phenomenon of the earth. They are an abstraction from the interview transcripts, representing six different or 'alternative' conceptions that exist in this group of students, and they can be found in other similar groups. (Nussbaum's research was replicated with samples in the USA and Israel).

Clement (1982) asked students on a pre-engineering course about the forces acting on a coin that is thrown upwards from a hand. The students were asked to mark the forces on a diagram, using longer arrows for longer forces. The students were then interviewed using their diagrams as stimuli. Clement identified an alternative conception based on a notion of forces which 'die out' or 'build up'. Based on this and other work, Clement has produced a catalogue of students' conceptual models in mechanics (Clement, 1983). Equivalent research has been described for an extensive range of science concepts, predominantly but not exclusively in secondary education. (A good review is Driver and Erickson, 1983; Pfundt and Duit, 1985, have compiled a bibliography; the proceedings of a Cornell conference on Misconceptions in Science and Mathematics [Helm and Novak, 1983], are another good source.)

Clement's work and that of Johansson, Marton and Svensson (1985) (see also Chapter 8) illustrate another aspect of the findings in alternative frameworks research. Such preconceptions appear to be resistant to instruction. After completing a course in physics, many students retain their alternative conceptions, despite being able to perform well in the examination. Hewson (1987), in a different context, highlighted this distinction by saying that physics students learned well to 'Newtonize' even if they were not converted 'Newtonians'.

Within this general approach, the descriptive phase has slowed down. Having demonstrated that there are serious defects in learning outcomes which escape examination filters, and the existence of persistent alternative conceptions, researchers have turned to potential solutions. This has seen the development of conceptual change theories, asking the question: How can we encourage students to change their minds? Strike and Posner (1982), following a series of empirical studies by them and others, theorize that there are four elements in conceptual change:

(1) There must be dissatisfaction with existing conceptions.
(2) The new conceptions must be minimally understood.
(3) The new conceptions must be plausible.
(4) The new conceptions must be fruitful.

Along with such studies has developed a range of teaching procedures that all seem to involve:

(1) an awareness phase in which alternative conceptions are articulated and identified in the students;

(2) a disequilibrium phase in which anomalies, discrepancies, etc, are introduced;
(3) a reformation phase in which a conceptualization that resolves the anomalies is presented and discussed.

One of the lessons from this research is that conceptual change is not as easy as one might expect. Champagne, Gunstone and Klopfer (1985) described the reactions of some science graduates to a week-long programme of conceptual change in physics:

I'm shattered! Didn't realise how devastating it could be to have a deep rooted belief proved wrong. Can I blame my physics teacher? It would be all right if some dummy didn't pose a question which could be used to support the opposite argument. Seriously though, very instructive. I don't know if I'm going to be able to last the distance. I'm mentally exhausted after each session and the effort to hold out when I'm wrong is very draining. Great fun so far even if I hate it at odd times.

(p 176)

Cognitive structures – some examples

West, Fensham and Garrard (1985) conducted a series of studies aimed at describing students' knowledge at the end of self-contained classes in chemistry. Their interest was partly in the things that students knew, but also on how that knowledge was integrated and differentiated. They produced two-dimensional representations of individual students' knowledge which contained two types of 'nodes'. Student-generated propositions were organized into an overall relational structure joined by lines. On the lines were written the student's description of the nature of the relationship between two nodes. Added on to this propositional skeleton were skills (procedural knowledge), examples and images that the student related to specific propositional nodes. The overall structure, which is different for different students, is generated by an algorithm based on student rating of the degree of relationship between the concepts or ideas represented by the propositions.

Much simpler procedures, in which the students construct their own concept maps, have been used. Novak (see, for example, Novak and Gowin, 1984) has used student–constructed concept maps extensively – mainly as a 'metalearning' technique (a technique that helps students to reflect on their own learning) – but also as a means of describing what students know. Champagne *et al.* (1981, 1985) have used a card-sorting procedure, which they call ConSAT (concept structuring analysis technique), to help students construct graphic representations of their cognitive structures. These descriptions of what students know have revealed that they tend not to relate learned concepts, skills, etc, either to each other or to knowledge they already have. Students tend to compartmentalize their knowledge without relating it to other knowledge.

This has led to research focusing on developing and encouraging integration and differentiation. Novak's use of concept maps and vee maps are procedures with these as goals (see, for example, Gurley, 1982). A related approach has been to attempt descriptions of the content as integrated wholes rather than as lists of discrete bits of knowledge. Fisher and others (1986) have developed microcomputer software to describe the content of a set of biology courses. These consist of concept maps of eight to ten concepts at any one time on the screen, which can be searched up so that a more general concept can become the centre of a more general map, or down so that a more specific concept can become the centre of a more detailed map. For example, a map that has 'nucleus' as its central concept has 'chromosome' as a subordinate concept. By calling up 'chromosome', a new map will appear with chromosome as the central concept, nucleus as a superordinate concept, and DNA as a subordinate concept. One can repeat this process with DNA, etc. Each map (of eight to ten concepts) describes an arrangement of concepts and their interrelationships. These programs are meant for both teachers and students, their aim being to emphasize and demonstrate the nature of the relationships that exist and that can be built between the new concepts to be met in the course. They are, in a sense, 'cognitive objectives'.

The elements of this research movement

The short descriptive overview given above is not meant to be a review; it fails to mention many of the important contributions. It is included to provide a skeleton for understanding the following elements of this research movement:

(1) The methodology is qualitative, with the data being extended student discourse, which even in its transformed state is readily understood by people outside the research movement. In most instances the methodology can be, and has been, adapted by teachers for use with their own students – not so much as research but as part of teaching.
(2) The conclusions are descriptive. Descriptions of students' knowledge are what are communicated; and this has been done without any attempt to blame teachers, since the findings tend to be reported for populations of learners. There are few attempts to tell teachers what they should do.
(3) The research questions are of interest and relevance to teachers; they concentrate on knowledge of content. To the extent that they deal with pedagogy, they deal with the pedagogy of that content. (I have borrowed the term 'pedagogy of content' from Marton, 1986).
(4) The findings imply a view of learning as the development of personal knowledge rather than as the ability to repeat other people's knowledge. This element will be discussed further in the next section.

A new view of learning

Concurrent with this research movement, and I think to a considerable extent because of it, a new view of learning (sometimes called 'constructivist') has developed. Let me begin with what learning is *not*, and echo some of the arguments developed in previous chapters. It is not repeating teachers' knowledge or textbook knowledge. Learning involves constructing one's own understanding of reality; making one's own sense of other people's understanding of the world. Learning involves constructing (Wittrock, 1985, uses the term 'generating') meanings. In the process of learning in school, the learner must seek a meaningful relationship between his or her own intuitive understanding of some phenomena (see Pines and West, 1986, for a discussion of this relationship from a Vygotskian perspective). In this regard, Fensham (1980) made a useful distinction between children's science, teacher's science and scientist's science.

This view of learning presents a particular dilemma in science learning. On the one hand are the scientific orthodoxies: the scientists' views of the world have developed over a long period and, although not fixed for ever, are certainly shared by an influential community. On the other hand are children's intuitive beliefs, which are based on their experience in the world and which seem real to them. A classic example is the Newtonian concept of the relationship between force and movement and the widespread common-sense concept that a body stops moving when an applied force 'wears out' or is 'used up'. Reconciling these conceptions so that the learner's generated meaning converges with the scientists' meaning is not a simple task, and it is not achieved by demanding only that students are able to repeat faithfully textbook knowledge and carry out a group of set 'problem' tasks.

It is not true that all science learning involves such a gulf between a student's conventional meaning and that of the scientist, although there has been a tendency for those taking a constructivist perspective to concentrate on conceptual change of this kind. Pines and West (1986) described three kinds of learning constructions, although they used the term 'conceptual understanding'. Rather than repeat their analysis here, I will give illustrative examples. It is very difficult to observe someone in the process of constructing meaning (how can we observe what is going on in someone's mind?), so the first example is drawn from my personal learning experience. Pines and West labelled this kind 'conceptual development'.

Conceptual development
When I was learning physical chemistry, I learned about two-component phase diagrams, that is, the temperature and composition conditions under which one or two phases can be present (phases are solid, liquid and gas). There are three types: solid-liquid systems, gas-liquid systems, and liquid-liquid systems. Typical examples are shown in Figure 2. I must point out that these three types were taught in different sections of the course and were not actually related together. It is a curious phenomenon that liquid-liquid systems can occur as a U-shape, an inverted U-shape or as an enclosed oval (in Figure 2 only the latter is shown).

While studying one day I tried to draw the solid-liquid, the gas-liquid and the liquid-liquid systems on the same diagram (something I have

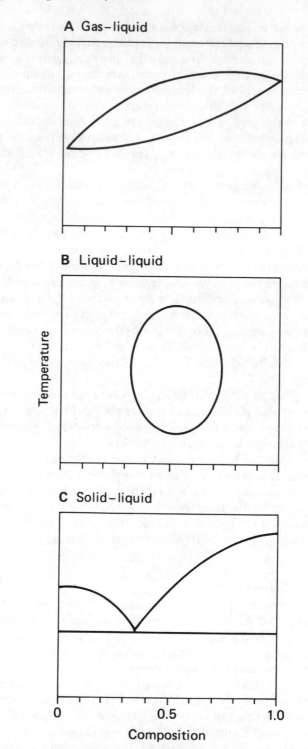

Figure 2. *Two-component phase diagrams (idealized)*

never seen done in a book). I drew the first two to start with, then as I tried to add the liquid-liquid system it became obvious why it might sometimes be a U-shape, sometimes an inverted U, and sometimes a full oval, depending on the relative positioning between the other two (see Figure 3). The oval sometimes ran into the other diagrams. If this was true, there

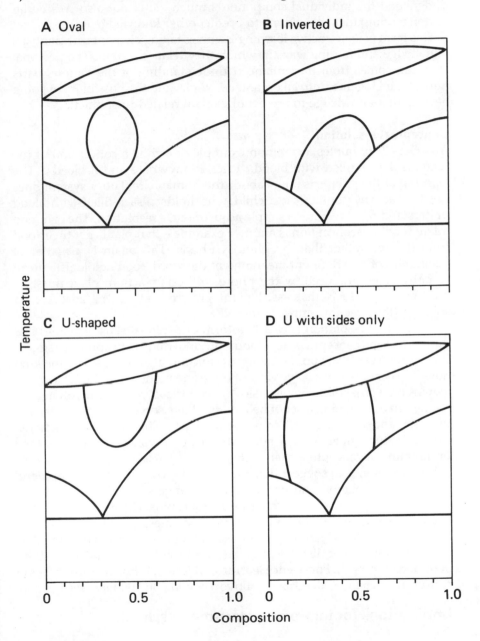

Figure 3. *Different ways of combining the three idealized phase diagrams*

may be some system that has a shape like that in shown in Figure 3 (*d*) – an oval with both top and bottom missing. This prediction turned out to be correct.

What had happened for me here was that I had brought together different components of knowledge and in combining them had not only understood the individual components much better but also created an understanding that allowed me to predict other knowledge.

This form of constructive learning involves taking elements of scientist's knowledge and finding ways in which they relate together. The personal meaning comes from the enhanced understanding of the various parts now related together into an organized whole, and the possibility of going beyond that knowledge to predict or explain related phenomena.

Conceptual resolution
Ausubel (1975) quotes a common example of a child's conception of the body as a sack filled with blood: 'Prick it anywhere and it bleeds.' The learning of the scientists' view about the human circulatory system does not lead to any conflict for a child who holds a sack-filled-with-blood understanding. It requires a simple adjustment, a resolution. The common 'plant food' misconception is another example – that plants get their food from the soil rather than by photosynthesis. This again is a matter of resolution, of two different meanings of the word 'food': biologists mean carbohydrates produced by the photosynthesis reaction; plant nursery-men mean products that assist plant growth and can be absorbed in solution (they use the term 'plant food').

Conceptual resolution is clearly a form of personal sense-making. It is different from conceptual development, and from conceptual change – Pines and West (1986) prefer the term 'conceptual exchange' – of the kind noted earlier between a naive view of force and motion and the Newtonian view. Conceptual exchange is a slow and difficult process, involving the student in abandoning a set of beliefs that have served him or her well in the past, and adopting a different set of beliefs. The difficulty was noted earlier in the quote from a student teacher involved in a week-long programme of conceptual change in physics (p 57).

I do not intend to suggest that these three – conceptual development, conceptual resolution and conceptual exchange – exhaust the ways in which we can differentiate such terms as 'conceptual change' or 'qualitative changes in a student's conceptualizations'. My message is that these latter terms do not refer to a unitary process, and there is much to be gained by searching for further discriminations (dare I say 'further understandings of understanding'?). For science learning, at least, I think the three types of conceptual change described above would be widely recognized.

Implications for improving learning in schools

The two movements described so far in this chapter occurred surprisingly easily, new research having grown and become legitimized remarkably quickly. Education research journals, once dominated by tightly designed 'laboratory' studies now contain many reports of qualitative investigations of student knowledge and conceptual change, sometimes even based on single cases. The new views of learning have risen quickly, like the phoenix, from the ashes of demonstrated failure in learning that dominated the early research findings. A plethora of books and articles describing the new views of learning, with various emphases, appeared during 1982-86 (eg, Marton, Hounsell and Entwistle, 1984; Osborne and Freyberg, 1985; West and Pines, 1985; Driver and Erickson, 1983; Gilbert, Osborne and Fensham, 1982).

The realization that learning is not just repeating other people's knowledge, and the evidence that many students can do very well in school examinations (even graduate from university in science) without having acquired personal meanings for the knowledge they can state, brings with it new responsibilities. Armed with this knowledge, can teachers simply leave it to the students? Are their responsibilities met if they present scientists' knowledge and test that students can repeat that knowledge? Or should they change their methods of teaching to help the students generate their own meanings?

Among researchers in this area there is general agreement that such changes should occur. We are poised, one might think, to lead a revolution in teaching and learning practice. Research studies are beginning to appear that seem to point the way (Brown, 1987 and Hewson, 1987 are two examples from last year's American Educational Research Association meeting). White and Horwitz's chapter in this volume is an excellent example. Their ThinkerTools approach had impressive effects: for example, sixth-grade students performed better than high school physics students (six years older on average) on a physics transfer test.

Yet I conclude on a pessimistic note. The next steps will be much more difficult. Changing the nature of the learning that goes on in schools demands changing teaching practices, changing conceptions of teaching, changing teachers', students', and society's perceptions of what schools should do – for example the perception that the transfer of information, often by students copying teacher's notes from the blackboard, is normal and appropriate school behaviour. Can we look to educational research and researchers to lead that revolution? History does not fill me with confidence. I have a picture of educational researchers on a train; we can move around inside, we can look out of the windows, some of us might be in a position to slow it down a bit, but the train's direction is set and we can do little about changing that. That sort of change will need to come in schools.

Several researchers within this movement have recognized this. Marton (1986) argued that we cannot generalize the findings, only the methodology (see also the last chapter in this book). His point, as I understand it, is that only by involving teachers in the process of understanding their pupils' conceptions will change occur in teachers' conceptions of teaching and learning. He sees it, correctly I feel, as a teacher–led, not a researcher-led, revolution. Researchers can bring their programmes into schools for a week, a month, perhaps longer, and teachers and students will tolerate, even enthusiastically embrace, the 'experiment'. When the researchers are gone, classroom practices will continue in their normal way, hardly perturbed by the experience. I am not convinced that such forays into schools, nor exhortation by researchers, will do much to change teaching and learning practices in schools. I am so convinced of this social momentum of classroom practices that I want to complete this chapter with some evidence of how difficult it is to change. I do this not with a sense of hopelessness, but with a sense of reality. If we want to create changes in the nature of teaching and learning in schools, then we need to recognize the extent of the obstacles.

The evidence to be presented in this last section derives from an action research project at a suburban high school in Melbourne, Australia. The project is known as PEEL – Project for Enhancing Effective Learning; a project aimed at improving the quality of teaching and learning. PEEL is a two-year project involving ten teachers and five classes across three grade levels (Years 7, 9 and 10) and six subject areas (English, Integrated Studies, Geography, History, Commerce and Science) in a single secondary school (Years 7 to 12). It is a different type of research, for it is a teachers' project. The project was initiated by teachers who had come under the influence of researchers at Monash University. The teachers set up the project, gaining the co-operation of, initially, a total of 13 teachers in one school and support from the Principal and Vice-Principal. Educational researchers acted as consultants or 'friends', but both the initiation and the conduct of the project were undertaken by the teachers.

The aims of the project were to create an environment where learning is independent and effective, where students learn how to learn, where learners are active not passive, where they learn with understanding and with control over the process – and where the teaching fosters such outcomes. I cannot do justice to the full meaning of the aims; they grew and changed as the different teachers and students interpreted them in their own way. To give a flavour I quote one of the teachers, Damien Hynes:

There is a subtle difference between telling students to ask questions, telling them to think about what they did last lesson, telling them to find problems in the topics being studied and teaching them to perform these activities, or creating an atmosphere in which they can take more initiative for their own learning.

(Hynes, in Baird and Mitchell, 1986, p 28)

The teaching strategies used by the teachers were varied but have included most of the following: reflection on what learning has occurred, generating student questions, interpretive discussions, extended wait-time, concept maps, reflective thinking. Again, a list such as this does little justice to what teachers actively did: a feeling for that can be obtained by reading the teachers' chapters in Baird and Mitchell (1986).

The origins of PEEL lie very much in the findings of the movements described in the earlier sections of this chapter. 'Instances of poor under-standing by apparently successful learners', research on 'children's science' and 'alternative conceptions' are cited explicitly as influences, and an inspection of any of the teachers' chapters in Baird and Mitchell (1986) will highlight these influences. The participant teachers' constructivist conception of learning is obvious. The PEEL project was aimed at changing the nature of learning as noted above. As such, the project's goals were similar to those of many of the authors of this volume, but that is not crucial to my argument. What we have at the school is a comprehensive action research project that aimed to change, in the mainstream of the school, the nature of teaching and learning. The decisions of what changes to make were in the hands of teachers, not researchers. Since these teachers talk to each other, they will obviously try similar techniques in their different subjects.

If the above smacks of general cross-discipline 'theories of instruction' that are heresy to some of us, then herewith lies our problem. For in the process of action research where teachers have control of events, researchers have given up their rights of veto.

And what of the outcomes . . . ? A reading of the reports of progress after the first year leaves me with strong impressions. The first is of difficulties. This was an extremely difficult experience for the teachers and the students. Highly motivated teachers imbued with a conviction that what they were doing was right were shattered by their lack of initial success and by self-doubts about their teaching abilities. Even though it turned out well in the end for most of them – and there are some wonderful anecdotes of achievement of the kinds of success they were seeking – one cannot help forming the impression from their stories that they had been to hell and back in the process.

For the students I can do no better than quote from Linda Dibley, a student of grade 10A:

Originally, when we were told that, through PEEL, we could be in more control of our learning, it was hard for us to comprehend. We couldn't see any way we could be in control of our learning, simply because we never had been. So, right from the start, we were sceptical as to the amount of success this project would have. After all, teachers still had a syllabus to follow, so how could we be in complete control of our learning? We needed something to show us we could have this control. But, there were no short-term benefits so we were quite agreeable to tossing out PEEL entirely.

Now, though, reflecting back on the whole year, it is easier to see the long-term benefits:

— an understanding that learning is many things: from asking questions and partaking in discussion, to understanding what you are doing and why;
— improved question-asking;
— awareness of lesson tasks and information covered. This understanding and awareness is necessary so that, in future, we may continue to improve our learning habits.

These benefits are more than simply benefits of this project. They are now a part of our learning strategy which will be carried on with us in years to come. Yet it was not an easy task. Coupled with the pluses of the project are the minuses, the major ones being:

— boredom;
— repetitiveness through tasks performed in consecutive classes (eg, a concept map in commerce during Period 2 and then again in science, Period 3), and through teachers using the same tasks in several of their lessons (eg, a learning checklist once a week);
— difficulty in understanding the information;
— time wasted on PEEL tasks and PEEL discussions . . .

I was glad at the end of the year to see PEEL disappear from my immediate life, due mainly I think to the way I had been swamped by it that year. Yet, at the same time, I was sorry to think PEEL would disappear forever. It helped me throughout the year and definitely inspires a new, and I think better way of teaching and learning in schools. Now, in May 1986, I have retained much of what I learned through PEEL. Picking up on what teachers are saying, thinking more about notes from the board as I write them down and hence understanding them, querying any answers or statements I don't understand or agree with, all have become habit for me.

(Dibley, in Baird and Mitchell, 1986, pp 96-7)

My second impression is of a powerful social momentum (hence my train metaphor). Teachers, students, parents, society, have clear expectations of what teachers should do in schools and what students should do, and these expectations are not easily challenged. I cannot capture it better than one of the PEEL students: 'We are doing too much thinking and not enough work' (Mitchell, in Baird and Mitchell, 1986, p 56).

The direction of the train will not be changed easily, but PEEL shows that it can happen. I am not sure how easily PEEL can be repeated in other contexts; nor whether the action research mode is crucial to achieving such changes. What is clear, however, is that PEEL had so much going for it – ten committed teachers, supported internally and externally; regular weekly meetings for mutual support; a charismatic innovator urging them on; a feeling that they were in control, and many other positive aspects – and PEEL experienced immense difficulties. The lesson is that change will not result from the urgings of educational researchers, no matter how sure their ground; change will not come from committed individual teachers defying the conventions. It is a depressing lesson, but one we need to embrace if we want to go anywhere other than where the present train is taking us.

References

Ausubel, D (1975). Private communication during a visit to Cornell University.

Baird, J R and Mitchell, I J (eds) (1986). *Improving the Quality of Teaching and Learning*. Melbourne: Monash University Printery.

Brown, D E (1987) Overcoming misconceptions in mechanics: A comparison of two example-based teaching strategies. Paper presented at the AERA Annual Meeting, Washington, DC.

Champagne, A B , Gunstone, R F and Klopfer, L E (1985). Effecting changes in cognitive structures among physics students. In: L H T West and A L Pines (eds), *Cognitive Structure and Conceptual Change*. New York: Academic Press.

Champagne, A B, Klopfer, L E and Anderson, J H (1980). Factors influencing the learning of classical mechanics. *American Journal of Physics*, **48**, 1074-9.

Champagne, A B, Klopfer, L E, DeSena, A T and Squires, D A (1981). Structural representations of students' knowledge before and after science instruction. *Journal of Research in Science Teaching*, **18**, 97-111.

Clement, J J (1982). Students' perceptions in introductory mechanics. *American Journal of Physics*, **50**, 66-71.

Clement, J J (1983). Students' alternative conceptions in mechanics: A coherent system of preconceptions. In: H Helm and J D Novak (eds), *Proceedings of the Misconceptions in Science and Mathematics Conference*. Ithaca, New York: Cornell University.

Dibley, L, Chapter 6 (1986). In: J R Baird and I J Mitchell, *Improving the Quality of Teaching and Learning*. Melbourne: Monash University Printery.

Driver, R and Erickson, G (1983). Theories-in-action: Some theoretical and empirical issues in the study of students' conceptual frameworks. *Studies in Science Education*, **10**, 37-60.

Fensham, P J (1980). A research base for new objectives of science teaching. *Research in Science Education*, **10**, 22-3.

Fisher, K, and others of the University of California Davis SEMNET group (1986). Paper set: Semantic network analysis of biology knowledge. Presented at the Annual Meeting of the National Association for Research in Science Teaching, San Francisco.

Gilbert, J K, Osborne, R J and Fensham, P J (1982). Children's science and its consequences for teaching. *Science Education*, **66** 4, 623-33.

Gunstone, R F and White, R T (1981). Understanding of gravity. *Science Education*, **65**, 291-9.

Gurley, L (1982). Use of Gowin's vee and concept mapping strategies to teach responsibility for learning in high school biological sciences. Unpublished PhD thesis, Cornell University.

Helm, H and Novak, J D (1983). *Misconceptions in Science and Mathematics*. Ithaca, New York: Cornell University.

Hewson, M (1987). The restructuring of classical textbook knowledge for problem solving: A conceptual change approach. Paper presented at the AERA Annual Meeting, Washington DC.

Hynes, D, Chapter 4 (1986). In: J R Baird and I J Mitchell (eds), *Improving the Quality of Teaching and Learning*. Melbourne: Monash University Printery.

Johansson, B, Marton, F and Svensson, L (1985). An approach to describing learning as change between qualitatively different conceptions. In: L H T West and A L Pines (eds), *Cognitive Structure and Conceptual Change*. New

York: Academic Press.

Marton, F, Hounsell, D and Entwistle, N (eds) (1984). *The Experience of Learning*. Edinburgh: Scottish Academic Press.

Marton, F (1986). Some reflections on the improvement of learning. In: J Bowden (ed), *Student Learning: Research into Practice – the Marysville Symposium*. Melbourne: Centre for the Study of Higher Education, University of Melbourne.

Mitchell, I J (1986). Establishing PEEL. In: J R Baird and I J Mitchell (eds), *Improving the Quality of Teaching and Learning*. Melbourne: Monash University Printery.

Novak, J D and Gowin, D B (1984). *Learning How to Learn*. Cambridge: Cambridge University Press.

Nussbaum, J (1979). Children's conception of the earth as a cosmic body: A cross age study. *Science Education*, **63**, 83-93.

Osborne, R and Freyberg, P (1985). *Learning in Science*. Auckland: Heinemann.

Pfundt, H and Duit, R (1985). *Bibliography: Students' Alternative Frameworks and Science Education*. Kiel, West Germany: Institut für die Pädagogik der Naturwissenschaften.

Pines, A L and West, L H T (1986). Conceptual understanding and science learning: An interpretation of research within a sources-of-knowledge framework. *Science Education*, **70**, 583-603.

Strike, K and Posner, G (1982). Conceptual change and science teaching. *European Journal of Science Teaching*, **4**, 231-40.

West, L H T, Fensham, P J and Garrard, J E (1985). Describing the cognitive structures of learners following instruction in chemistry. In: L H T West and A L Pines (eds), *Cognitive Structure and Conceptual Change*. New York: Academic Press.

West, L H T and Pines, A L (eds) (1985). *Cognitive Structure and Conceptual Change*. New York: Academic Press.

White, R T and Gunstone, R F (1980). Converting memory protocols to scores on several dimensions. *Proceedings of the Conference of the Australian Association for Research in Education*, Sydney.

Wittrock, M C (1985). Learning science by generating new conceptions from old ideas. In: L H T West and A L Pines (eds), *Cognitive Structure and Conceptual Change*. New York: Academic Press.

Chapter 4

Computer Microworlds and Conceptual Change: A New Approach to Science Education

Barbara White and Paul Horwitz
BBN Laboratories, Cambridge, Massachussets, USA

Introduction

Research has demonstrated that students can succeed in high school, and even on college physics courses, while still maintaining many of their misconceptions and without acquiring an understanding of the physical principles addressed in their programmes (Caramazza *et al.*, 1981; Clement, 1982; diSessa, 1982; Larkin *et al.*, 1980; McDermott, 1984; Trowbridge and McDermott, 1981; Viennot, 1979; White, 1983; and many others). For example, they make incorrect predictions about what will happen to the motion of a ball when it emerges after passing through a spiral tube (McClosky *et al.*, 1980). Such questions do not call for computation or the algebraic manipulation of formulae; rather, they require an *understanding of the implications* of fundamental tenets of Newtonian mechanics. Students' failure to answer such questions correctly reveals a lack of knowledge of the causal principles that underly the formulae they have been taught.

We believe that at an early age students need experiences that will enable them to acquire accurate causal models for how forces affect the motions of objects (White and Frederiksen, 1986). This will inhibit the development of misconceptions and foster the type of understanding that many older students appear to lack. In contrast to our view, many cognitive and educational theorists believe that attempts to teach children physics will inevitably fail (see, for example, Shayer and Adey, 1981). They argue that understanding physical principles requires formal operational thinking (Piaget and Garcia, 1964), and that many students have not reached this stage of cognitive development at high school or even college level, let alone at elementary school level. Consequently, such students cannot be expected to master physical principles. We have found this not to be the case. This chapter will describe an instructional approach that enabled sixth graders (aged about 11 years) to understand important aspects of Newtonian mechanics. Further, it will illustrate how they also began to learn about the nature of science – what are scientific laws, how do they evolve, and why are they useful?

The progression of microworlds and subject matter

Our objective was for students to evolve a mental model of sufficient sophistication to enable them to analyse projectile motion problems (ie problems involving motion under a constant, uniform gravitational force). The desired model would incorporate such fundamental concepts of Newtonian mechanics as force, velocity, and acceleration, as well as causal principles, such as forces cause changes in velocity. In order to enable the students to acquire such a causal model, we created a progression of increasingly complex microworlds. Associated with each microworld is a set of problem-solving activities and experiments designed to help the students discover the laws governing the microworld. The design of the curriculum was based on careful studies of the students' conceptions of phenomena related to projectile motion. This chapter illustrates how teaching can be improved by applying our knowledge of students' conceptions.

The microworlds gradually introduce the full set of principles needed to analyse projectile motion problems. All of them require students to control the motion of a computer-generated graphic object via the application of forces. Within these simulations, the complications introduced by friction and gravity can be selectively eliminated, allowing students to encounter first simpler situations obeying Newton's first law (objects do not change their velocity unless a force is applied to them), and later to analyse more complex situations in terms of such basic laws. In addition, the microworlds incorporate a number of different representations for the application of forces and for the motion of objects. For example, there is the datacross (see Figure 1), which is essentially a pair of crossed 'thermometers' that register the horizontal and vertical velocity components of an object via the amount of 'mercury' in them. And there are wakes (also shown in Figure 1) that provide a record of an object's past speed and direction of motion by leaving a mark on the screen at fixed time intervals. These representations allow the effects of forces on an object's motion and velocity components to be directly observed, and thereby facilitate students' attempts to formulate the principles governing these causes and effects.

Microworld 1

At the beginning of the curriculum, we introduce a simple one-dimensional microworld which has no friction or gravity. In this world, students try to control the motion of an object (referred to as the 'dot') by applying fixed-size impulses to the right (→) or to the left (←). The students observe that whenever they apply an impulse to the dot, it causes a change in its speed: if the impulse is applied in the same direction as the dot is moving,

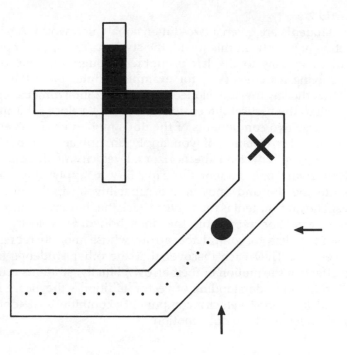

Figure 1. *The representation of motion within the microworlds.*

In this game, one must control the motion of the dot so that it navigates the track and stops on the target ×. The shaded circle in the middle of the angled path is the dot. It represents a physical object which may be given fixed-sized impulses in the left – right or up – down directions. In this diagram the dot has been given the (optional) property of leaving 'wakes' in the form of little dots laid down at regular time intervals. These denote, by their position and relative separation, the past history of the motion. The large cross in the middle of the figure is the 'datacross' – a device for displaying the instantaneous values of the X and Y velocity components. Here the datacross is depicting a velocity inclined at +45 degrees to the horizontal. The arrows at the bottom and right side of the diagram continually point to the dot, unless it leaves the screen, in which case they 'get stuck' at the edge of the screen. They represent the X and Y coordinates of the dot's position, and are useful for determining its location to within a quadrant when it is off the screen. Their motions, while the dot is on the screen, dynamically illustrate the X and Y components of the dot's velocity.

it adds to its speed; applied in the opposite direction, it subtracts from the speed. In this way, the students discover that a formalism they learned in second grade, scalar arithmetic (eg 3 – 2 1), will enable them to make predictions about the effect that a particular impulse, or sequence of impulses will have on the motion of the dot. As part of this process, the students have discovered a corollary of Newton's first law – whenever you apply an impulse to an object, you change its velocity.

Microworld 2

Next, the students are given a two-dimensional microworld. Again, there is no friction or gravity. In this world, the students can apply impulses up or down, as well as to the left or right. Through carefully designed problem-solving activities (see, for example, White, 1984) the students discover that the law they developed for the horizontal dimension applies equally well to the vertical dimension of the dot's velocity. Further, they learn that these two components of the dot's motion are independent of one another – for instance, if you apply an upwards or downwards impulse, it has no effect on the horizontal velocity of the dot. (This is learned by giving one student the capability to apply only horizontal impulses to the dot and another the capability to apply only vertical impulses. The first student is then given a task that requires controlling the arrow whose motion represents the dot's horizontal velocity, and the second student has to control the arrow whose motion represents its vertical velocity. They each discover that the other student's impulses have no effect on the motion of their arrow.) Finally, students acquire the foundation for an understanding of vector addition – they learn how the vertical and horizontal velocity components combine to determine the speed and direction of the dot's motion.

Microworld 3

The next step is to provide students with a microworld where the rate at which they can apply impulses can be varied. The purpose of this microworld is to introduce students to continuous forces via a limit process: the students can repeatedly double the frequency with which they can apply impulses, while at the same time the size of each impulse is halved. At the end of this process, the students are applying very small impulses at closely spaced time intervals. In this way, the students learn to think of continuous forces, such as gravity, as a lot of small impulses applied one after another. This enables students to apply their causal model, learned in the simpler microworlds, to understand the effects of continuous forces. For example, they are asked to think about what happens when you throw a ball up into the air. They learn that gravity is constantly applying an impulse that continually adds a small amount to the vertical velocity of the ball in the downwards direction. This causes the ball to go upwards at a slower and slower rate until it finally stops, turns around, and accelerates downwards. By analysing such problems, the students develop an understanding of acceleration and of Fma for the case where the mass and force are constant. In other words, they learn a simpler causal form of Fma, ie Fa.

Microworld 4

Finally, the students are presented with a microworld in which gravity is acting, and they can again apply impulses to the left and right, as well as up and down. In this world, in the absence of other forces, motion is characterized by constant acceleration in the vertical dimension and constant speed in the horizontal dimension. The students are given problems of the form: 'Imagine that you give two balls a horizontal push off the side of a table. One ball gets a soft push and the other gets a hard push. Both balls are pushed at the same time. Which ball hits the floor first?' Working in this microworld thus enables students to make connections to some interesting real-world situations. Solving such problems requires the students to apply the causal model they learned from interacting with the prior microworlds.

The instructional approach

The set of microworlds we have created focuses on, simplifies, and makes concrete certain aspects of Newtonian mechanics. The challenge was to devise instructional techniques, centred around the microworlds, that would facilitate students' acquisition of the desired mental model. A central aspect of the approach that we developed is to synthesize the teaching of subject matter with teaching about the form, evolution, and application of scientific knowledge. Students are given a variety of laws that have been proposed for a given microworld, and are asked to determine which laws are correct and which laws are incorrect (ie demonstrably false). Then, for the correct laws, they have to devise criteria for deciding which laws are better than others. Finally, they have to apply their laws to real-world contexts and thereby discover that the laws are general and enable one to make predictions about a wide range of physical phenomena.

Within each of the existing four modules of the curriculum (corresponding to the four microworlds described above), instruction was divided into four distinct phases.

The motivation phase

In the first phase, students are asked to make predictions about what they think will happen in simple real-world contexts. For example, in the first module of the curriculum, the teacher asks the students: 'Imagine that we have a ball resting on a frictionless surface and we blow on the ball. Then, as the ball is moving along, we give it a blow, the same size as the first, in the opposite direction. What will be the effect of this second blow on the motion of the ball?' The teacher simply tabulates the different answers and reasons for these answers without commenting on their correctness. This process demonstrates to the students that not everyone holds the same beliefs (cf Svensson and Högfors' confrontation technique in Chapter 8). For instance, some think that the second blow will cause the ball to turn around and go in the opposite direction, others think it will make the ball stop, and yet others believe it will simply cause the ball to slow down. Since not everyone can be right, students are motivated to find out who has correct explanations and who has misconceptions. Further, since the predictions are about the behaviour of real-world objects, this phase sets up a potential link between what happens in the computer microworld and the real world.

The evolution phase

In this phase, students solve problems and perform experiments in the context of the computer microworld. For instance, one of the problems in the first module requires the students to make the dot hit a stationary target while moving at a specified speed. Once the student succeeds, the dot returns to its starting location and a new target speed is specified. By attempting to solve this problem, the students learn how impulses affect the speed of the dot. As described in the previous section, the computer microworld increases in complexity with each new module of the curriculum. The problems and experiments are designed and sequenced to build upon the students' prior knowledge and to enable them to induce increasingly sophisticated concepts and laws relevant to understanding the implications of Newton's laws of motion.

The formalization phase

In this phase, the students are asked to evaluate a set of laws formulated to describe the behaviour of objects within the microworlds. Examples of such laws are: (1) whenever you give the dot an impulse to the left, it slows down; and (2) if the dot is moving, and you do *not* apply an impulse, it will continue moving at the same speed. Initially, students are asked to sort the laws into two piles – those they can prove wrong and those for which they cannot find a counterexample. Then, for the subset of 'true' laws, they are asked to pick the rule they like best: 'If you could only have one of these rules in your hand to base predictions on, which one would you pick and why?' This activity typically engenders discussions of: (1) the precision of a rule's predictions; (2) the range of situations to which it applies; and (3) its simplicity and memorability.

The transfer phase

In this phase, the objective is to get students to appreciate how the rule they have selected applies to real-world contexts. In the first stage of this process, students apply their rule to the predictive question that they were asked at the beginning of the instructional cycle. They then compare the answer that the rule generates to the set of answers generated by the class. For answers that differ, students go to the microworld and experiment, for example, by putting friction and/or gravity into the microworld, to see which of their 'wrong' predictions can become correct predictions under these more complex circumstances. In the second stage of the transfer process, students conduct experiments with real-world objects, or design their own experiments to illustrate how the rule they evolved in the microworld context holds in these real-world contexts.

Experimental results

The curriculum was implemented by a teacher who taught five science classes in the sixth grade of a middle school located in a middle-class Boston suburb. One of the five classes was used for a pilot trial of the first two modules of the curriculum. Of the remaining classes, two were used as a peer control group (containing 37 students), and the other two were given the ThinkerTools curriculum (containing 41 students). The curriculum took two months to complete. During this period, the students had a science class lasting 145 minutes every school day. The ThinkerTools curriculum occupied the entire class period. Students in the control classes received the standard curriculum which, at this point in the year, was devoted to a unit on inventions. All students had completed a physics unit earlier in the year which included material on Newton's Laws.

In addition to the control group of sixth-grade students, a second control group was employed, consisting of two classes of high school physics students (containing 41 students) drawn from the same school system as the sixth graders. These students had just completed two-and-a-half months studying Newtonian mechanics using the textbook *Concepts in Physics* (Miller, Dillon and Smith, 1974).

We utilized a variety of evaluation instruments to help us determine the effectiveness of the ThinkerTools curriculum. During the course we observed numerous classroom sessions and kept videotape and audiotape records of certain sessions. At the end of the course we administered three written tests measuring: (1) ability to translate between the alternative representations of motion (datacrosses and wakes – see Figure 1) employed within the curriculum; (2) subject matter knowledge in the computer microworld context; and (3) transfer of the underlying principles to real-world contexts. This third test was also given to the two control groups. In addition, following the administration of the written tests, seven of the ThinkerTools students were interviewed on an individual basis. These protocols allowed us to explore in depth the nature of the mental models they had acquired.

Since the first two tests were given only to the experimental students, we will focus in this limited space on the results of the third test. The findings will be discussed with respect to the two primary objectives of the course: (1) understanding the principles underlying Newtonian mechanics: and (2) learning about the form and evolution of scientific knowledge.

Understanding Newtonian mechanics
The experimental students did well on the first two tests, with a third of them getting more than 90% of the questions correct. Protocols of high-scoring students reveal that their pattern of correct answers was produced by the consistent application of the desired mental model for reasoning about force and motion problems. This is in marked contrast to the inconsistent and misconception-fraught reasoning that many sixth graders display prior to instruction (White and Horwitz, in preparation), and high school physics students exhibit following a traditional physics course (White, 1983).

The third test, administered to the experimental group and two control groups, measures students' understanding of Newtonian mechanics in real-world problem-solving contexts. It is composed of questions used by other researchers in studying misconceptions among physics students (Clement, diSessa, McClosky, McDermott, White). The particular questions used are simple predictive questions to which high school and college students frequently give wrong answers. They all require reasoning from basic principles, rather than constraint-based, algebraic problem solving.

In the first analysis of this transfer test, we compared sixth graders who had the ThinkerTools curriculum with those who did not. A three-way between-students analysis of variance was carried out with: (1) treatment (experimental versus control); (2) gender; and (3) ability (low, middle, and high, based upon California Achievement Test [CAT] total scores) as the three factors. With this design we could assess the effectiveness of the experimental curriculum for students of each gender and ability level. There was a highly significant main effect of instructional treatment (F [1,62] 62.9, p .0001). The average number of questions correct for the experimental students was 11.15 out of 17, while the average for the control students was 7.56. In addition, there was no significant interaction of gender with treatment or ability with treatment. The ThinkerTools curriculum was equally effective for girls and boys as well as for students of different ability levels as measured by the CAT.

With respect to the ThinkerTools students, the questions on the test can be classified into two categories:

(1) those involving the application of a principle taught in the course and which the students have applied in a context similar to the one presented in the problem; and

(2) those involving a principle addressed in the course but which the students have never applied to the particular context presented in the problem.

An item analysis revealed that the experimental students did better than the control students on both types of problems. This suggests that the ThinkerTools students not only learned the principles focused on in the course, but could also apply them to unfamiliar contexts. Finally, it is worth noting that the ThinkerTools students also did significantly better on this transfer test than the *high school* physics students (t [80] 1.7, p .005), who were on the average six years older and had been taught about force and motion using traditional methods. An item analysis revealed interesting differences between these groups. The ThinkerTools students performed better (in some cases dramatically better) than the high school physics students on problems that involved analysing the effects of forces in terms of velocity components. The high school students, however, performed better on problems that involved constraint forces (such as a fixed-length string constraining the motion of a pendulum bob). This latter result is not too surprising, since constraint forces were not dealt with in the ThinkerTools curriculum.

Acquiring scientific inquiry skills
In addition to teaching students principles underlying Newtonian mechanics, we had the symbiotic goal of helping them learn about the form, evolution, and application of scientific knowledge. In evaluating our success with respect to this second major objective of the curriculum, we relied partly upon observations of students' classroom performance. For instance, we examined the quality of the laws and experiments that they formulated for themselves, as well as the sophistication of the discussions they held when they were attempting to select the best law. In addition, we looked at the results of the written tests, particularly the transfer test, to aid in this aspect of the evaluation.

Understanding the form of scientific knowledge
Knowing the characteristics of a useful scientific law is an important aspect of understanding the form of scientific knowledge. The instructional technique we developed was to present students with alternative laws for each microworld, and have them select the best law. We observed that when students were evaluating these sets of laws, they spontaneously engaged in discussions concerning the simplicity of a law, the precision of its predictions, and its range of applicability. The set of laws was carefully constructed to elicit such discussions and this approach thus appears to have been highly successful.

Developing scientific inquiry skills
It is important to understand that falsification is part of the process by which scientific knowledge evolves. For a rule to be a potential scientific law, it must be capable of being proven wrong. Being able to develop and reason from counter evidence is an important scientific inquiry skill. We observed that when the students were evaluating the sets of laws given to them, they were adept at designing experiments that would falsify a particular law.

When we went on to look at what the students did when they formulated laws for themselves, there were clear limits to their scientific inquiry skills. For example, one group of students discovered the 'linear friction law' in the microworld: the effect of friction is linearly proportional to the speed with which the object is moving. The consequence is that whether you apply them one right after the other or whether you separate them further in time, the dot will come to rest at the same point. The students discovered this fact, but they did not fully explore its implications, nor did they go on to investigate whether it was true for the kind of real-world friction that affects, for instance, rolling balls or sliding hockey pucks.

If one looks at our instructional approach, this limitation in their inquiry skills is understandable. We gave the students activities to help them induce the laws, as well as sets of possible laws to evaluate, and real-world activities that illustrated the laws. This was clearly too abrupt a transition, and an important area of our future research will be the development of bridging activities that enable a more gradual transition to independent scientific discovery.

Acquiring scientific problem-solving skills
Students need to understand that the laws they are evolving are of increasing general applicability, and need to be able to apply them in new contexts. Based upon classroom observations and the results of the transfer test, we see that the students were indeed able to generalize principles derived in the microworld contexts to a variety of simple real-world contexts. This was achieved by the process of abstracting what they learned from the computer microworld into a set of laws and then learning how to map the laws onto different real-world problem-solving situations.

The general conclusion is that the ThinkerTools students learned that a useful scientific law is a concise principle that enables predictions across different contexts. In addition, they developed skills in designing experiments to falsify or show the limitations of a law, and applying a given law to a variety of different domains. This view of scientific knowledge and these inquiry skills are an important component of understanding what science is all about.

Discussion

The design of the curriculum was based upon extensive protocol studies of sixth graders' reasoning about force and motion problems. It was necessary first to learn about how students conceptualize these phenomena. Based upon this research, we determined which aspects of their prior knowledge we could build upon, and which misconceptions we could use to motivate their learning about Newtonian mechanics. The progression of increasingly complex computer microworlds was then designed to correspond to the desired evolution of the students' understanding of the phenomena. Further, the design of the microworld transformed abstractions, such as Cartesian components of displacement and velocity, into concrete observable data-objects, and introduced simplifications, such as quantized impulses, that enabled students to learn and make concrete what are normally regarded as abstract and difficult concepts.

Another aspect of the instructional approach that we believe was crucial to its success is the process of *reification*. Students were asked to consider alternative descriptions of what they learned from the computer microworld in the form of a set of laws, and had to evaluate the properties of the various laws. This enabled the students to develop a concept of what it was they were trying to learn – for example, rather than learning a set of facts, they were trying to induce a set of laws and learn about the properties of scientific laws. Further, the process of getting students to apply the laws they induced from the microworld to real-world contexts was important both for their understanding of Newtonian mechanics and for their perception of the nature of scientific knowledge. They learned that their laws apply in a wide range of contexts and they gained experience in transferring what they learned in one context (ie the computer microworld) to another context (ie a particular real-world situation). We conjecture that these formalization and transfer phases of our curriculum are responsible for the ThinkerTools students being able to apply their knowledge to unfamiliar contexts – a result that is rarely obtained in educational research.

Acknowledgements

This research was sponsored by the National Science Foundation, under award number DPE-8400280 with the Directorate for Science and Engineering Education. This chapter is a revised version of a paper that appeared in the proceedings of the Ninth Annual Conference of the Cognitive Science Society which was held in Seattle, Washington in July, 1987. For the interested reader, this approach to science education is more fully described in the research report by White and Horwitz (1987).

References

Carmazza, A, McClosky, M and Green, B (1981). Naive beliefs in 'sophisticated' subjects: Misconceptions about trajectories of objects. *Cognition*, **9**, 117-23.

Clement, J (1982). Students' preconceptions in elementary mechanics. *Amercian Journal of Physics*, **50**, 66-71.

diSessa, A (1982). Unlearning Aristotelian physics: A study of knowledge-based learning. *Cognitive Science*, **6**, 37- 75.

Larkin, J H, McDermott, J, Simon, D P and Simon, H A (1980). Expert and novice performance in solving physics problems. *Science*, **208**, 1335-42.

McClosky, M, Caramazza, A, and Green, B (1980). Curvilinear motion in the absence of external forces: Naive beliefs about the motion of objects. *Science*, **210**, 1139-41.

McDermott, L C (1984). Research on conceptual understanding in mechanics. *Physics Today*, **37**, 24-32.

Miller, F, Dillon, T J and Smith, M K (1974). *Concepts in Physics: A High School Physics Program*. New York: Harcourt, Brace and World.

Piaget, J and Garcia, R (1964). *Understanding Causality*. New York: Norton.

Shayer, M and Adey, P (1981). *Towards a Science of Science Teaching*. London: Heinemann Educational.

Trowbridge, D E , and McDermott, L C (1981). Investigation of student understanding of the concept of acceleration in one dimension. *American Journal of Physics*, **49**, 242-53.

Viennot, L (1979). Spontaneous reasoning in elementary dynamics. *European Journal of Science Education*, **1**, 205-21.

White, B (1983). Sources of difficulty in understanding Newtonian dyamics. *Cognitive Science*, **7**, 41-65.

White, B (1984). Designing computer activities to help physics students understand Newton's laws of motion. *Cognition and Instruction*, **1**, 69-108.
White, B and Frederiksen, J (1986). Progressions of qualitative models as a foundation for intelligent learning environments. BBN Laboratories Report No. 6277. Cambridge, Massachusetts.
White, B and Horwitz, P (1987). ThinkerTools: Enabling children to understand physical laws. BBN Laboratories Report No. 6470. Cambridge, Massachusetts.
White, B and Horwitz, P (in preparation). *Multiple Muddles: Novice Reasoning about Force and Motion.*

Chapter 5

The Phenomenography of the 'Mole Concept' in Chemistry

Leif Lybeck, Ference Marton, Helge Strömdahl and Aina Tullberg
University of Gothenburg, Sweden

Introduction

In this chapter we will illustrate how, by studying students' understanding of scientific concepts, and integrating the results with their theoretical context, we may contribute to a greater degree of conceptual clarity, thus contributing to the advancement of science. We argue that such conceptual improvements can be used as a basis for developing better presentation of the subject matter, thus improving students' understanding of it. Using Habermas' (1978) terminology, we could say that our work was inspired by three different 'knowledge interests'. We aim at three different kinds of knowledge as results. We would like to make a contribution to chemistry, to phenomenographic knowledge, and to education in chemistry.

The study we describe below depicts the qualitatively different ways in which secondary school students think about and deal with 'the mole concept' or, more correctly, about the quantity *amount of substance* and its SI unit the *mole*. The research approach exemplifies the phenomenographic model of description outlined in Roger Säljö's chapter.

Chemistry and the mole

The physical quantity known as 'amount of substance', together with its SI unit ('mole') is of central importance in chemistry. It is used in all chemical calculations. 'Mole' is a crucial quantitative bridge between the atomic model and the reality that students are faced with in the laboratory. Students do experiments and they observe chemical changes taking place in test tubes or crucibles. They are then expected to explain those changes in terms of atoms or molecules, and to describe the changes with chemical formulae. But in order to understand what a chemical formula stands for, and how it is used by chemists, it is necessary to comprehend the physical quantity called 'amount of substance'.

The quantity 'amount of substance' is, therefore, intimately related to chemistry. Unfortunately there is no way in which we can describe the results of our research without describing chemistry as well. We know that this may create difficulties for readers not familiar with chemistry. But we hope that general readers can appreciate the arguments, if not the chemistry. Having raised this issue of disciplinary content we want to stress that in research of this type the team needs to include researchers who have expertise in the specific content area. Our research team included people knowledgeable in chemistry and also in teaching chemistry.

The epistemological and pedagogical treatment of the quantity 'amount of substance' has been characterized by considerable conceptual muddiness. Even the use of the term 'mole concept' is misleading. The mole is the name of the unit (given the symbol mol) used for the quantity 'amount of substance' (in the same way as the metre is the name of the unit [symbol m] used for the quantity 'length'). In fact the mole, like the metre, is one of seven basic SI units defined by the international scientific community.

There are several reasons for the conceptual confusion referred to above. One problem is that amount of substance is treated by some chemists as a mass and by others as a number (Dierks, 1981), while in fact it is a quantity quite different from both mass and number (but related to mass and number by two simple mathematical relations that will be discussed later in this chapter). Secondly, even advanced chemists – like chemistry teachers – mix up the quantity ('amount of substance') with its unit ('mole'), a fact which may be very frustrating to students. The muddiness of the mole has obvious historical reasons too. 'Mole' was first introduced as a short form for gram *mole*cule (a mass quantity). The term 'mole' was then linked to the gas laws and Avogadro's hypothesis and thus became connected with a *number*. Another source of confusion is that the standard for atomic weight (which is basic in defining the mole) has been changed three times over the years (from hydrogen to oxygen to carbon).

There have been many studies showing that students have difficulties in learning to use the mole in calculations (eg Johnstone, Morrison and Sharp, 1971; Lazonby, Morris and Waddington, 1982). Other studies have identified frequent mistakes and misconceptions of students when they use the mole concept (eg Cervellanti *et al.*, 1982). The mole has also been a fruitful area for those who have wanted to apply general learning theories – in particular, Piaget's theory of intellectual development (eg Shayer and Adey, 1981) and Gagné's learning hierarchies (Gower, Daniels and Lloyd, 1977).

The study of science concepts and the phenomenographic approach

There is a rapidly growing field of research aimed at finding and mapping the different ways in which students understand concepts, principles and phenomena dealt with in school, primarily within science subjects. The differing understandings described have been referred to as misconceptions, pupil paradigms, alternative frameworks, naive theories, and so on (see, for example, Driver and Erickson, 1983). A major common element in the scattered research efforts seems to be a view of learning as a change from one way of understanding a phenomenon to another and qualitatively different way of understanding the same phenomenon. In accordance with this, 'cognitive structure and conceptual change' has been chosen as a label for the research specialization and as the title of a recent collection of studies originating from it (West and Pines, 1985).

One of these research approaches – the one which we have adopted in this study – is phenomenography. Its characteristics have been described in Chapter 2 and several contributions to this volume make use of it. In general terms, it is the study of the qualitatively different ways in which people experience and conceptualize the world around them. An experiential perspective, a view of conceptions of phenomena as relational (ie as describing relations between the conceptualizing individuals and the conceptualized phenomena) and a concern with both the 'how' and the 'what' of learning (ie the act of conceptualizing and the meaning of the phenomenon as conceptualized) are three of the basic features of phenomenography that we should like to remind readers about here.

In several studies using an approach similar to ours, students' understanding of phenomena appearing both in everyday and scientific contexts (eg weight, force, density) have been investigated (see Chapter 3). The students' differing conceptualizations are then seen as a function of a conflict between the two different ways of thinking (ie the common-sense and the scientific). In the case of the mole concept, however, the students have met the phenomenon in school only. The 'world around us' is thus limited to the world of school and hence differences in conceptualization logically originate from differences in the students' interpretation of the content of teaching, rather than from a conflict between frameworks of science and of everyday life.

Didactics of chemistry

Just as a conception is not a simple sum of a kind of thinking and a kind of object, but reflects a specific way of thinking about a specific object, the field of knowledge we aim at contributing to cannot be described as a sum (or intersection) of two separate fields of knowledge (such as educational psychology and chemistry). What we refer to here as the *didactics of chemistry* is an autonomous domain of knowledge concerning how chemistry is taught and how chemistry is learned. It is autonomous in the sense that it cannot be derived by simply combining knowledge from these two fields separately. It has to be developed on its own terms from knowledge that results from research studies of the teaching and learning of chemistry (Lybeck,1979).

When we say that the didactics of chemistry presuppose insights into chemistry, we mean that in order to investigate students' understanding of concepts in chemistry, we have to have an understanding of those concepts ourselves. The relationship between the two domains of knowledge (chemistry and didactics of chemistry) is not one-directional, however. In this chapter, we show that studying students' understanding of conceptions in chemistry can contribute to conceptual development in chemistry itself.

Details of the study

The investigation involved individual interviews in which students undertook several tasks. Only one of these tasks is considered here. All the results originate from analysis of the transcripts of the interviews. Thirty students aged 16–19 (9 girls, 21 boys) specializing in science in one Swedish secondary school participated. (One student's interview could not be analysed because of a recording failure.)

Figure I shows the task configuration used for the 'mole' question, adapted from Novick and Menis (1976). The plexiglas cylinders were marked 1a, 1b, 1c, . . . , IIIc. The students were first asked to inspect the plexiglas cylinders and their contents. We told students that the elements were (a) tin; (b) aluminium; and (c) sulphur. The tin and the aluminium were in finely granulated form while the sulphur was in powder form. Students were allowed to lift the cylinders and feel or smell their contents, and they were supplied with paper and pencil. There were no other aids (such as a table of the periodic system or a balance).

The principle of the task is as follows: in group I, the *amount* of substance is constant: there is 1 mol of each element (in the case of sulphur, 1 mol of the elementary entity S, not of the elementary entity S_8 –in fact, only one of the students considered the case of S_8). In group II the *volume* is constant, and in group III, the *mass* is constant. Students were asked: 'Which group contains 1 mol of each element?' (In most cases, we made the question clearer by adding that there was 1 mol of each element in either group I, group II, or group III).

Students were asked to explain their choice of group. We asked questions such as 'How did you think?', 'How did you reason?', 'How did you arrive at that answer?' During the interview, we followed up the students' answers in different ways in order to find out how they reasoned. The interviewer used only such concepts and terms as had been introduced by the students themselves. If the students so wished, they were told the numerical values of the 'atomic weights' or 'molar masses' (119, 27 and 32 for tin, aluminium and sulphur respectively). Note that the interviewer did not specify the unit. When the student had reached a conclusion, the interviewer said either yes or no to the experimental conclusion but made no comment on reasoning. When the task had been completed, we asked: 'When I say (the word) mole, what do you think of?'

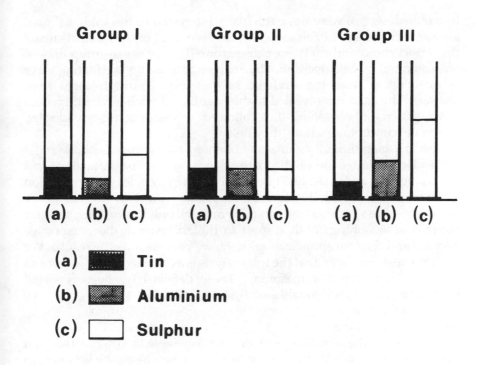

Figure 1. Test configuration for the 'mole' question

Expected responses to the task

One expected response might have been: 'I cannot answer the question because I don't have a balance, nor do I know what the molar mass is.' The question could have been answered by reasoning as follows: We have 1 mol in the group where the mass of each element corresponds with the element's molar mass. Since the molar mass of each element is different, one can rule out the group where the masses are the same (by lifting the cylinders in order to compare their weights). Since their bulk density is different, it would be a pure coincidence if 1 mol of each element were to have the same volume ($V_m = \frac{M}{\rho}$). Consequently, the group where the columns appear to be similar should be ruled out. We are then left with group I which contains 1 mol.

An approach by a student based on visual perception (of volume) can 'obscure' the relevance of mass. Also, an approach based on the acquired assumption that number is equal to amount of substance can 'obscure' the relevance of mass.

Results of the study

In our analysis, we were not particularly interested in the students' final answer to the task itself, although for the record, 14 of the students made the correct choice (group I). Six chose group II, eight chose group III, and one could not reach a decision. The analysis focused on elucidating ways of categorizing what the students said as they argued towards their answers. The students revealed highly significant qualitative differences in the patterns of reasoning they followed, in the perspectives adopted and in the conceptualizations they held.

Since the analysis is qualitative and phenomenographic it is necessary, if the reader is to judge the validity of the claims, to describe the analysis and results together and in detail. This would involve a very lengthy exposition and it would place high demands on the reader with respect to chemistry knowledge. We shall therefore describe in detail only the first analysis, for patterns of reasoning. With respect to the analyses of the perspective adopted and the conceptualizations held, we provide only the results. We wish to stress, however, that the full analysis is as detailed in these cases as it is for the patterns of reasoning. These details have been reported elsewhere (Lybeck, Strömdahl and Tullberg, 1985).

Patterns of reasoning

On the basis of the students' answers, we were able to describe the path each individual student's reasoning followed when he or she brought up one concept after another. It became obvious, however, that the students picked the concepts and the relations between the concepts from the same 'universe of concepts and relations'. That is, they all used combinations of a limited set of concepts and relations. Our problem thus became: Was there a comprehensive structure of reasoning, a kind of collective map, within which each individual reasoning pattern could be characterized? This comprehensive structure would not correspond with any of these individual reasoning patterns. All of them would, however, be subsets within it.

This created an analytical problem. We wanted to characterize the parts in terms of a whole, which was supposed to emerge from the parts. The parts were 'parts', however, only in relation to the whole yet to emerge. This dialectical constitution of the whole and its parts in relation to each other is at the heart of phenomenographic analysis. Transcripts of the individual interviews from the group of students are dealt with collectively. The description eventually arrived at is a result originating from the analysis of the entire range of interviews. There is a kind of 'hermeneutic circle' connecting the whole and its parts, consisting of a great number of iterations between the description of the whole and the characterization of the individual interviews, and vice versa.

There is another dimension in which a different kind of iteration takes place. In the interpretative analysis, the researcher has to rely on his or her knowledge of the content and previous experience of students' thinking.

In this dimension, this competency has to be 'bracketed' in order to be maximally open to what the students say, without imposing one's judgement on it. Yet one's own understanding of the field has to be used in order to grasp the students' ideas in depth and to relate them to each other.

As these processes are inherent in the results, we shall try to illustrate them in the description of the way we arrived at the collective map of the patterns of reasoning.

After scrutinizing the transcripts again and again, a basic structure gradually emerged where the focus was on the amount of substance (n) surrounded by the quantities mass (m), volume (V) and number (N). A simple diagram of the collective structure of reasoning began to take shape (see Figure 2).

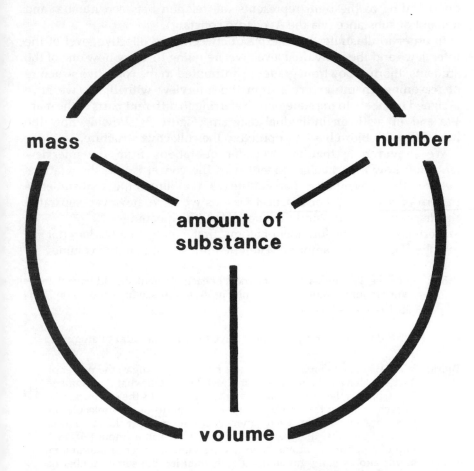

Figure 2. *The basic structure of the collective map of patterns of reasoning*

It is now appropriate to present the more complete collective map that builds on the one in Figure 2 by including the connections between relations that were found in the interview. The basic structure of the complete collective map in Figure 4 consists of three arcs and three lines. Each arc represents a non-molar relationship. The lower left arc represents the relation (via density) between mass and volume. The lower right arc represents the relation (via 'atomic' volume or, more generally, via the volume of a specific elementary entity) between volume and number. The upper arc represents the relation (via 'atomic' mass or, more generally, the mass of a specified elementary entity) between mass and number.

The three lines emerging from the centre of the complete collective map in Figure 4 represent three molar relationships. The line pointing to the left represents the relation between mass and amount of substance (via the molar mass). The line pointing downwards represents the relation between volume and amount of substance (via the molar volume), and the line pointing to the right represents the relation between number and amount of substance (via the Avogadro constant).

In order to illustrate the interplay between the collective level of the interviews and the individual level, we are going to show how one of the students, Björn, a boy from grade 2, contributed to the collective structure of reasoning. In the excerpts from the interview with Björn, we have assigned numbers to the statements referring to different parts of the map. We end up with an individual diagram (Figure 3) showing how the interview with Björn has contributed to the collective structure.

We should note that we consider quotations from the interview (showing how a particular student uses the concepts and the relations between them) as inherent parts of the diagram illustrating that student's pattern of reasoning. For practical reasons we have, however, separated the diagram (structure) and the quotations (the meanings).

Björn considers the 'number of atoms' first. Notice that he does not say 'number' but, rather, 'amount'. Then he thinks about atomic volume:

Björn: Let's see, I'll think aloud. One mole of each element should have the same amount of atoms or molecular units, or units, what should I say? (1) . . . Then it's a matter of . . .

I: What do you mean by 'It should have the same amount of atoms'?

Björn: Well, 1 mol is defined as . . . what is it . . . something to the power of 23, right? It's a certain number anyhow. I can't tell what that number is yet, but it's the same for all elements, right? So it's the same amount (1) in each case, but then it's a question if the atoms or the molecules in them are larger than each other. Sulphur, number 15 . . . I was thinking anyway, that it's obvious that it's the same amount, if it's 1 (2) mol of sulphur . . . atoms, then it's the same number of aluminium atoms and as many tin atoms. Right, then it's the same number of atoms, isn't it, but . . . The atoms are successively larger according to (2) the periodic table (atomic volume).

He is unsure as to whether the volumes should be equal or unequal in the required group. He knows that atomic volume varies (he assumes the atomic volumes increase steadily with increasing atomic number). But he is unsure of the relationship between volume and number. He then goes on and considers mass and derives the relationship between amount of substance and mass.

Björn: Well, I guess the mass should be larger the higher it gets (atomic number), in comparision to . . . even if it's the same number of . . .   (3)

I: Larger mass? What do you mean by mass?

Björn: Molar mass. So the further you go in the periodic table, the more 1 mol   (3) weighs. So then you need . . . Let's see here, the more 1 mol weighs . . . that would mean . . . it can't mean that . . . Right, it should have a larger mass, but the same amount (our interpretation: volume), let's see, the amount should be the same . . .

Björn is picturing the periodic table in his head in order to 'see if I can remember the molar masses'. 'Chlorine is 35.5' and it is '30g for each sulphur'. And '1 mol of aluminium weighs more than 1 mol of sulphur'. He receives at this point the molar mass numerical values: 119, 27, and 32. It is possible that the choice of group III occurred earlier to Björn, but the new information excluded group III.

Björn: It's the same then (27 and 32) . . . it should be about as much in each one would think, so that one, group III, I guess I would eliminate.

He concentrates heavily on the volume (the observable variable) and tries to relate it to the mass. He mentions density:

Björn: On the other hand, yes . . . The same mass means that . . . It depends a little on what their densities are, that's clear.   (4)

I: Okay, what is 'density'?

Björn: It's what they weigh per gram, or per kilo, yeah, I didn't think it was so difficult (the '1 mol' task).   (4)

Our student suggests group II because 'the amounts are equal':

Björn: Then the weight wouldn't make much difference. It's just that it's a little heavier, but not much, so it's probably group II. It seems as if there's as much (volume) in each one, and that should be the amount (number).

I: What do you mean by 'amount'?

Björn: The amount (number) of atoms. So that if it's a lot, then it's . . .

I: Why do you choose group II then?

Björn: Well, because it should be 1 mol, and 1 mol is the same (number of atoms) no matter what element it is. The difference ought to be very slight anyway.

Björn is still considering the atomic volumes. He means partly that the atomic volumes vary, and realizes that (the continuous) volume should also vary, and partly that the amounts (the volumes, in the sense of continuous volumes) should be the same because the numbers of atoms are the same. He does not get it to work out, but decides on group II.

Björn: The difference ought to be slight, then. Let's see, the size, that's the only thing you . . . I would think . . . but yes . . . it's

I: What do you mean by 'size'?

Björn: Well, if the atoms are larger, then they take up more . . . No, never mind . . . more space, but it . . . No, it's probably group II, because there should be as much (volume) in each tube. (5)

During the follow-up, we get to know how Björn thought about volumes.

I: Do all the atoms of all the elements take up the same amount of space?

Björn: Yes . . . in principle . . . Yes, it's obvious, they get bigger . . . but it's . . . Everything is so small, the atoms get bigger as you go up the periodic table (increasing atomic number) . . . (5)

Björn actually knows how to solve the problem:

I: If you were to go to a lab and solve this problem, how would you do it?

Björn: Well, then you could go and simply weigh it. And one would also know how much 1 mol weighs. (6)

He had earlier received the molar mass numerical values but still weighs the tubes with his hands. Group III is eliminated because 'they weigh the same – then it can't be 1 mol'. He hesitates between group I and group II.

Björn: IIa is heavier than IIb, and Ia is heavier than Ib, but the difference between Ia and Ib is larger than the difference between IIa and IIb, so that . . . so it should be . . . It's a little difficult to decide simply according to how they feel, but I would wonder if there was something else to go by.

He is thinking of density. In other words, the relationship between mass and volume.

Björn: So that . . . On the other hand it is . . . We have the density as well. The smallest (density), I guess, is sulphur . . . maybe not . . . That's probably right, I believe it's group II. (7)

I: You choose group II. Why don't you choose group I?

Björn: No, because if it had been group I, you would be able to think that it would have . . . If we say that sulphur is lighter, then you would be able to fill up . . . but then it would have to be filled up to be the same as the others and then it should . . . they ought to have different weights, because it should be 119, 27, and 32. So it ought to be the same . . . They ought to have about the same amount (volume) but different masses.

Finally, Björn chose group II.

In Figure 3, we see the part of the collective map referred to in Björn's statements. Björn's pattern of reasoning constitutes a subset of the collective map – a subset which includes the quotations made. Thus, Figure 2 – the empirical collective map – is a holistic description of all the individual subsets and it includes all the quotations assigned to all parts of it.

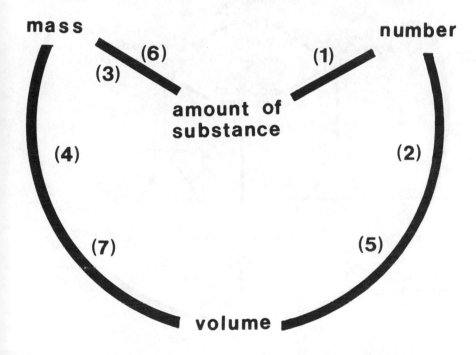

Figure 3. Björn's pattern of reasoning. The numbers give the chronological order of statements made in the interview and marked in the text

Students also reasoned about relationships between the relations that have been mentioned above. Two quotations demonstrate this point:

Erik: Density is closely related to molar mass, if I am not mistaken.

Eskil: You learn a routine for finding out the molar weight, and one does that by looking up the atomic weight in u and then taking it in grams instead. The only thing is . . . I get confused when I have to work out what I've actually done here.

Thus, in each of the three sectors of Figure 2, one non-molar relationship (arc) can be combined with two molar relationships (lines). Together these constitute three specific relationships which are also important aspects included in the collective map.

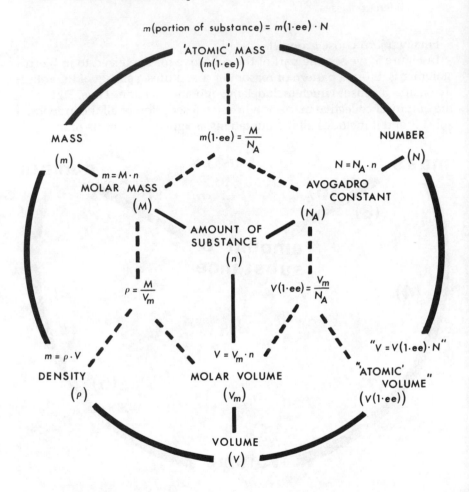

Figure 4. *The complete integrated and multidimensional collective map of patterns of reasoning (the abbreviation 'ee' in m (1· ee), is short for elementary entities (atoms, etc))*

It is important to notice that the collective map is a result of the empirical study. Our data base does not allow us to give a detailed description of each student's understanding of the relationships. But we have enough data to discuss some qualitative aspects concerning the main relationships. Let us give two examples. Some students expressed the relation (correctly or incorrectly) between mass and amount of substance mathematically. For example:

Alf: Mole is the number of grams times the molar mass.

Evert: . . . and then you divide the mass in grams by the mass in u (units), and get the number of moles.

Other students mentioned the quantities they operated with, but they did not express the relationships clearly. For example:

Bengt: Use a formula, weigh it, find out the mass and compare with the molar mass.

Bruno: If I know the number of grams per mol, then I can get the number of grams and then I can find out the number of moles.

Berit: The substance with the largest molar mass has the largest mass.

Enok: Then I'll think about its molar weight.

The relation described by the quantity equation $m = M \cdot n$ needs to be considered here. This equation describes a proportionality (a well-known mathematical relationship, compare $y = k \cdot x$) in which M, the molar mass, is the proportionality constant. It has the dimension of mass divided by amount of substance, ie it has the SI unit mol $g.mol^{-1}$. The derivation of this equation from this relation can be directly compared with the derivation of the SI unit for velocity, $m.s^{-1}$. Among the students the molar mass was frequently referred to as the mass of 1 mol of a portion of substance. For example:

Arne: You have to find out the molar mass, how much 1 mol of the substance weighs.

Enok: Molar weight says how much 1 mol weighs.

This is like saying that velocity is metres travelled in one second, rather than that it is the distance divided by the time it takes to travel the distance (with the SI unit $m.s^{-1}$). It implies that the quantity molar mass is assigned the dimension of mass, just as the notion of velocity in terms of metres implies that the quantity velocity is assigned the dimension of length.

In other phenomenographic studies, Lybeck (1981, 1985) has observed the same use of proportionality leading to problems of the same nature. The quantity density (the constant of proportionality in the quantity equation $m = \rho.V$) is comprehended by many persons not as a constant of proportionality (with the dimension of mass divided by volume, with the unit $g.cm^{-3}$) but as the mass of 1 cm^3 of a body. While this is not wrong in itself it often leads to conclusions about units that are wrong (eg the use of the gram in both cases above), and so to confusions about the nature of the quantities themselves.

There is a subtle yet very important issue here. It includes but goes beyond the confusion about units noted above. If you think about molar mass in the way that Arne and Enok do, not only are you likely to get the units wrong, but since you might not have grasped the general form of the relationship, your ability to calculate in this area is restricted. In particular, since the proportionality constant is seen as a number, it has to be deduced anew in each calculation rather than used as a general constant. We make a distinction, which is explained in more detail later, between two forms of thinking about proportionality in these contexts, which we call the A-form and the B-form. Arne and Enok are using the B-form of thinking, in which the constant of proportionality (molar mass, M) is thought of as a *number*, and probably as a number with units of gram. In the complete collective map (Figure 4), we have included the A-form, in which the constant of proportionality is thought of as a *constant*, with units $g.mol^{-1}$.

The collective map in Figure 2 does include statements about the relationships in the B-form of comprehending proportionality but a few quotations pointed to the A-form, so we decided that relations corresponding to an A-form of proportional reasoning were important even if they were only rarely found in the interviews. We thus integrate outcomes of the present study with the outcomes of previous studies (Lybeck, 1981, 1985), and by doing so we combine what is observed with what is possible in the more complete collective map shown in Figure 4. This integration of theoretical relations with the outcomes of phenomenographic studies is a widening of our didactic research approach which fulfils criteria of relevance and validity to be discussed later. By means of this kind of work, we achieve a connection between chemistry and the students' understanding of chemistry.

Perspectives
In this analysis of the students' answers, we have tried to describe the strategies they used to arrive at a solution. The main features are that the students *thematize* the task from a *continuous perspective* (c) or from a *discontinuous perspective* (d). One group of students pursued a continuity-type line of reasoning with the help of continuous quantities such as mass, volume and density, while another group pursued a discontinuity-type line of reasoning with the help of the quantity number. These lines of reasoning were more or less well developed, but their emphasis was always either on the continuous (c) or the discontinuous (d). A third group of students coordinated both the continuous and the discontinuous aspects of the problem in their line of reasoning (c&d). (Chemists do make observations at a macroscopic level, ie they observe colour changes, gas bubbles, etc, but they explain the phenomena observed at a microscopic level, ie in terms of atoms, etc. The macroscopic observations correspond to a *continuous* perspective on matter and the microscopic model of explanation corresponds to a *discontinuous* perspective on matter).

We classified Björn's way of thinking as a combined line of reasoning (c&d). He started with a discontinuity-type of reasoning according to the statements (1), (2), and (5) (see Figure 3 above). Then he made use of discontinuous quantities. But he also used a continuous perspective, applying the continuous quantities in his statements (3), (4), (6) and (7). In fact, Björn oscillated between the two perspectives, and he chose the discontinuous perspective when answering the following question:

I: If I say 'mole', what comes to mind?

Björn: An amount.

I: What do you mean by 'an amount'?

Björn: A certain number of something.

I: Yes, can 'amount' mean anything else?

Björn: Do you mean other than a number of something? Well, 1 mol can be a mass also, a certain number of grams of an element.

I: When I say 'mole', you think of the fact that it is a number of something, then?

Björn: Yes, hum. If you say 1 mol of a certain element, perhaps I would think of mass.

I: And when I say amount?

Björn: Then, perhaps, I would think of 1 mol, if you were talking about an element.

I: You've used the word 'amount' occasionally. Is that the mass?

Björn: No, it's the number.

The students' answers reflected different conceptions of matter. Answers reflecting a continuous perspective concerned compaction of the solids, their grain size, 'space between (the grains)', etc. Answers reflecting a discontinuous perspective contained thoughts about the atoms' compaction and volume. Many of the students had problems in combining continuity with discontinuity, ie the real, visible world with the explanatory model (the atomic theory). According to our classification, 13 of the students displayed a continuous (c), 4 a discontinuous (d), and 12 a combined (c&d) perspective.

Conceptions
The two previously used ways of describing the students' thinking, 'patterns of reasoning' and 'perspectives' were aimed at characterizing how the students dealt with the actual task they were facing. We were then able to reveal the conceptual network in terms of which one can think

about the mole. But they also revealed to a certain degree the *conceptualizations of 'mole'* underlying the task or expressed by the students' handling of it. The knowledge of the students' conceptualization of the mole can be deepened, however, by also considering holistic impressions of the entire interview, and especially the answer to the question: 'When I say mole, what do you think of?' We refer to this more intuitive and holistic characterization as their 'conception'. While 'perspectives' refer to a global and comprehensive aspect of the students' reasoning, 'conceptions' refer to a focal and central aspect. Needless to say, these two aspects are closely related to each other. Indeed, they are linked to two related questions: 'How do the students solve a mole problem?' and 'What is the meaning of the mole to them?'

We found five qualitatively different ways of conceptualizing 'mole' in the group of students participating in our investigation:

A. Mole as something to be used in calculations. In this case, the mole is seen only as an object of calculations. It belongs to chemistry classes without much reference to any reality outside them. This conception is linked with or originates from what has been described as a surface approach to learning tasks (see, for instance, Marton and Säljö, 1984; see also Chapter 1). It means that the learner's attention is focused on the pages of the textbook or on the numbers in a problem, without much orientation towards the reality that the text or the problem is supposed to denote.

B. Mole as mass. Here, and in the case of the following conceptions, mole is seen as referring to some aspect of matter as concrete substance and not only as something involved in calculations in chemistry. As far as this particular conception is concerned, 'mole' is seen as being identical with mass.

C. Mole as a number. This conception also reflects an identity relation with matter of wider meaning. In this case, the mole is dealt with as a number (and not identified with mass as in conception B).

D. Mole as a number and as related to mass. 'Mole' is seen as a number. But in this case it is understood that the mole is related to mass as well. Furthermore, while the relation to number is an identity relation, 'mole' is seen as being related to mass 'in some way' without claiming an identity relation between the two.

E. Mole as related to number and mass. As is obvious from the discussion section below, 'mole' is a *unit* by means of which a property of matter, 'the mole concept', is measured. This unit *corresponds to* a certain number of elementary entities of a substance. The difference is thus between 'corresponds to' and 'is'. The latter means an identity relation which leads to the collapse of the distinction between the measure (unit) and the measured (attribute).

Some of the students did seem to see the mole as a property of matter both in relation to number and mass. The distinction between the measure and what is measured was not stated explicitly, but was understood in an intuitive way in these conceptions.

The outcome space of conceptions
The five conceptions described above can be understood as if they had been generated by the underlying structure illustrated in Figure 5. Consider conception A first. It is different from the others in that it represents an understanding of 'mole' in the context of calculations only (not 'real'; $\sim R$) and not in terms of real-life entities ('real'; R). Secondly, conception B is distinguished from C, D and E by the absence of the mole–number relation ($\sim N$). Thirdly, conception C is distinguished from conceptions D and E by the identity relation between 'mole' and number (number identity; $N(I)$). And finally, conceptions D and E are distinguished from each other in terms of the difference between an identity and a non-identity mole–mass relation (mass identity; $M(I)$ and not mass identity; $M(\sim I)$ respectively).

A central idea in phenomenography is that we can find logical relations between categories of description corresponding to different conceptions of the same phenomenon. The set of conceptions constitutes the *outcome space*. The structure in Figure 5 is the logical structure of the outcome space.

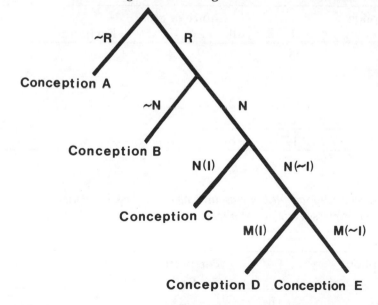

Figure 5. The outcome space of conceptions

Relations between various descriptions
We characterized the 29 students' patterns of reasoning in terms of the collective map. We categorized all the protocols in three different ways: in terms of the solution of the task (the final choice of group of cylinders), the

perspective adopted in reasoning about the choice of continuous (c), discontinuous (d), or combined (c&d), and the conception expressed in the entire interview (A, B, C, D or E). What are the relations between these three different ways of describing the individual students' thinking? We can see the three possible comparisons in Tables 1, 2, and 3.

Table 1. *Solution of the task (choice of group) in relation to perspective adopted in reasoning about it*

| Perspective | Choice of group | | | | Total |
	I	II	III	No group	
C	8	1	4		13
C & D	6	4	2		12
D		1	2	1	4
Total	14	6	8	1	29

Table 2. *Solution of task (choice of group) in relation to conception expressed*

| Conception | Choice of group | | | | Total |
	I	II	III	No group	
A	3	2	4		9
B	2				2
C			2	1	3
D	4	3	2		9
E	5	1			6
Total	14	6	8	1	29

Table 3. *Perspective adopted in reasoning about the task in relation to conceptions expressed during the interview*

| Conception | Perspective | | | Total |
	c	c&d	d	
A	6	2	1	7
B	2			2
C		1	2	3
D	2	6	1	9
E	3	3		6
Total	13	12	4	29

As far as Table 1 is concerned, we can point to the fact that the task cannot be solved within a discontinuous framework (one obviously has to pay attention to macroscopic properties available to the senses) and consequently, none of the students who adopted a discontinuous perspective made the correct choice (ie chose group I).

In Table 2, we see that five of the six students showing conception E made the correct choice in the task, while only nine of the other 23 students did so. Table 3 has some interest from the point of view of principles. In phenomenography, a central distinction is made between logical relations that can be found between categories of description, and empirical relations that can be found between conceptions. In this particular case, conceptions D and E imply that the student relates 'mole' to both number (which represents a discontinuous perspective) and mass (which represents a continuous perspective). In consequence, we could expect all the students who exhibit conceptions D and E to adopt a combined perspective (c&d) in their reasoning. (In practice nine out of 15 did so.)

This seems a very reasonable expectation, especially if we restrict ourselves to looking at how the categories of descriptions are related to each other logically. As far as the individuals' real acting and reasoning are concerned, other factors – in addition to the logical connections – have to be taken into consideration. Above all, there is a difference between the task given and the concluding question about the mole in the interview. The former invites the adoption of continuous perspective. As was pointed out, it is in fact necessary in order to solve the problem. A majority of the students answered the mole question by referring to number. More specifically, it is the Avogadro constant that most of them have in mind. The categorization of the protocols into perspectives was made on the basis of the students' accounts of their solutions of the task, while the categorization into conceptions was made on the basis of the entire interview – including the question about 'mole' at the end. Now, as we have pointed out, these two contexts of thinking differ in important respects and thinking in general is profoundly contextual. This accounts for most of the deviation between the pattern of logical relations between categories of description and the pattern of empirical relationships between conceptions in Tables 1, 2, and 3.

The empirical relationships in Tables 1, 2, and 3 are, however, only by-products of this research, the main aim of which is to reveal the qualitatively different ways in which people think about the world around them (in this particular study, how they think about the 'mole concept'). The categories of description arrived at are seen as the main result of the phenomenographic research enterprise.

Contribution to phenomenography

We mentioned earlier the growing interest within the research community in describing the ways in which students understand and misunderstand scientific concepts. In this respect, our study is similar to a great number of others. We would, however, like to point to some methodological differences between the approach adopted by us and approaches adopted by other researchers having interests similar to ours.

We have used three different, though related, models of description. These were the collective map of patterns of reasoning, the perspectives and the outcome space of conceptions. In our view, it is the first of these that comes closest to the models of description used by other researchers in the field of science students' conceptual understanding.

A relatively common methodological solution of the question of how to study students' understanding of various content domains is the use of concept maps. These include, as West (1985) says:

Some form of description of knowledge elements or 'bits' (concept labels, for example) and some ways of describing the relationship between these elements.

West gives examples of some differing approaches (Shavelson, 1974; Sutton, 1980; Champagne *et al.*, 1980; West *et al.*, 1985), concluding that:

Concept maps have been used to describe discipline knowledge (eg a section of subject matter) and an individual's private understanding.

We might add that the mean distance between concepts is often calculated by means of some psychometric procedure. By doing this, the researcher can construct a kind of average structure for the group of subjects participating in the investigation.

In our collective map of patterns of reasoning there is a number of concepts corresponding to a domain of knowledge and they are seen as components of a structure comprising the concepts and relations between them. This is similar to the approach used in concept maps. There are several differences, however. One concerns they way in which the description is arrived at. In some of the studies using concept map methodologies, the actual construction of the structure is the students' task. In our study, as in some other studies using this methodology, it was the handling of a task by students which gave us the opportunity to derive a structure from the way in which they dealt with that task.

A second difference concerns ontological assumptions. In concept map studies, the observable structure constructed by the individual usually seems to be assumed to correspond to the students' representation of the domain. We, however, have tried to describe the structure of the students' actions, experiences or conceptualizations without any assumption of the exact nature – or even the existence of – an internal representation they hold.

The third (and perhaps most obvious) difference concerns the fact that in concept map studies there are, in principle, as many structures as there are individuals, while the structure in our case is of a collective character. Of course, in our case there are individual patters of reasoning, but they are seen as subsets of the collective map. This difference stems from our method of analysis. All the protocols together make up the basis of the analysis which proceeds in a dialectical manner. That is, it aims at describing the whole in terms of its parts and the parts in terms of the whole at the same time.

This mode of analysis is typical for phenomenographic analysis. But in one important respect, the description arrived at is not typical. If we consider the diagram of the collective map (without quotations), the meaning of the concepts appears to be taken for granted, as is the meaning of the relations between them. Possible qualitative differences in the understanding of the various concepts or the various relations are not revealed in the diagram as such. In this respect, our diagram of the collective map is similar to the concept maps used as models of description by some other researchers.

As we pointed out in our account of how we arrived at the description of patterns of reasoning, excerpts from the interviews were, however, seen as inherent parts of the individual diagrams. This means that in the more detailed technical report of the investigation, we characterized each individual case both in structural terms (which concepts and which relations have been used) and in terms of the varying meanings individuals associate with them (ie in what sense the concepts and the relations were used).

In order to illustrate how the different concepts are related to each other on the collective level, we have to 'freeze' the variation in their meaning. On the other hand, we can focus on one single concept at a time and describe the variation in its meaning among the students. This is exactly what we do when we describe conceptions. In this case, the outcome space does not denote relations between different concepts, but between different conceptions of the same scientific concept.

We now turn to another central aspect of phenomenography. In the case of the collective map (without quotations), the *content* (in terms of the concepts) and the *acts* (going from one concept to another) are described separately. In the case of the conceptions, act and content represent two inseparable aspects of the same whole. In each conception, there is an act of conceptualization and there is something conceptualized; the two aspects are simply inconceivable without each other. The idea of phenomenography is to describe the world as it appears to persons engaged with it. This cannot be done in the language of psychology without reference to what is acted upon, nor in the language of subject matter without reference to the act of conceptualization. Conceptions must be described in the form 'something (x) is seen as something (y)'. The answers to the questions 'What is conceptualized?' and 'How is it conceptualized?' should coexist.

Contribution to chemistry

We have noted earlier that many student misconceptions arise from conflicts between students' naive conceptions (developed outside school) and those in accepted use in science. The case of the mole is quite different. There are few out-of-school experiences to do with amount of substance as it concerns chemists. The confusions experienced by students seem, instead, to have their roots in chemistry itself. We have used the task from the investigation described in interviews with teachers of chemistry. We have also analysed a number of textbooks in chemistry. The same kind of conceptual confusions are found with teachers and in textbooks. This strongly suggests that these are the sources of students' confusions. If we want to improve student learning we may well need to turn our attention towards chemistry and chemistry teaching. Conceptual clarification needs to be achieved in these two areas in order to improve student learning. The results of phenomenographic research on students provide a key to how this conceptual clarification should proceed.

On the basis of our empirical findings we will now present some equations that may help to eliminate existing conceptual muddiness. Readers unfamiliar with chemistry and mathematics may wish to skip the derivation that follows. For those readers, we provide the essence of the argument in the mathematical presentation, together with its implications, in the next few paragraphs.

A set of six equations is derived to help clarify the relations between the quantities. In the derivation, three principles have been followed: (1) the equations originate from the collective map obtained from the research on students' conceptions; (2) the A-form is used throughout; and (3) the IUPAC conventions concerning use of the quantity calculus are used. In addition, the intention of this development was to provide a bridge between the discontinuous and continuous reasoning described in Figure 4. Thus we are careful to specify whether the quantities used refer to elementary entities or to the total system.

The development begins with two equations, (1) and (2), drawn from the collective map, and written in the A-form. Equations (3) – (6) follow directly, keeping in mind the second and third principles given above. Two things emerge. Equations (1) – (6) represent an unequivocal development of the quantities mass, number, molar mass and amount of substance, and of the unit ('mole') of the latter. This set of equations provides a way of avoiding the confusions inherent in most current treatments – and a way, it should be noted again, that is consistent with SI conventions. We do not intend that the derivation should be used directly for teaching. But it does provide the prerequisites for developing a consistent didactic presentation of a central component of chemistry.

Secondly, a need emerges from these equations for both an Avogadro constant (N_A, which is already widely used in chemistry) with units of mol^{-1}, and an Avogadro number, N_0, which is a dimensionless number, defined by equation (3) and having the further relationship with N_A given by equations (5a) and (5b). This use of N_0 is new and derived as a result of this research, but we think it is necessary to avoid the confusion, often found in textbooks, whereby N_A is referred to as Avogadro's number but is then given units (mol^{-1}). That is nonsense if it is a number.

And now to the equations themselves. Let us start from certain assumptions concerning continuous (c) and discontinuous (d) perspectives on the properties of a portion of substance. Table 4 shows a number of quantities within the two perspectives.

Table 4. *Quantities within the countinuous (c) perspective and the discontinuous (d) perspective respectively*

Continuous (c) (Property of portion of substance)		Discontinuous (d) (Property of the specified *elementary entities, eg* an atom)	
mass	m	mass	$m(1 \cdot ee)$
volume	V	volume	$V(1 \cdot ee)$
density	ρ		
amount of substance	n	number	N (Specifies the number *of elementary entities* that are 'countable' in the microscopic world, eg by means of mass spectrometric methods.)

In the continuous perspective on matter, we face the quantities mass (m), volume (V), density (ρ), amount of substance (n), etc, which are all continuous quantities regarded as abstract properties of a concrete portion of substance. In the discontinuous perspective on matter, the properties of specified elementary entities (ee), eg atoms, etc, are mass ($m[1 \cdot ee]$), volume ($V[1 \cdot ee]$), number (N), etc.

Consider N elementary entities of a system that can interact and form a portion of substance with the mass m and the amount of substance n. We then obtain two direct proportionalities:

(1) $m = m(1 \cdot ee) \cdot N$

(2) $N = N_A \cdot n$

The relation in equation (1) quite simply shows that the masses of the elementary entities are added together to constitute the mass of the portion of substance. It is the crucial bridge that connects the continuous (c) and the discontinuous (d) perspectives of comprehending matter. The introduction of the relation (1) as a fundamental relation is an implication of our empirical findings.

The unit of N is 1, so

(2a) $N = N_0 \cdot 1$

From (2) and (2a) we get

(3) $N_A = N_0 \cdot \text{mol}^{-1}$

The constant of proportionality, N_A, is a quantity called the *Avogadro constant*, which is general ($N_A - 6.022\,097\,9 \cdot 10^{23}\,\text{mol}^{-1}$). The number N_0, the numerical value of the Avogadro constant, which is the logical result of the definition of the basic SI unit 'mole', is here called *Avogadro number*. Note that N_0 is *not* included among SI's current quantities.

Use of (2a) and units from (1) suggests

(4) $1g = N_0 \cdot 1u$ or $\frac{\lg}{1u} = N_0$

The relation (4) expresses a change of unit that is based on quantity identity. Consequently it appears as a numerical factor of transformation between the mass units 1g and 1u. This factor is the Avogadro number, N_0. The value of N_0 depends on what nuclide is chosen in the definition of 1 mol. The definition of an SI unit stipulates the conditions for an experimental comparison when carrying out measurements.

If we combine the proportionalities (1) and (2), the following relation is obtained:

(5a) $m = m(1 \cdot ee) \cdot N_A \cdot n$

As $m(1 \cdot ee)$ and N_A are constants, the product $m\,(1 \cdot ee) \cdot N_A$ is also here denoted $M(ee)$. The proportionality (5a) can now be written:

(5b) $m = M(ee) \cdot n$

Note that $M(ee)$ is an elementary entity-specific constant of proportionality since $M(ee)$ includes $m(1 \cdot ee)$ as a factor, as seen in (5a). $M(ee)$ is called *molar mass* and has the SI unit $kg.\text{mol}^{-1}$. Chemists, however, normally use the unit $g.\text{mol}^{-1}$.

When the identity $M(ee) = m(1 \cdot ee) \cdot N_A$ (see equations (5a) and (5b)) is combined with equations (3) and (4) we get

(6) $M(ee) = m(1 \cdot ee) \cdot \frac{\lg}{1u} \cdot \text{mol}^{-1}$

Provided the formula mass, $m(1 \cdot ee)$, is known, and that it is substituted with its unit, u, into this equation, calculation of the molar mass for a specific substance is easy. The presence of the units in the equation helps clarify the meaning of molar mass. The use of this sixth operation was not clear for most of the students in our empirical study.

Contribution to didactics of chemistry

We will now comment on the educational implications of the equations above. We are not suggesting that students should be presented with these six equations in this form, but that they should be used to guide the design of the curriculum. We agree that the relation (1) 'is readily understood by the learner due to everyday experience' (Dierks, Weninger and Herron, 1985, p 1021). Relation (1) is a quantification that intellectually follows directly from the conceptions of matter taught at grade 1 of the upper secondary school in Sweden. Relation (2) expresses the simple quantitative fact that the amount of substance of the new portions of substance is doubled at the same time as the number of the elementary entities is doubled, etc. (This line of reasoning is based on the view of proportionality that we called the B-form. It is one aspect of how students comprehend the concept of proportionality. Our departure from earlier considerations is that we emphasize a meaning of the relationships (1) and (2) in the sense of the functions' A-form, another aspect based on empirical findings of students' understanding of the relationships to be encountered in contexts involving this function.)

The proportionality (5b) is well known in chemistry literature and textbooks, where it is mostly written as $m = n \cdot M$, ie the constant of proportionality, M, takes the place of x and the amount of substance n takes the place of k in the well-known relation used in mathematics $y = k \cdot x$. From a mathematical point of view, these alterations naturally do not matter in the slightest, other than that when the form $y = k \cdot x$ is used, the denotations y, k and x are usually given certain meanings. The very fact, however, that the proportionalities mentioned are not stated explicitly, and that the order in (5b) is not changed, reveals that there is no natural integration between chemistry and mathematics teaching. In physics teaching, thought patterns of this mathematical type concerning quantities and units are logically developed. We can see no reason whatsoever for developing different patterns of mathematical thought in physics and in chemistry. In general, one can say at present that B-form thought patterns are used in chemistry teaching when it comes to using proportionality, while in physics instruction, A-form thought patterns are used.

Chemistry textbooks mostly define the molar mass M as the mass of 1 mol of a substance with a unit of 1 g per mol. This is a B-form definition. From the student's standpoint, it is not obvious that it is a question of *division* (of quantities of different qualities) when the unit is given as 1 g *per* mol. Our presentation above explains why the units are given the forms they have as derived units.

The B-form definition of molar mass can lead to the implication that molar mass has the dimension of mass – an incorrect statement. Furthermore, use of the word 'molar' before the name of an extensive quality is restricted to the meaning 'divided by amount of substance' (eg molar volume $V_m = \frac{V}{n}$) (IUPAC, 1979). In a similar way 'linear', 'arear' or 'volumar', are restricted to the meaning 'divided by length, area or volume', respectively. In the last sense, a quantity is divided by another quantity and a new quantity is derived. This is also valid when dividing by amount of substance, but in the denotation 'molar mass' the work 'molar' refers to an SI base *unit* and not to an SI base *quantity*. Thus the term 'molar mass' might carry with it a meaning not acceptable to the intention of SI's conventions.

Our presentation also explains the difference between the Avogadro constant (N_A) and the Avogadro number (N_0). In some textbooks, N_A represents a number, and in the same textbooks, N_A is also assigned the unit mol^{-1} without any explanation being given. A presentation of this type does seem to create unnecessary conceptual confusion. According to SI, N_A represents the Avogadro *constant*. The symbol N has the connotation of number. That is confusing, because N_A is *not* a number. This is evident from equation (2). Nobody would suggest that density, ρ in the quantity equation $m = \rho \cdot V$, has the connotation of mass. Consequently, it is not denoted by a mass symbol. In a similar way the Avogadro constant N_A is a derived quantity. A source of existing conceptual confusion might be this lack of clarity concerning the symbol N_A used in textbooks.

We suggest the introduction of a new symbol, A_L, named the Avogadro-Loschmidt constant, to replace N_A. This would be an improvement within SI and chemistry. In fact, the introduction of A_L and N_0 are didactic contributions to chemistry as well as to the teaching of chemistry.

We also suggest the introduction of molar mass tables in textbooks. Recently, we have found two handbooks including molar mass tables (Meueendorf *et al.*, 1982; Ellis, 1984). In the empirical study, the students used the periodic system as a molar mass table: 'All you have to do is add the unit g.' Alternatively, the atomic mass table is used: 'All you have to do is to change the unit from u to g.' These algorithms make it difficult for the students to learn the concepts involved. For instance, in the periodic system the atomic weight of sulphur is given by the number 32.1 (in fact, relative atomic mass with the unit 1 and the dimension 1). In textbooks and tables, atomic mass has the unit u.

We advocate the introduction of the number N_0 in connection with the definition of the unit 'mole'. This helps us to derive the quantity equation (3) which explains the unit of the Avogadro constant. We also obtain the relation (6) which makes the nature of the quantity molar mass conceptually clearer to the students. Thus, we avoid in a simple way the muddiness found in textbooks.

In textbooks, the definition of 'mole' is often given such a prominent position that it obscures the quantity 'amount of substance'. In our presentation, we started with the quantities, not with the definition. In SI, quantities are fixed. The definitions of the base units in SI are, however, altered from time to time. Accordingly, however important the definitions of the base units are, it is the quantities that are important in the learning process.

This chapter has investigated students' conceptual difficulties related to amount of substance and has demonstrated a number of prerequisites for instruction and learning. It is our hope that the results we have outlined here may contribute to reducing the difficulties.

Acknowledgements

The experimental task employed in our investigation was taken from Novick and Menis (1976). The late Shimshon Novick was extremely helpful in supplying us with unpublished information about the work carried out at The Hebrew University of Jerusalem. We feel a deep sense of gratitude to his memory.

The editor and authors would like to express their thanks to John Bowden, Peter Fensham, Harry Sisler, Keith Trigwell and Leo West for valuable comments on earlier drafts of this chapter. The editor has introduced many of their suggested revisions into the original text and any errors which may thereby have arisen are his responsibility alone.

The research reported here was financially supported by the Swedish National Board of Education.

References

Cervellati, R, Montuschi, A, Perugini, D, Grimellini-Tomasini, N and Pecori Balandi, B (1982). Investigation of secondary school students' understanding of the mole concept in Italy. *Journal of Chemical Education*, **59**, 852–6.

Champagne, A B, Klopfer, L E, Desena, A T and Squires, D A (1981). Structural representation of students' knowledge before and after science instruction. *Journal of Research in Science Teaching*, **18**, 97-111.

Dierks, W (1981). Teaching the mole. *European Journal of Science Education*, **3**, 145–58.

Dierks, W, Weninger, J and Herron, J D (1985). Mathematics in the chemistry classroom. Part 2. Elementary entities play their part. *Journal of Chemical Education*, **62**, 1021-3.

Driver, R and Erickson, G (1983). Theories in action: Some theoretical and empirical issues in the study of students' conceptual frameworks in science. *Studies in Science Education*, **10**, 37–60.

Ellis, H (ed) (1984). *Nuffield Advanced Science*. Revised book of data. Harlow: Longman.

Gower, D M, Daniels, D J and Lloyd, G (1977). The mole concept. *School Science Review*, **58**, 658-76.

Habermas, J (1978). *Knowledge and Human Interest*. London: Heinemann.

IUPAC (1979). *Manual of Symbols and Terminology for Physico-chemical Quantities and Units*. Oxford: Pergamon.

Johnstone, A H, Morrison, T I, and Sharp, D W A (1971). Topic difficulties in chemistry. *Education in Chemistry*, **8**, 212–13 and 218.

Lazonby, J N, Morris, J E and Waddington, D J (1982). The muddlesome mole. *Education in Chemistry*, **19**, 109–11.

Lybeck, L (1979). A research approach to science education at Göteborg.

European Journal of Science Education, **1**, 119–24.

Lybeck, L (1981). *Arkimedes i klassen*. Gothenburg: Acta Universitatis Gothoburgensis.

Lybeck, L (1985). Research into science and mathematics education at Göteborg. In: *Proceedings of the Nordic Conference on Science and Technology Education: The Challenge of the Future*. Karlslunde, Denmark, 8–12 May.

Lybeck, L, Strömdahl, H and Tullberg, A (1985). Students' conceptions of amount of substance and its SI unit 1 mol: A subject didactic study. Paper presented at the Nordic Conference on Science and Technology Education. Karlslunde, Denmark, May 8-12, 1985.

Marton, F and Säljö, R (1984). Approaches to learning. In: F Marton *et al.* (eds), *The Experience of Learning*. Edinburgh: Scottish Academic Press.

Meueendorf, G *et al.* (1982). *Chemie. Lehrbuch für Klasse 7*. Berlin: Volk and Wissen Volksegner.

Novick, S and Menis, J (1976). A study of students' perceptions of the mole concept. *Journal of Chemical Education*, **53**, 720-22.

Shavelson, R (1974). Methods for examining representations of subject-matter structure in a student's memory. *Journal of Research in Science Teaching*, **11**, 231-49.

Shayer, M, and Adey, P (1981). *Towards a Science of Science Teaching: Cognitive Development and Curriculum Demand*. London: Heinemann.

Sutton, C R (1980). The learner's prior knowledge: A critical review of techniques for probing its organization. *European Journal of Science Education*, **2**, 107-20.

West, L H T (1985). Concept mapping. Paper presented at the AERA Annual Meeting, Chicago, March 31-April 4 1985.

West, L H T, Fensham, P J and Garrard, J (1985). Describing the cognitive structures of learners following instruction in chemistry. In: L H T West and A L Pines (eds) *Cognitive Structure and Conceptual Change*. New York: Academic Press.

West, L H T and Pines, A (eds) (1985). *Cognitive Structure and Conceptual Change*. New York: Academic Press.

Chapter 6
Promoting Conceptual Change Learning from Science Textbooks

Kathleen Roth and Charles Anderson
Michigan State University, USA

They always tell us, you know, don't use the textbook, but why *not*? I mean it's there.

(*Sarah, a student teacher, in Ball and Feiman-Nemser, 1986*)

This student teacher had learned in her teacher education courses, including her science methods course, that textbooks were bad and that good teachers do not use them. Yet faced with the demands of student teaching and the necessity to plan for five subject areas daily, Sarah relied heavily on textbooks (Ball and Feiman-Nemser, 1986). Experienced elementary and middle school teachers have also received the message (through in-service programmes and science teacher conferences) that textbook teaching in science is undesirable. Many of these experienced teachers have tried to teach without the textbook, using activity-based, textbook-free science programmes. Unlike Sarah, however, who assumes she will be able to move away from textbooks as she gains experience, many of these teachers are moving in the opposite direction. They are abandoning the activity approach and returning to the science textbook.

It is clear that preaching to Sarah and other teachers about the limitations of science textbooks and the virtues of activity-based teaching is not particularly useful. It may make them feel guilty, but it is not a solution to the problems they face in teaching elementary school science. It would be better to help them become critical and intelligent *users* of science texts, aware of both the limitations of textbooks and their potential for aiding student learning.

What do we know that will help teachers use textbooks intelligently? How should teachers use textbooks? What are the consequences if they use textbooks inappropriately? These are questions about which most educators have opinions, but few can produce arguments based on empirical evidence.

In this chapter we try to construct such an argument, drawing on two studies we have conducted that focused on the use of science textbooks. In common with other chapters, our argument begins not with teachers but with students. We describe the results of a study that examined what, and how, middle school students learn from science textbooks. We then describe the instructional strategies of two different fifth-grade teachers as they used science textbooks in their classrooms, and consider the consequences of those strategies for student learning. Finally, we come back to Sarah and her question, and draw on our two studies to make recommendations about what she should consider when she uses a textbook to teach science.

Students using textbooks

We begin by considering students as users of textbooks. Most teachers ask their students to read textbooks and expect them to learn from their reading. At the same time, though, most teachers are aware that the nature of that learning is problematical. Students often seem to read science texts without fully understanding them, but what goes wrong, and how? Recent research on text comprehension and science learning provides some answers to these questions and serves as background to the study we conducted on students' reading strategies.

Research on text comprehension

One indication of what happens when students read science texts comes from studies of comprehension of texts in general. These studies indicate that what we understand from our reading is not a straightforward interpretation of the contents of a text. Rather, it is the result of a complex interplay between the content of the text and the reader's prior knowledge.

Cognitive psychologists and other researchers investigating reading comprehension have emphasized that the reading process requires active involvement of the reader in sense-making. The meaning of a text is not simply contained in the explicit words on the next page. Instead, the reader must create, or construct, meaning in response to the text, and the reader's prior knowledge plays a central role in guiding and shaping interpretations and understandings of the text. In this view, reading is a constructive, interactive process where what is in the reader's head is used to make sense of what is written on the page.

A large number of text comprehension studies have shown that prior knowledge can both facilitate and constrain learning from text (eg Anderson, Spiro and Anderson, 1978; Bower, Black and Turner, 1979). This body of research provides compelling evidence for the critical role of the reader's prior knowledge in reading comprehension.

Studies of misconceptions and student learning in science

A second line of research also investigates how prior knowledge affects comprehension, but it focuses more particularly on how prior knowledge influences science learning. These studies indicate that the prior knowledge on which students must depend to interpret science texts is often in conflict with scientists' understandings and ways of explaining phenomena.

For example, consider what happens when school students learn about photosynthesis, the process by which green plants use the energy from sunlight to make their food (glucose) from carbon dioxide and water. In three different studies, we have administered pre-tests to probe upper elementary and middle school students' ways of thinking about how plants get their food (Smith and Anderson, 1984; Roth, 1985a; Anderson and Smith, 1986). These tests, as well as clinical interviews conducted in one of the studies (Roth, 1985a), revealed that while none of the students knew about the concept that plants make their own food during photosynthesis, the students had *rich* prior knowledge about plants. They had developed this knowledge from their everyday experiences with plants, and they were convinced that their experience-based explanations were sensible and correct. But the students' conceptions contrasted sharply with the scientific explanations they were given during instruction. In this sense, we call the students' explanations misconceptions.

Scientific explanations emphasize that plants are critical in the ecosystem because they *differ* from animals and humans in their ability to use sunlight to make their own energy-containing food internally out of non-energy-containing raw materials (water and carbon dioxide). Students, on the other hand, held misconceptions that plants eat food just *like* people eat food. Almost anything that a plant takes in, they called food for the plant: water, fertilizer, plant food, soil, air, sunlight. Thus, students saw plants as having many external sources of food which they could choose from, just as people do. They had no idea that plants could manufacture food. For example, Michelle described plants' food as basically the same as food for humans except 'plants don't have as good food as we do . . . they don't eat steaks'. According to this student, plants eat like people, but from a more limited menu. Thus, students' prior knowledge about plants was rich and personally meaningful, but it differed in critical ways from the scientific conceptions of photosynthesis presented in science class.

While prior knowledge can often facilitate learning, these students' incompatible prior knowledge about plants made learning a much more difficult task. Despite 6–8 weeks of instruction, only 7% of the 229 fifth-grade students we tested in one study were able to explain that plants get their food only by making it themselves (Roth, Smith and Anderson, 1983). Instead, students clung to their initial conceptions that plants have multiple external sources of food. At best, some students added plants' ability to make food to their list of sources of food for plants. Students' experientially based conceptions were strongly held, personally satisfying and sensible, and instruction was ineffective in helping them change these ideas (for some other examples of differing conceptions of science phenomena, see especially West's chapter in this book).

111

A study of students' reading strategies

What happens when students are asked to read texts that are based on assumptions about the world that are incompatible with their own? How do they cope with the problems posed by this situation? We attempted to answer these questions through a study of middle school students' reading about photosynthesis (Roth, 1985a). The 19 students in this study each read a 3500-word chapter on photosynthesis over a three-day period. In addition to pre-tests that confirmed that all the students started with the misconceptions described above, every student engaged in a detailed clinical interview after each day of reading and took a post-test at the end. The clinical interviews focused both on students' understanding of the section of text they had just read and on their ideas of how plants get their food. Each student read one of three alternative texts. Two were commercial middle school textbooks (Blecha, Gega and Green, 1979; Brandwein et al., 1980); the other was an experimental text developed for this study (Roth 1985b). Our discussion below focuses on the 12 students who were reading the commercial texts. In this discussion, we describe five different strategies that students used to read these commercial texts.

Because all the students began with naive theories that were incompatible with the ideas explained in the texts, meaningful learning from text would not occur if students simply added to their own ideas the notion that 'photosynthesis is a process by which plants make food'. For meaningful learning to occur, the new knowledge had to be linked to prior knowledge. But these students faced a tremendous task in making such links. They first had to recognize that the new concept was related to their personal notions about plants and plants' sources of food. They had to link new information not only to prior knowledge that was *consistent* with the scientific notions but also to *incompatible* prior knowledge. Then they needed to realize that their own notions were at least partially in conflict with the scientific explanation. They also had to recognize that their own ideas were not complete or satisfying explanations and that the scientific explanation provides a more convincing and powerful alternative to their own ideas. In this chapter we will refer to the learning that results when students can make such changes, using scientific explanations and experimental evidence to change their conceptions, as *conceptual change learning*. Only one of the 12 students reading from the commercial texts achieved this conceptual learning.

Strategy 1. Reading for conceptual change. Susan was the only student in our study who used the text to *change* appropriately her experientially based ideas about how plants get their food. She integrated ideas presented in the text with her 'real-world' ideas about plants. Recognizing key statements in the text that conflicted with her own ideas, Susan gave up her misconceptions and began to think about photosynthesis as plants' only source of food.

Like the rest of the students, Susan finished the first day of reading continuing to talk about multiple, external sources of food for plants:

I: What do you think would be food for this plant?

S: Well, air, water, sun and the stuff the cells get . . . I think it said from the soil
. . . minerals, air or oxygen or whatever . . . what also happens at home, when
the leaves get all crinkled up and junk, we always give it and my Dad says it's
like fertilizer.

However, after the second day of reading, the first thing Susan described
in her recall of the text was an accurate summary of a text statement that
conflicted with her own ideas:

Well, the water *isn't* food and it gets food out of – I mean it gathers stuff out of the –
it gathers water and materials out of the soil and it's *not* food.

Susan recognized that the statement was different from her own ideas,
and she used key statements such as this to change her ways of thinking
about plants' food. Throughout the rest of the interviews she consistently
talked about plants getting food *only* by making it and *not* by taking it in
from the soil. Even when the interview questions were framed in ways
designed to elicit her experientially based thinking, Susan continued to
abandon her old ideas and to explain phenomena using ideas she learned
from the text:

Day 2

I: Can you tell me how this plant here on the table gets its food?

S: Yeah. Under there, down in the soil it gets water and nutrients from the soil
and it takes it up to the leaves and the sunlight goes on the leaves and changes
it to food through the hydroplates, or whatever. And then, from there it gets
into the cells network and it goes back down to the rest of the plant, feeds it
like, and it gets to everything by the roots, branches.

Day 2

I: If I were to cover up all but one of the leaves of this plant, do you think that
would change the way that it grows?

S: Yeah, that would, because there's only one leaf that can change the materials to
food and regularly you have much more – and I don't think that it could feed
the whole plant. I just don't believe it.

Instead of giving a typical student response that the plant is dying because
it's not getting enough light, Susan used the concept of food-making by
the plant as presented in the text to develop a reasonable explanation of
the problem.

We describe Susan's reading strategy as a conceptual change reading
strategy. This strategy is characterized by:

(1) the student's efforts to link text ideas with their experiential knowledge; to apply text ideas to explain real-world phenomena;
(2) the student's ability to recognize and actively think about text statements that are central and are in conflict with personally held naive ideas;
(3) the student's willingness to change misconceptions to resolve the conflict using text ideas.

How did the rest of the students read the two commercial texts? These students used four different reading strategies, *none* of which helped them use text information to change their misconceptions that plants have multiple sources of food that they take in from the outside environment.

Strategy 2. Overrelying on prior knowledge and ignoring text knowledge. Some students relied almost entirely on their incorrect experiential knowledge about plants and food in interpreting the text. When asked to recall what the text said, for example, they frequently attributed statements to the text which were not in it at all but which came from their prior knowledge. Although they reported that the text made sense, these students appeared to avoid thinking about the text itself as much as possible. If they could decode the words and understand enough of the gist of the text to call up a well-developed real-world schema, the text 'made sense'. Unlike Susan, these students did not attempt to use text ideas to shape their thinking.

For example, Maria read a section of one text that used milk as an example of how all foods can ultimately be traced back to green plants, the food producers. Maria announced that 'most of this stuff I already knew' and that this was the easiest section to understand. 'It was about milk.' When probed, she expanded her summary of the 'text': 'It's just about milk . . . how we get our milk from cows.' In fact, the text did not discuss people at all in this example. Maria never picked up any notion of the main ideas the text was developing – that plants make food. This is typical of her pattern of reading to find familiar ideas, ignoring the rest of the text, and relying on prior knowledge to fill in the details.

The students using this strategy often successfully answered questions posed in the text by thinking about their real-world knowledge about plants rather than using text knowledge. Without thinking about plants' role in producing food, for example, Maria came up with the right answer to the following question by thinking about her prior knowledge:

Question: All the foods we eat can be traced finally back to the

(1) green plants
(2) cows.

Maria: Correctly picked (1) and explained: 'I don't know . . . I just circled green plants because *everybody* eats green plants.'

Thus, the text 'made sense' if students had a source of information (prior knowledge about vegetarians, in this case) to answer the questions in the text and in the interview. Performance of the assigned task and compliance with school expectations was the reading goal of these students. Their strategy of overrelying on prior knowledge enabled them to reach this goal without developing an understanding of the content.

Strategy 3. Overrelying on details in the text – separation of prior knowledge and text knowledge. Other students paid much more attention to the text. But their way of paying attention did not help them to understand the concepts outlined in the text and to relate those concepts to what they already knew. These readers were 'bottom-up' processors of text (Spiro, 1979) or, in the terminology of Marton and Säljö (1984), used a surface approach. They focused on the details in the text but failed to attach any meaning to them. The details, most often specialized science vocabulary, were just isolated words that students saw as having no relationship to each other or to any prior real-world knowledge. They felt they 'understood' the text if they were able to decode the words and to identify details in the text that satisfactorily answered the questions it posed. And they learned that using the big words can often get you by in school. They saw this school exercise as having nothing to do with their own ideas about how real plants get their food. They never changed their conceptions about how plants get food, and they never used the big words they had picked up from the text when they were talking about real plants. 'School knowledge' in text was seen as something totally separate from real-world understanding.

When asked to relate what she had read, Tracey described the book as being about particular words or phrases ('It was about chlor-something and an ecosystem'). She could not attach any meaning to these words or relate the words to each other. In spite of this lack of attention to meaning, she felt she understood the text. That this strategy of focusing on words in the text was never used to make sense of it became clear when Tracey answered text-posed questions. Her strategy for answering questions was to look for the big word in the question, find the big word in the text, and copy the surrounding words or sentence. Using this strategy, she was able to answer many of the test-posed questions accurately. What is photosynthesis? Tracey put: 'Photosynthesis is a food-making process.' But when asked to reread a paragraph that defined photosynthesis and then to describe photosynthesis, Tracey did not have any meaning for the word. She described photosynthesis vaguely as 'some kind of chemical or name or something'. The final interview question after three days of reading was, 'can you tell me anything about photosynthesis?' Tracey replied: 'No, I don't remember it (the text) saying anything about it.' The question-answering process had been meaningless for Tracey in the sense of developing an understanding of the text content. It *was* meaningful to her, however, because it enabled her to complete a school task successfully.

When asked what she knew about how a real plant sitting in the classroom got its food, Tracey relied totally on her prior knowledge, giving the same description after each day's reading. She never linked the text

115

content with her prior knowledge about plants. She used her knowledge about schooling and science classrooms to 'make sense' of the textbook without ever recognizing that it conflicted with real-world thinking about plants. Students using Tracey's approach did not recognize that the text ideas had anything to do with real plants. Despite their failure to look for meaning in text, they were rarely confused about the reading. They were not cognitively engaged with text ideas and, as a result, it was impossible for them to use the text to change their misconceptions.

Strategy 4. Overrelying on facts in the text with an additional notion of learning – separating prior knowledge and text knowledge. Other students went beyond the focus on words but still kept their understanding of ideas presented in the text separate from their knowledge about real plants. These students held the view that school science learning is all about developing a list of facts about natural phenomena. Their prior experiences with schooling had convinced them that memorization of unrelated facts is satisfactory learning (cf Säljö, 1984, p 88). They accumulated facts from the text but never attempted to relate the facts to each other or to their real-world knowledge about plants. This strategy is also a type of surface approach and it makes reading for conceptual change impossible.

While students like Tracey tended to recall single words, which they listed without reference to any meaning, they often had fairly accurate and complete recall of explicit text material. They might recall, for example, that 'plants make their food' and that 'chlorophyll is what makes leaves green'. However, they remembered ideas in no particular conceptual order; they placed equal emphasis on trivial details and on main concepts (they 'horizontalized' the text: cf Eizenberg's students in Chapter 9), and they did not link facts together to develop a picture of the main concepts. For example, Myra remembered a lot of details about an experiment that had been described in the text she was reading:

Myra: She had some fish and she had some plants in there and one day she was looking at them and a bubble came out of one of the plants. And she started experimenting a little, and she noticed they were giving off oxygen, they asked us what we thought. I put one time it did and one time it didn't . . . They said the first time it wasn't sunny all the time. The first time it was out for one week and every day it was sunny.

However, when the interviewer asked Myra about whether the girl doing the experiment had made a conclusion about the role of the sun, Myra said, simply, 'no'. Although she remembered a lot of details, she missed the critical reason for the experiment being included in the text.

Students using this strategy answered questions about real plants without making reference to any of the facts they had read about in the text and included in their recall. Their view of science learning as an accumulation of memorized facts from textbooks prevented them from linking those facts to real plants.

Strategy 5. Overreliance on prior knowledge and distorting text to make it compatible with prior knowledge. Five of the 12 students genuinely tried to make sense of text and to integrate text ideas with what they already knew about plants. They used a more sophisticated strategy of attempting to link prior knowledge and text knowledge. This is critical for conceptual change learning. However, because the students' real-world knowledge was so strongly held and because it was often in conflict with the content of the text, the students using this fifth strategy distorted or ignored some of the text information to make it fit with their ideas. Thus, these students did make some attempts at integrating real-world and disciplinary knowledge, but they expected that the text would basically confirm what they already knew. They read to add more details to what they already knew, not to change what they knew. With prior knowledge in the driver's seat, students' interpretations of the text were often quite different from those intended by the authors of the text.

Kevin was an above-average reader who almost anyone would have predicted would have no trouble making sense of the text. However, Kevin began with a strong conception that plants have multiple sources of food. On his pre-test he wrote:

Food (for plants) can be sun, rain, light, bugs, oxygen, soil and even other dead plants. Also warmth or coldness. All plants need at least three or four of these foods. Plus minerals.

Nevertheless, Kevin claimed that he had had all this 'stuff' before, that this was all 'sort of like a review for me with some detail'. And, indeed, Kevin did pick up a lot of details, especially about plant structures. However, he described these plant structures in ways more consistent with his prior knowledge than with what the text had said. For example, the text makes the point that roots and root hairs take in water but that this water is not food for the plant. It describes the water as being taken to the leaf where it combines with carbon dioxide to produce food. Kevin described root hairs this way:

Root hairs, they go, it goes further than the roots . . . and it goes further into the soil to get water and minerals and stuff like that, food.

He said that the main idea of this section of the text was that 'it told about the food from the soil, like minerals and water'. He interpreted the text as saying just the opposite of what it actually did say.

In the end, Kevin developed a pretty good definition of photosynthesis. What middle school teacher would not be pleased with this explanation?:

Well, in the leaves, in the green plants, they have little chloroplasts which inside that have chlorophyll. When the sun shines on it it does photosynthesis which changes, well it doesn't really change, but the plant has certain chemicals that change the sunlight . . . well, they have certain chemicals that the sunlight changes into food which is energy for the plant.

But this was not the only way plants get food, according to Kevin. When asked to summarize how a plant gets its food, Kevin replied:

Whew, from lots of places. From the soil for one, for the minerals and water, and from the air for oxygen. The sunlight for sun and so it would change chemicals to sugars. It sort of makes its own food and gets food from the ground. And from air.

Kevin had a fascinating way of distorting ideas from text and mixing these with his ideas from prior knowledge. He decided photosynthesis was the leaves' source of food and described water and minerals as food for the roots. The stem could use both sources. Unlike students using the other strategies, he did not keep prior knowledge and text knowledge separate. He tried to link the two, and he changed his ideas in a way he thought was consistent with the text.

Conclusion

This study of students' text-processing strategies describes the situation confronted (usually unknowingly) by Sarah as well as by more experienced science teachers. In order to learn science with comprehension, their students must go through a process of *conceptual change*, but this rarely happens when students are asked to read commercial texts on their own. Instead, students typically cope with the task by using reading Strategies 2–5 described above.

In all these ineffective strategies, conflicting prior knowledge hindered rather than helped students in making sense of text. While the students using these strategies had reading test scores ranging from grade level equivalents of 3rd grade to post-high school, all failed to develop meaningful understandings of photosynthesis and food for plants. In this sense, they were all poor readers.

However, these students were reading the texts in the absence of any instruction. Could classroom instruction help students use the text to change their preconceptions appropriately?

Teachers using textbooks

In this section we consider what happens when teachers use science textbooks as part of their classroom instruction. The case studies of Ms Lane and Ms Ramsey both come from a two-year study of fifth grade science teaching in which teachers were using commercial science text as they taught a unit about light and seeing. The study included teacher and student interviews, classroom observations of a unit of teaching, and pre- and post-tests of student learning.

Ms Lane is representative of five teachers we observed during the first year of the study who used the texts in reasonable ways but were ultimately unsuccessful in helping students through the process of conceptual change. These teachers were thoughtful and experienced. But, in fact, they unintentionally *encouraged* students to use the ineffective reading strategies described in the last section. Ms Ramsey is representative of six teachers observed using the same textbook during the second year of the study. With the help of supplemental material developed by us, she and the other second-year teachers were much more successful in helping the students through the process of conceptual change.

Ms Lane: a typical pattern of science textbook use

Planning and content coverage. In planning what she would teach about the concepts of light and seeing, Ms Lane relied on what was covered in the text. While she thought about what her students might already know of light, she did not consider what they might *misunderstand* about light. The *Teacher's Guide* to the textbook did not suggest to her that students might have ideas that would pose critical barriers to their understanding of the main concepts in the unit. Her planning and lesson content were determined by the page numbers in the text that were to be covered. Since the text presented one idea after another without emphasis on important ideas, without relating one idea to another, and without challenging students' common misconceptions, Ms Lane's lesson plans and unit organization followed the same format. In one class period, for example, Ms Lane introduced the following concepts: light as energy, light for seeing, light travels fast, the speed of light, atoms, photons, sources of light (artificial v. natural), bioluminescence, uses of light, animals that give off light, reasons light travels fast, lightning, amplitude, wavelengths, light travels in straight lines, intensity of light, pioneer uses of candles, electricity provides artificial light, watts, volts, fluorescence, and light cannot curve.

It is easy to imagine that students would fall back on inappropriate strategies to make sense of all this information. Some students probably ignored the text and relied on prior knowledge to get by (Strategy 2 above). Many others clearly succeeded on the textbook-produced unit test by memorizing words and facts. For example, they could match the words *transparent, translucent* and *opaque* to their definitions. However, it was clear from the researcher-constructed post-tests, which required students to explain everyday phenomena, that they had failed to link the memorized facts together or to change their everyday ways of thinking about light. For example, they could not explain how light enables a person to see a tree. The breadth of content coverage and the once-over-lightly coverage of this mountain of information communicated to these students that learning in science is memorizing facts and/or big words that have nothing to do with real life (Strategies 3 and 4 above).

Questions. Ms Lane's usual instructional pattern was to have students take turns reading aloud from the text, pausing to answer orally questions posed at the end of paragraphs in the text. Unfortunately for Ms Lane's students, the questions posed in the text were often not the most important ones in terms of helping them learn key concepts. The text-posed questions were problematic in two ways. First, they did not help students think about the ideas most likely to posit difficulties for them. Many questions were asked but they were wide ranging in content and predominantly fact-oriented. Students could answer this type of question easily by finding big words or facts in the text (Strategies 3 and 4 above).

Secondly, while some of the questions did encourage students to think about their everyday experiences with light, they did not elicit students' misconceptions or challenge students to use scientific concepts or explanations to *change* their naive ways of thinking about those everyday experiences. Rather, many questions were of the sort that invited everyone to tell a story about some personal experience with light. Thus, the text questions encouraged students to rely on their prior knowledge about light without requiring that they link the ideas presented in the text to that prior knowledge. As a result, the use of Strategy 2 above, overreliance on prior knowledge, was encouraged.

For example, pre-tests showed that Ms Lane's students did not have any idea that light enables us to see because it bounces off objects to our eyes. Rather, students held the idea that light shines on objects, and we then directly perceive the objects. The difference between the students' conception and the scientific conception is illustrated in Figure I.

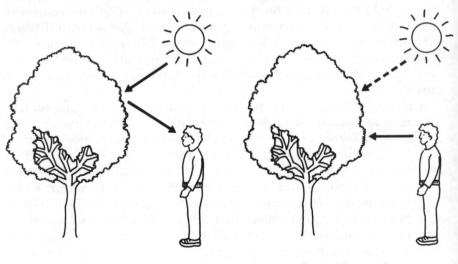

Scientific conception   Students' conception

Figure 1. The difference between (a) the scientific conception, and (b) the students' conception

One paragraph in the book begins by talking about the necessity of light for seeing. However, instead of posing a question to focus students' thinking on this important scientific concept, the question at the end of the paragraph drives the discussion and student thinking away from the central issue by asking: 'When do you think lights made by people are helpful?' The resulting discussion in Ms Lane's class focused on why we need to see rather than on why *light* is needed for us to see. It was a lively discussion with lots of students coming up with tales of what would happen if we had no light. But the discussion did nothing to help students gain a new understanding of why light enables us to see. The students felt they were comprehending the text because they could answer this question, but in fact the question only encouraged them to think about their prior knowledge. The question did nothing to help reveal students' misconceptions to the teacher, and it did not suggest to students that their ideas about light and seeing might be different from those held by scientists. It also did not create the conceptual conflict or confusion that would suggest to students that they might need to change some of their ideas about how light helps us to see.

Thus, the questions posed by Ms Lane were usually taken from the textbook, were generally easy for students to answer using facts from the book or their everyday experiences, and did not serve a diagnostic role in helping Ms Lane understand her student's thinking. They did not challenge students to think about the contrasts between scientific ways of thinking about light and their own. In fact, the questions posed in the text often misled students into thinking that this was all stuff they already knew (Strategy 5 above) and that to learn it they simply needed to memorize a long list of facts. The students were not asked to link their stories of everyday experiences with light with the facts presented in the book.

Responding to students. In listening to student responses to questions, Ms Lane waited to hear the answer given by the *Teacher's Guide* to the text. She would call on students until she got a correct answer, politely passing over or rejecting incorrect student answers. By failing to attend to the thinking behind students' incorrect answers, Ms Lane missed the opportunity to discover students' misconceptions and to structure discussions in ways that would help them change their ideas. When students had difficulty coming up with the right answer, she would change the question and rephrase it to help them produce the right answer. Notice in the following example how an initial question that asks for a student explanation is changed into a series of factual-level questions in which text language is used to give students hints about the desired answer:

Ms Lane: What is the function of the optic nerve? (waits, no response) What is it that a nerve does? What do they do?

Heidi: Tells whether it is hot or cold.

Ms Lane: Uh . . . , OK, they send what?

Students: (calling out) Messages.

Ms Lane: Where do they send them?

Students: (calling out) To the brain.

Ms Lane: Without the optic nerve, could you see?

Students: (unison) No.

Ms Lane: Because it sends messages of the image to the brain. (She writes on the board: Optic nerve from the back of the eye to the brain.)

Once the students gave a correct answer, even when the wording of the question had already given it away, Ms Lane proceeded to a new topic as though these correct answers signified that the students had understood. Students' one- or two-word responses to a series of questions were accepted as evidence that they understood how to put these answers together to explain the function of the optic nerve. And students quickly learned that using isolated words or phrases from the text (Strategy 3) would more often lead to satisfactory answers than trying to make sense of text ideas.

At other times, Ms Lane accepted incorrect answers if they were close enough to the response she wanted. She would indicate approval that the answer was correct and restate the answer. However, her restatement might be quite different from the student's answer:

Ms Lane: Then there are cells that contain pigments (in the retina). What do you think they do?

Jim: They store.

Ms Lane: What might they do? What does pigment have to do with?

Bob: The colour of the eye.

Ms Lane: So you think they might help us to see colour?

Students: Yeah.

(Ms Lane goes on to next type of cell, light-sensitive cells.)

Bob's answer was referring to the colour of the *iris* of the eye; he was talking about something very different from the pigment-containing cells in the retina that Ms Lane was discussing. But Ms Lane heard something about colour and accepted an inappropriate answer as if it were correct. She did not probe to elicit improvement of this answer or of other incorrect or half-correct student answers. Bob's strategy of relying only on prior knowledge to answer the question was not challenged.

Ms Lane also allowed students to use everyday definitions of scientific terms. For example, the students had learned from the text that the scientific definition of 'transparent' is something that light can pass through. However, each time the term came up in classroom discussions, the students talked about transparent as 'something you can see through'. By not insisting that they think about what happens to light and by allowing them to talk of 'seeing through' things, Ms Lane allowed the student misconception to persist, ie that we see by directly perceiving objects (see Figure 1 above). And students received the message that their everyday ways of thinking and talking about light and seeing were correct. In attaching 'big words', such as 'transparent' to their naive ways of thinking, students were distorting the text meaning, just as Kevin did with the text on photosynthesis (Strategy 5 above). The students thought they were adding details to what they already knew. The text and Ms Lane never helped them recognize that there was any problem with what they already knew.

Explanations. Ms Lane generally depended on reading the textbook out loud to give explanations of scientific concepts: 'Let's read what our book says about what makes the sky blue or other colours'. And there were *many* explanations! Ms Lane rarely even rephrased these explanations unless it became necessary for answering one of the questions posed in the text. Only once throughout the whole unit did she give an explanation in her own words about the critical issue of how light enables seeing. Thus, students were quickly exposed to many explanations, but were rarely challenged to struggle with making sense of them. All explanations were treated as equally important and as straightforward presentations of fact that required only passive acceptance by the students.

Even when students raised issues that were confusing to them, Ms Lane did not take the opportunity to encourage them to use a conceptual change reading strategy. One day, for example, after reading an explanation from the textbook about how the eye inverts images, the students confronted Ms Lane with their confusion:

Ms Lane: Would you read, Scott, that little section near the illustration?

Scott: The lens of each eye bends light so that the images of things you look at form upside down on the retina. But your brain 'reads' the messages about these images in a way that lets you see things right side up.

Pat: I don't get it.

Ms Lane: OK, so actually if you look at the second picture, when you look at something it is upside down.

Heather: Why?

Ms Lane: (comes over to Heather's desk and points at the diagram in her book) I think it is because of the way light bends. See how the light comes in at two angles from the bottom part. It's rather confusing, isn't it? To think that we see everything upside down. (She walks to the front of the room and directs the students to close the books and look at an overhead).

123

Ms Lane appeared uncomfortable giving this explanation and clearly was not intent on her students' understanding of the concept. Instead of encouraging them to struggle with their confusions, she quickly moved on to a new topic. Thus, Ms Lane used explanations as a way of presenting lots of information to students and did not encourage them to grapple with any confusions or conflicts the explanations might raise.

Activities. Ms Lane infused her lesson with many hands-on activities. She used almost all the activities suggested in the text, except the ones that another teacher had told her 'don't work'. She also found activities from other sources that were related to light, colour and seeing. During the 15 lessons in the light unit, Ms Lane conducted 20 hands-on activities (teacher demonstrations, student experiments), and she told the interviewer that she had found a new book of experiments she would draw from in teaching the unit next time.

Student learning in Ms Lane's classroom. Although Ms Lane and the other five teachers in this study ended the unit feeling all had gone well, both post-tests and clinical interviews revealed that students' misconceptions had persisted. Ms Lane's students became aware of idea after idea about light, but they were not stimulated to think about the meaning of these ideas. They viewed learning science as a mass of information to be memorized. Ms Lane's absorption with the textbook and the suggested answers to questions given in her teacher's edition took her attention away from focusing on what her students were really saying, thinking, and misunderstanding.

How textbooks help teachers

The difficulties experienced by Ms Lane and her students might seem to lend support to the argument that commercial science textbooks do more harm than good, and that Ms Lane and her students would be better off with no textbooks at all. This is the message that Sarah (quoted at the beginning of this chapter) was getting from her methods professors. Could it be that they are right?

There are a number of reasons for arguing that Ms Lane would *not* be better off without a textbook. Some of our arguments are based on the problems experienced by teachers we observed using an activity-based science programme (Knott *et al.*, 1978; Smith and Anderson, 1984). In this curriculum, students participate in the gathering, recording, and analysis of experimental data in order to develop understanding of central concepts and processes in science. A *Teacher's Guide* provides background information and details about the experimental procedures and suggested questions for discussion, but there is no student textbook.

We observed nine teachers using this curriculum to teach a unit about plants' ability to produce food. While the teachers were quite skilful at the challenging task of managing students as they carried out hands-on activities, they had difficulties helping students understand the *meanings* to be drawn from the activities. Some teachers became so involved in the activities that they failed to provide opportunities to explore the ideas behind the activities (Smith and Sendelbach,1982). Others led discussions to elicit students' explanations of the activities but were frustrated that students clung to their misconceptions (Roth, 1984; Smith and Anderson, 1984). These teachers were unsure about how to explain ideas about photosynthesis or how to respond to students' misconceptions. They believed that the activities themselves should have helped students 'discover' the need to change their ideas.

In the end, student learning in these activity-based classrooms was just as disappointing as in the textbook-centred classrooms. Although the teachers did not bombard students with lots of facts, but instead focused on central concepts, their students failed to develop understandings of these concepts. After 6–8 weeks of such instruction, only 7% of 229 students changed their misconception about how plants get food and understood that plants get food by making it in the process of photosynthesis. Replacing the textbook with hands-on activities is not a solution to teachers' problems.

We conclude that even in cases like Ms Lane's where there are many problems with student learning, the textbook is still performing a number of important functions. First of all, textbooks help teachers make *curriculum decisions* about what topics to teach, what to emphasize, and how to order topics. This is a particularly important function of textbooks for elementary teachers, who generally do not have strong science backgrounds. They rely on the text to define the content to be taught and the appropriate depth of coverage for a particular grade level. As one of the teachers explained:

I decided to start at the beginning and just go straight through the text . . . If you don't have any logical reason for juggling the units, then why do it? I still think, well somebody must have known something when they wrote the text. Laidlaw is an old established textbook company and if they include something in a text, it must be pretty well written.

(*Slinger, Anderson and Smith, 1982*)

Textbooks also help simplify *planning and the selection of teaching strategies* for teachers. Textbooks can greatly reduce the cognitive demands placed on teachers, especially when the texts are used not just to guide curriculum decisions but to guide daily teaching strategies. For Ms Lane, planning consisted primarily of identifying and reviewing the pages in the text to be covered. This type of planning and teaching is certainly less demanding than that required for activity-based teaching. In activity-based programmes, for example, teachers must plan and manage the handing out and cleaning up of materials, be prepared for a variety of difficulties students might have in carrying out the experiments, keep students on task as they work with material, and lead discussions that can take a number of different turns depending on how the experiment goes and how students interpret it. Textbooks reduce such management and planning demands and result in more orderly, predictable lessons. Teachers also rely on textbooks to provide *scientific explanations* and information in a clear, straightforward way for students. Giving good explanations is a very difficult task. Ms Lane, for example, explained ideas by simply repeating the text explanations. On the few occasions when she tried to develop her own explanations, she ended by confusing both herself and her students.

Given these functions of textbooks, it not surprising that teachers use them so heavily. But what about the students' failure to learn from such text-centred teaching? Don't teachers care about student learning?

Teachers are unaware of students' misconceptions

A decisive finding from our studies is that teachers are often unaware of the ways in which students misunderstand and misinterpret textbooks. Teachers using the textbook chapter about light ended their units expressing satisfaction that students had learned. One teacher, for example, pointed to her students' performance on the unit test provided in the *Teacher's Guide*. All the students had received marks greater than 50%, with all except three having 70% or better. Unfortunately, the tests assessed students' abilities to match terms such as 'transparent', 'translucent', and 'opaque' to their definitions, but did not test students' understanding of those concepts in real-world contexts. Thus, students could recognize that 'transparent' matched up to the definition 'object that light can pass through', but would explain on the researcher-constructed post-test how a boy can see a tree through the window without referring to the behaviour of light, saying that 'the boy can see through the window because the window is transparent'. Students thus ended their instruction still holding on to their naive beliefs about how light helps us see. Because teachers did not ask questions that would reveal students' persistent misconceptions, they remained in the dark about their students' misunderstandings.

Ms Ramsey: using the textbook to promote conceptual change learning

In the second year of this classroom study, we attempted to help teachers to use the textbook more effectively by developing new curricular materials. Five teachers using the textbook to teach about light, including Ms Lane, were given a set of transparencies and accompanying *Teacher's Guide* (Anderson and Smith, 1982) to use as a supplement to the regular text. Using these materials, the teachers were much more successful in helping students develop understandings of the scientific explanations than they had been in Year 1 when we observed most of them teaching the same unit using only the text.

In this section we will describe ways in which one of these teachers, Ms Ramsey, used the text differently from all the teachers we had seen in the first year. We will point out how this encouraged students to use the text to change their conceptions and to develop scientific understandings of the presented concepts. Ways in which these teaching strategies *discouraged* the use of the four ineffective reading strategies will also be described.

Ms Ramsey was using the same text chapter about light and seeing as Ms Lane. However, she also used the set of researcher-developed transparencies which were designed to focus instruction on a few key ideas that were problematical for students who had misconceptions about light and seeing. Each transparency first presented a problem for students to answer. Each problem consisted of an everyday situation that *could* be explained using concepts from the text. However, students who had not yet linked text ideas with everyday phenomena would be likely to explain these problems by relying only on their prior knowledge and everyday ways of thinking about light (Strategy 2). The transparencies each included an overlay showing a scientific explanation of the problem (see Figure 2). Thus students could immediately contrast their own answer with one more consistent with ideas in the text. The *Teacher's Guide* to the transparencies described common student misconceptions, predictable explanations that students might use to answer the problems, and explanations of the relationship between students' common misconceptions and the scientific conceptions of light and seeing.

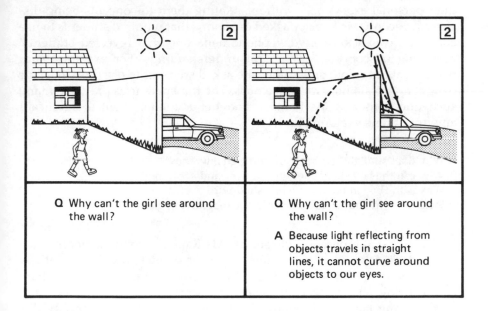

Figure 2. Page from 'Transparencies on Light Teacher's Guide' illustrating the transparency used by Ms Ramsey

Planning and content coverage. Ms Ramsey's teaching focused on getting key concepts across rather than on covering all the pages in the text. Unlike Ms Lane, Ms Ramsey focused on the key issues that seemed to represent critical barriers to student learning. Her content coverage could be described as narrow and deep compared to Ms Lane's. This focus conveyed to students that science was about understanding and making sense of a few ideas, rather than a process of collecting and memorizing facts and words (Strategies 3 and 4).

Because of this focus on key ideas, Ms Ramsey chose not to have students read the whole text chapter. Instead, she focused on certain key passages in the text and had students use the text much less frequently. For example, the only part of the first section of the text that the students read in class was the paragraph that explained how light bounces off objects to people's eyes. This was the paragraph that had no question at the end of it to indicate its importance. While Ms Lane had skimmed over the paragraph, Ms Ramsey focused on this section with a ten-minute discussion of how light bounces. Instead of *following* the text, she *used* the text to help students develop the central ideas.

Questions. Like Ms Lane, Ms Ramsey asked a lot of questions. However, the nature and function of her questions were very different from those of Ms Lane. First, her questions were focused more on the key issues. She tried to avoid questions that would encourage students to tell stories about their personal experiences without relating them to concepts being discussed. Second, Ms Ramsey asked questions that required students to use concepts to explain everyday phenomena and that revealed students' persisting misconceptions and misunderstandings. For example, after teaching about colour and vision, she asked students to use the behaviour of light to explain how we see colours. The transparencies provided many such questions and Ms Ramsey and her students spent a significant amount of time exploring them:

Why does sunlight reach a plant through a window?
Why can the boy look out of the window and see a tree?
Why is the boy in the picture in a shadow?
Why does the thumb look bigger in the magnifying glass?

In asking such application questions, Ms Ramsey would sometimes tell the students to answer the question 'using what you know about light'. By asking many application questions, Ms Ramsey reduced students' chances of being able to 'get by' using the strategies of picking out and regurgitating facts or big words from the text (Strategies 3 and 4). She encouraged them to link text ideas and real-world phenomena, fostering the use of a conceptual change strategy. Students might have succeeded in answering these questions by overrelying on prior knowledge (either Strategy 2 or 5), but Ms Ramsey's ways of listening and responding to students discouraged the use of these strategies.

Responding to students. An important way in which Ms Ramsey's verbal behaviour differed from Ms Lane's was the way she responded to student answers to her questions. She not only frequently required students to explain phenomena, she also listened carefully to these explanations and frequently readdressed questions to a student to get a clearer idea of what the student was saying or to challenge the student to give a more complete, accurate explanation. In contrast with Ms Lane's class, student answers were lengthier, and the teacher was more likely to interact with a student repeatedly before posing a new question or moving on to another student. She would also come back to a student after other students had spoken to see if she could get the student to restate a position more precisely, based on what other students had said. She constantly pushed students to clarify their explanations, and she pointed out to them the limitations of their answers and contrasts between different student answers. This careful probing of student answers enabled Ms Ramsey to uncover student misconceptions even when the students' initial answers sounded pretty good and could easily have been accepted as close enough approximations of the 'correct' answer. The following classroom excerpt illustrates how Ms Ramsey followed up on students' statements. The discussion is focused on the overhead transparency illustrated in Figure 2.

Ms Ramsey: (Puts up transparency) Why can't the girl see around the wall?

Annie: The girl can't see around the wall because the wall is opaque.

Ms Ramsey: What do you mean when you say the wall is opaque?

Annie: *You can't see through it. It is solid.*

Brian: (calling out) The rays are what can't go through the wall.

Ms Ramsey: I like that answer better. Why is it better?

Brian: The rays of light bounce off the car and go to the wall. They can't go through the wall.

Ms Ramsey: Where are the light rays coming from originally?

Students: The sun.

Annie: *The girl can't see the car because she is not far enough out.*

Ms Ramsey: So you think her position is what is keeping her from seeing it. (She flips down the overlay with the answer.) Who was better?

Students: Brian.

Ms Ramsey: (to Annie) Would she able to see if she moved out beyond the wall?

Annie: Yes.

Ms Ramsey: Why?

Annie: *The wall is blocking her view.*

Ms Ramsey: Is it blocking her view? What is it blocking?

Student: Light rays.

Ms Ramsey: Light rays that are doing what?

Annie: If the girl moves out beyond the wall, then the light rays that bounce off the car are not being blocked.

In this interchange, notice how Annie has first tried to demonstrate her understanding of the concepts presented in the text by using a 'big word' (*opaque*). Although her answer sounds good, and some teachers might have ended the discussion with that answer, Ms Ramsey probes to be sure Annie has attached some meaning to the word. Annie has indeed attached some meaning, but it is not the meaning explained in the book. Instead, she fits the text word 'opaque' into her everyday way of thinking about how we see: we see by looking out and directly perceiving objects. Annie's emphasized responses all reflect this misconception about seeing. For example, when she says, 'You can't see through the wall', or 'the wall is blocking her view', she is not applying ideas from the text about the role of light in seeing. In fact, she is not thinking about *light* as being involved at all. She is only thinking about the girl and the car and the object blocking the girl's view. She is using her everyday knowledge about seeing, and attaching a text word, *opaque*, in a way that has nothing to do with light – it is just something you cannot see through.

Annie is using a strategy of integrating text knowledge and prior knowledge in a way that distorts text information to make it fit her preconceived view (Strategy 5). Ms Ramsey asked questions that challenged students to develop more appropriate answers.

Ms Ramsey also responded to students with very careful feedback. She praised students for precise, careful use of language: 'I like that word better. Why is it better?' When students made incorrect statements, Ms Ramsey would often directly point out the inaccuracies or limitations of the student's statement:

Ms Ramsey: The pigments absorb the green light so no green light is reflected. What will the plant look like in the green light?

Amy: The plant will appear green, because the object is already green.

Ms Ramsey: No, the *object* isn't green. The *light* is green and the object reflects . . .

Amy: Green light.

Another key feature of Ms Ramsey's questioning pattern was the repeated opportunities she gave students to work with a single concept. Several different application questions were asked addressing each key concept, so that students had repeated opportunities to work on developing explanations of everyday events using text ideas. In addition, different students were given opportunities to answer the same question.

Ms Ramsey's emphasis on developing explanations communicated to students a valuing of sense-making over content coverage and encouraged the use of a conceptual change strategy. Ms Ramsey's questions could not be answered by ignoring text ideas (Strategy 2), or by repeating big words or facts from the text (Strategies 3 and 4).

Explanations. Ms Ramsey did not rely on the textbook as the only source of explanations about concepts. She did not have students read an explanation and then move on to the next paragraph simply because the text had not posed a question at that point. Instead, Ms Ramsey represented and explained concepts to students in a variety of ways, including reading and discussing text explanations, discussing the problems posed in the transparencies, and completing teacher-designed worksheets. Ms Ramsey often repeated and rephrased explanations and used key transparency questions to emphasize important concepts. There was a regular end-of-the-lesson classroom activity of developing 'summary statements' of important ideas which students then copied into their notebooks. Finally, explanations were clearly linked to activities and demonstrations.

Activities. While Ms Ramsey taught exactly the same number of lessons as Ms Lane, she used only five experiments/demonstrations. Like Ms Lane, Ms Ramsey liked to use activities to motivate students. However, in addition to emphasizing the 'fun' aspects of such activities, Ms Ramsey also described their importance as stimulators of student thinking. One of the reasons she used fewer activities is because she had students *think about* and discuss each experiment much more thoroughly than Ms Lane. Observations were only a first step in 'doing' experiments in Ms Ramsey's class. The activities represented another occasion (in addition to the application question) for posing everyday problems and phenomena for students to explain using new concepts presented in the text.

Ms Ramsey talked with students on three different days about one experiment in which a pencil appeared bent as it sat in a glass of water. The students first made careful observations, but the heart of the discussion focused on Ms Ramsey's 'why' questions: What is happening to make the pencil look that way? Do opaque objects bend light? What does a magnifying glass do to light rays? Why will sunlight passing through a magnifying glass make a bright spot on a piece of paper? Why does a thumb look bigger under a magnifying glass? Students had a chance to use text ideas to answer such questions because this experiment was done the day *after* students had read about and completed worksheets about reflection and refraction. Following the experiment, students filled out and discussed a worksheet about the experiment which required them to record both observations and explanations. These ideas were discussed in class on two different occasions, with Ms Ramsey consistently asking students to clarify their explanations and to use ideas about light rays from the text to explain. Thus, concepts that the activities demonstrated were explored in depth, and the activities were used to encourage students to link text ideas and real-world phenomena. In this way, the activities supported conceptual change learning. Students could not rely on facts or big words in the text or overrely on prior knowledge to answer Ms Ramsey's questions about the experiments.

Student learning in Ms Ramsey's classroom

Did these differences in teaching style make a difference in terms of student learning? On the post-test, 64% of Ms Ramsey's students understood how light enables seeing and could apply that concept to everyday phenomena. Only 15% of the students in Ms Lane's class (in Year 1) had developed this kind of understanding. Because her students were challenged to think about and state their ideas clearly and to give evidence for their ideas, Ms Ramsey learned a lot about their thinking. This knowledge helped her to elicit, analyse, and respond to students effectively. Ms Ramsey was not giving students new ideas to memorize; she was diagnosing their misunderstandings and using this knowledge to guide them in the difficult process of changing their ideas about light and seeing. Ms Ramsey could be characterized as a conceptual change teacher.

Discussion: using textbooks effectively

Our studies of students and teachers as they use textbooks have helped us to construct some empirically based answers to Sarah's questions. Yes, textbooks *are* there, and they will continue to be there in the foreseeable future. They also perform useful and necessary functions for teachers. However, textbooks are typically structured in ways that do not help students read for understanding. Students often use reading strategies that enable them to complete assignments and pass tests without developing conceptual understanding. In addition, most teachers follow patterns of textbook use that, though reasonable, do not help students overcome their reading difficulties. Understanding the limitations of textbooks as aids to conceptual change learning can help teachers appreciate their students' learning difficulties, but it does not tell them what to do about it. We conclude this chapter by suggesting some principles that Sarah and other teachers can follow to help students understand concepts presented in textbooks. We stress that the recommended teaching strategies cannot be used meaningfully without a thorough understanding on the teacher's part of student learning and thinking in her classroom (see also Chapter 14).

Principles for effective use of science textbooks

The principles for effective textbook use suggested below (and summarized in Table 1) are drawn from our study of text-based science teaching and learning, including the case of Ms Lane and Ms Ramsey and five other teachers. In that study, we observed strikingly similar teaching approaches being emphasized among teachers who were more effective in helping students undergo conceptual change learning.

Each principle grows out of understandings gained from our study of students' reading strategies and their difficulties in learning from text (Roth,1985). In that study, we documented ways in which textbooks are currently structured which do not help students read for conceptual understanding and conceptual change. In addition, we found that texts were often structured in ways that encouraged students to use ineffective reading strategies.

Focus on a few critical issues. Textbooks typically cover *many* ideas and emphasize many specialized vocabulary words. To cope with the barrage of ideas presented, students are forced to rely on strategies that emphasize memorization of facts and definitions of lists of 'big words' rather than on strategies that foster conceptual understanding. To use such texts to promote conceptual change learning, teachers must define the content to be covered in ways that differ substantially from most textbooks.

Instead of covering everything in the text, those teachers in our study who were more successful in promoting conceptual change learning focused on the central issues that were most problematical for students. They kept lessons closely tied to these issues and resisted going off on interesting tangents that only resulted in pulling student thinking away from the central concepts. These conceptual change teachers did not overload students with lots of specialized vocabulary words to define and memorize. Recognizing the difficulty of reading for conceptual change, they focused on helping students make real sense of a few ideas, the relations between these ideas, and the relations between these ideas and student's inaccurate or incomplete ideas. In selecting issues on which to focus, the conceptual change teachers in our study focused on ideas they knew were difficult for students and on the critical 'whys' of science. The supplementary curriculum materials we provided played a critical role in helping teachers to understand student thinking and to select central issues.

In contrast with this approach, students in Ms Lane's class became acquainted with concept after concept at a factual level, but they were never challenged to understand the concepts at a meaningful level. Information was presented without making explicit the importance of each piece of information and how the pieces fit together. Science was presented as a string of seemingly unrelated abstract ideas or observations, and this context encouraged students to use surface approaches (Strategies 3 and 4).

Table 1. *How suggested principles for effective text use grow out of knowledge of student difficulties with textbooks*

Common features of science textbooks that are problematic for conceptual change learning	Ways in which text features cause difficulties for students	Principles for effective use of textbooks
Content coverage is broad and shallow, with emphasis on specialized vocabulary words. Many concepts are 'covered', but they are addressed superficially, not in ways that promote real understanding.	Encourages students to approach learning science as memorizing lists of unrelated facts and 'big words'.	Focus on a few critical issues.
Science textbooks are written from scientists' perspectives and do not seriously consider students' alternative ways of thinking.	Students fail to change their ideas because they either do not see the connections between their own ideas and ideas in the text, or because they distort the text to make it fit with their prior knowledge.	Ask questions to elicit and challenge students' thinking and misconceptions.
Questions posed to students in textbooks are primarily fact-oriented; they rarely require students to construct explanations.	Students think they understand science because they can answer fact questions, but they may continue to hold critical misconceptions that have not been challenged.	Ask questions that give students repeated opportunities to apply text concepts to explain real-world phenomena
Teacher's guides for textbooks give correct answers to questions and do not anticipate or discuss alternative student responses.	Students develop inappropriate strategies for getting right answers and continue to hold critical misunderstandings. They view learning science as a process of getting right answers, even if the answers don't make sense to them.	Probe student responses and give clear feedback to students about their ideas.
Explanations of concepts are given in only one way, and explanations of related concepts come in rapid succession.	Students holding alternative explanations cannot link the text explanation to their own ideas. They view text explanations as things to be memorized that have nothing to do with their own understandings of the world.	Construct alternative representations of text explanations that make explicit the contrast and connections between scientific explanations and students' misconceptions.
Activities/experiments are optional supplements to the text and are not closely linked to concepts presented in the text.	Students learn that 'doing' science has little to do with reading and thinking about science concepts; that text ideas are separate from the real world. Activities are fun for students but don't help them develop better understandings of concepts.	Select and use activities to create conceptual conflict and to develop conceptual understanding.

An important part of focusing on key issues is the significant amount of redundancy built into lessons. Ms Lane had students read through the text once. Reading the textbook explanations once, especially explanations that conflict with students' everyday ways of thinking about phenomena, is not sufficient to help students recognize the contrasts between the text and their own ideas. Ms Ramsey repeated key explanations and provided numerous opportunities for students to use central concepts to explain everyday problems and situations.

Ask questions to elicit and challenge students' thinking and misconceptions. Textbooks are written from scientists' perspectives; students' alternative ways of thinking about topics are rarely seriously considered in organizing text content. However, because students will interpret the text in terms of what they already know, it is critical that *teachers* find ways in which student thinking differs from concepts in the text. It is critical that *students* learn that their ideas about plants, light, or whatever, are related to and sometimes different from statements made in the text. Otherwise, students will view ideas in the text as a separate world of knowledge from what they already know from experience (Strategies 2, 3, 4), or they will distort text ideas to make them fit with their prior knowledge (Strategy 5).

It is therefore important to reiterate here one of the unifying themes of this book: good teaching and curriculum design require asking questions that elicit and challenge students' current conceptions. Teachers like Ms Ramsey asked questions that invoked students' misconceptions. These teachers continually considered how the misconceptions were influencing students' responses to the text and to instruction, and they challenged these misconceptions. This actively supported students in using a conceptual change strategy. Students, as well as teachers, became better able to trace the changes in their thinking. Ms Lane, on the other hand, was so absorbed with following the textbook and getting students to give right answers to factual-level questions that she failed to track her students' thinking. She did not become aware of students' conceptual difficulties or listen to students' ideas. Her students learned facts and definitions (Strategies 3 and 4), but they never became aware that these facts were in conflict with their everyday ways of explaining light and vision. In fact, many students probably never realized that these facts had anything to do with their everyday experience of light and seeing.

Ask questions that give students repeated opportunities to apply text concepts to explain everyday phenomena. Textbooks pose many questions for students that simply ask them to repeat or recognize facts and definitions. They rarely ask students to construct explanations that connect concepts being presented to the students' real-world experiences. When such questions *are* posed in textbooks, they are likely to be framed as enrichment or optional questions. In response to the kinds of questions they are asked, students develop strategies for finding facts and 'big words' in the text (Strategies 3 and 4). Learning science becomes a largely passive process of repeating a bunch of facts and vocabulary words that do not seem to have anything to do with everyday experiences.

The conceptual change teachers largely avoided the factual-level memorization questions. Instead they focused on questions that required students to think about text ideas and to link those ideas to their everyday experiences. They encouraged students to compare each others' explanations, to challenge each others' explanations, and to debate. The process of asking such questions and discussing them in depth helped teachers become more aware of the particulars of their students' misconceptions. This questioning pattern communicated to students that relying on prior knowledge or memorizing facts from text were not effective strategies. Instead, the teachers demanded that students answer these questions by thinking about and linking textbook knowledge and prior knowledge. Changes had to be made in students' everyday ways of thinking about phenomena, which required some struggle on the part of the students. However, it was a productive kind of struggle that resulted more often in conceptual change understanding.

Probe student responses and provide clear feedback to students about their ideas. Textbooks present content and pose questions in ways that suggest that learning is a fairly simple process of adding new information to memory. If students 'understand', they will give correct answers to the questions. But students can answer text-posed questions correctly and still have important misunderstandings (see Maria, above). The typical way of responding to student answers – praising good answers and passing over incorrect answers – encourages students to use ineffective strategies to find the right answer.

Teachers need to go beyond the search for correct answers and listen and respond to student statements in ways that will shape, guide, and support their thinking. For example, Ms Ramsey's probing for clarifications when her students' responses were incorrect or incomplete, or even when they sounded 'correct', helped her make important instructional decisions. By listening for student thinking rather than for right answers, teachers can gather information that will then guide students towards thinking more carefully about the meaning of the science content.

Another important part of responding to students is clear feedback about the strengths and limitations of responses. Ms Ramsey's response: 'I like that answer better. Why is it better?', communicates to students not only that some explanations of phenomena are better than others but also that students can figure out why some explanations are better than others.

Conceptual change teachers can also respond to students in ways that will enable them to understand better scientists' ways of thinking and constructing explanations. For example, one of the effective teachers in our study, Ms Kain, talked to students about the characteristics of good scientific explanations and the importance of going beyond descriptions of observations to explain *why*. When students' explanations were merely descriptive, she would ask them what was missing from their explanations. Thus, she told students about the kind of thinking needed to construct good explanations and coached students as they attempted to use similar thinking processes.

Construct alternative representations of text explanations that make explicit the contrasts and connections between scientific explanations and students' misconceptions. Most science textbooks are packed full of explanations of scientific concepts. Each concept is presented in one way and then the text moves on quickly to an explanation about a different concept. Students reading explanations of one concept after another do not have time to make real sense of all of them. If they did take the time, students might find that the one explanation given in the text does not make sense given their own naive ways of thinking about the concept. Students like Kevin (see above), who take the time to try to link text explanation to their own understandings of the world, often resolve such confusion by distorting text explanations to make them fit with their misconceptions (Strategy 5). Reading textbook explanations once, especially textbook explanations that conflict with students' everyday ways of thinking about phenomena, is not sufficient to help students like Kevin recognize that they need to change their thinking.

To help students understand key explanations in the text, teachers must first give them *time* to grapple with the text explanation. In addition, they need to help students recognize ways in which the text explanation differs from their own explanations. However, this one way of explaining a concept will often still not be enough. Teachers also need to construct different ways of representing the explanation. The representations will be most effective if they make clear the contrast and connections between students' ideas and scientific explanations. Ms Ramsey repeated key explanations in several ways. She stated ideas simply and made contrasts with common student misconceptions clear.

Select and use activities to create conceptual conflict and develop conceptual understanding. Some activity-based science programmes, such as the Science Curriculum Improvement Study (SCIIS), closely integrate hands-on activities with the conceptual understanding that students are to develop. However, such programmes pose difficult planning and management demands for teachers. Because of these difficulties, teachers often look for textbooks in which activities are optional. In response to this demand, science textbooks provide a variety of activities that teachers might use to accompany reading of the text. However, the contribution of the activities to the development of students' understanding is not usually made clear in the teachers' guides. As a result, teachers like Ms Lane often get caught up in doing activities because it's *fun* for kids or because it seems important to *do* experiments in science classes. In these classes, kids 'learn' that *doing* science is fun, but they also learn that doing science is a separate part of science that has little to do with reading and thinking about scientific explanations, facts, definitions and concepts. Ms Lane had students involved in many activities with light, lenses, and prisms, but they still did not understand what the text said about how light enables us to see or why we can see colours.

Conceptual change teachers typically select activities that will contribute to students' understanding of the central science concepts. For example, activities or experiments whose results differ from students' predictions (discrepant events) can provide very convincing evidence to students that there may be better explanations for phenomena than their own 'theories'. Activities should challenge students' ideas and provide opportunities for them to acquire new evidence that could help them change their own explanations.

Doing activities is not as important as helping students make sense of the activities. Therefore, in using experiments and activities, teachers need to emphasize the meaning that can be drawn from them. Ms Lane overemphasized the procedural and observation phases of such activities. Ms Ramsey, in contrast, engaged students in discussions about activities that clearly linked the activities to concepts they had been reading about in the text.

Promoting effective patterns of textbook use

The principles for textbook use suggested in that last section are not easy for teachers to implement. They require a lot of knowledge about students and science. How can we help student teachers like Sarah and experienced teachers like Ms Lane to use these principles? In our work we have been addressing this issue both through the development of curriculum materials and through pre-service and in-service teacher education.

Development of curriculum materials. In our curriculum development efforts, we have developed two types of curriculum materials. In both kinds of materials, critical information is provided about (1) key concepts of a given unit and relationships among the concepts; and (2) students' typical misconceptions and ways of going wrong in learning these concepts. The curriculum materials also provide questions that require students to apply concepts to everyday situations. The materials are designed to give teachers specific knowledge about the topics being taught that will support them in using the principles for conceptual change teaching.

One type of curriculum materials we have developed and tested is the transparency set and *Teacher's Guide* used by Ms Ramsey and other teachers in Year 2 of the study reported in this chapter. These materials, which *supplemented* the textbook, helped teachers to select critical issues to focus on, provided questions to elicit students' misconceptions as well as application questions, suggested to the teachers likely student responses to the questions, and provided alternative ways of explaining key concepts that clearly contrasted student conceptions with scientific explanations.

Both our curriculum development efforts suggest that better classroom materials can be written. But what can we do to help teachers follow our suggested principles using currently available texts?

Pre-service and in-service teacher education. In working with both pre-service and in-service teachers, we have found that teachers are often unsuccessful in implementing conceptual change strategies effectively. They have difficulties because they hold conceptions about the nature of science, about the nature of science learning, and about science teaching that are not consistent with conceptual change notions.

In order to teach effectively for conceptual change learning, for example, science teachers have to understand the explanatory nature of science and appreciate the close interaction between process and content in the development of increasingly satisfying explanations of phenomena. However, many teachers think about science as consisting of two distinct components – as a body of knowledge and as a set of processes used to investigate phenomena. In translating this two-pronged view of science into thinking about teaching and learning, teachers often overemphasize one or the other, fostering either a 'science is acquiring facts' view or a 'science is messing about' view. Teachers should also understand student learning in a particular way. They must understand it as a difficult and complex process of conceptual change, rather than as a process of acquiring and memorizing facts. Instead of blaming learning failures on students' lack of effort, teachers need to explore and understand the difficulties students have in changing their ideas. Finally, teachers should understand teaching as a process of supporting and guiding students in constructing increasingly sophisticated understandings of phenomena, rather than as a process of telling students all about phenomena.

Teachers often need to go through their own version of conceptual change before the teaching strategies we are recommending will make any sense and be useful to them. Simply telling teachers about the research findings in the usual 'one-shot' in-service sessions or as part of a science methods course is not an effective way to help them undergo such conceptual change. Like learners in classrooms, they must perceive a need to change their ideas before they can find this alternative model of instruction more powerful.

Such changes do not happen rapidly and cannot occur without struggles with both the theoretical and practical issues involved. We have had the best success in fostering such changes when we have worked with either pre-service or in-service teachers over time and in conjunction with their own teaching of a specific unit. Such topic-specific efforts enable teachers to develop understanding both of the complexity of teaching and learning and of the kinds of knowledge that are needed to teach effectively for conceptual change. As they look in detail at their students' understanding of one topic, teachers develop a better understanding of how much they need to know about this topic, about science, and about students, in order to make appropriate decisions about teaching strategies. We have found that curriculum materials that have conceptual change teaching strategies built into them can play a critical role in helping teachers begin the process of rethinking their conceptions of science learning and thinking. However, we as teacher educators need to think harder about ways to build on that beginning and to support and guide teachers in undergoing such conceptual change. The fundamental issue of how to help teachers change their conceptions will be taken up in the last chapter of this volume.

Conclusions

While science textbooks are indeed difficult for students to make sense of, simply telling student teachers and practising teachers to avoid textbooks is not a reasonable message to communicate. Textbooks can be helpful tools when teachers understand when and how they can be used to promote students' conceptual learning. An understanding of the kinds of ineffective strategies that students resort to in order to 'read' textbooks can help teachers make predictions about potential student difficulties with text. By appreciating the contrasts between students' everyday ways of thinking about natural phenomena and the explanations presented in science texts, teachers can begin to develop some ways of thinking about the use of the textbook that *will* help students make better sense.

Some key features of such instructional strategies have been described. In the studies reported here, specially developed curriculum materials provided critical information to teachers about students' thinking and about the content that should emphasized. Without the support of such materials, teachers must develop the kinds of deep understandings of both the students and of the content that will enable them to use the suggested teaching strategies effectively. Helping teachers develop such understanding of the differences between content as understood by scientists and content as interpreted by students needs to be a major focus of pre-service and in-service teacher education. It is this understanding that will enable teachers to become conceptual change teachers.

References

Anderson, C W and Smith, E L (1982). *Transparencies on Light: Teacher's Manual* (Research Series No. 130). East Lansing, Michigan: Institute for Research on Teaching, Michigan State University.

Anderson, C W and Smith, E L (1986). *Science Teaching Project: Final Report.* East Lansing, Michigan: Institute for Research on Teaching, Michigan State University.

Anderson R C, Spiro, R J and Anderson, M C (1978). Schemata as scaffolding for the representation of information in connected discourse. *American Educational Research Journal,* **15,** 433-40.

Ball, D L and Feiman-Nemser, S (1986). The use of curricular materials: What beginning elementary teachers learn and what they need to know. Paper presented at the annual meeting of the American Educational Research Association, San Francisco.

Blecha, M K, Gega, P C and Green, M (1979). *Exploring Science,* Green book (second edition). River Forest, Illinois: Laidlaw Brothers.

Bower, G H, Black, J B, and Turner, T J (1979). Scripts in memory for text. *Cognitive Psychology*, **11**, 177–220.

Brandwein, P F , Cooper, E K, Blackwood, P E, Cottom-Winslow, N, Giddings, M G, Romero, F and Carin, A A (1980). *Concepts in Science* (Brown). New York: Harcourt, Brace, Jovanovich.

Knott, R, Lawson, C, Karplus, R, Their, H and Montgomery, M (1978). *SCIIS Communities Teacher's Guide*. Chicago: Rand McNally.

Marton, F and Säljö, R (1984). Approaches to learning. In: F Marton *et al.* (eds), *The Experience of Learning*. Edinburgh: Scottish Academic Press.

Roth, K J (1985a). *Conceptual Change Learning and Student Processing of Science Texts* (Research Series No. 167). East Lansing, Michigan: Institute for Research on Teaching, Michigan State University.

Roth, K J (1985b). *Food for Plants Teacher's Guide* (Research Series No. 53). East Lansing, Michigan: Institute for Research on Teaching, Michigan State University.

Roth, K J (1984). Using classroom observations to improve science teaching and curriculum materials. In: C W Anderson (ed), *Observing Science Classrooms: Perspectives from Research and Practice*. 1984 Yearbook of the Association for the Education of Teachers in Science. Columbus: ERIC Center for Science, Mathematics, and Environment Education.

Säljö, R (1984). Learning from reading. In F Marton *et al.* (eds), *The Experience of Learning*. Edinburgh: Scottish Academic Press.

Slinger, L, Anderson, C W and Smith, E L (1982). Studying light in the fifth grade: A case study of text-based science teaching. Paper presented at the annual meeting of the National Association for Research in Science Teaching, Fontana, Wisconsin.

Smith, E L and Anderson, C W (1983). *The Planning and Teaching of Intermediate Science Study: Final Report*. East Lansing, Michigan: Institute for Research on Teaching, Michigan State University.

Smith, E L, and Anderson, C W (1984). Plants as producers: A case study of elementary science teaching. *Journal of Research in Science Teaching*, **21**, 685–98.

Smith, E L and Sendelbach, N B (1982). The programme, the plans and the activities of the classroom: The demands of activity-based science. In: J K Olson (ed), *Innovation in the Science Curriculum: Classroom Knowledge and Curriculum Change*. London: Croom Helm.

Spiro, R J (1979). *Etiology of Reading Comprehension Style* (Technical report No. 124). Urbana, Illinois: University of Illinois, Center for the Study of Reading.

Part 3
Research into Practice:
Learning in College

Chapter 7
Different Worlds in the Same Classroom

William G Perry
Harvard University,USA

Introduction

This chapter departs from the conventions of this book in that I do not report directly the research from which it derives. Rather, I attempt to translate the findings of the research into a form in which young college teachers may recognize their experience of the classroom. Of the research itself – a longitudinal study of hierarchical evolution in the form of students' thought in the college years – I give only an informal description in the early pages. A full account is available in my *Forms of Intellectual and Ethical Development in the College Years: A Scheme* (New York: Holt, Rinehart and Winston, 1970). For a bibliography of researches building on the original study, see Copes (1984).

In Figure 1 I present a summary of the nine-step scheme couched in the phenomenological outlook of the student, together with definitions we assigned to the characteristics of the forms of thought in each of the nine 'positions' or steps. As will be evident, the distinction between the approaches to learning of students whose thinking is described in Positions 1 through 9 parallels the differentiation between qualitatively different processes of studying and conceptions of reality that is a theme running throughout this book.

I wrote this particular translation, or dramatization, in the context of Harvard College, but I trust that such localisms as 'mid-term' (a time of assessment half-way through a semester), 'mid-years' (examinations in February) and 'blue books' (in which examinations are written) will not seriously detract from the understanding of cosmopolitan readers.

Enigmas in explaining differences in student learning

I want to describe an orderly variety in the ways students in your classroom make sense – including their sense of what you should be doing to be a good teacher. We labour among our students' individual differences

Figure 1. Scheme of cognitive and ethical development

Position	Description	Label
Position 1	Authorities know, and if we work hard, read every word, and learn Right Answers, all will be well.	Basic duality
Transition	But what about those Others I hear about? And different opinions? And Uncertainties? Some of our own Authorities disagree with each other or don't seem to know, and some give us problems instead of Answers.	
Position 2	True Authorities must be Right, the others are frauds. We remain Right. Other must be different and Wrong. Good Authorities give us problems so we can learn to find the Right Answers by our own independent thought.	Multiplicity pre-legitimate
Transition	But even Good Authorities admit they don't know all the answers yet!	
Position 3	Then some uncertainties and different opinions are real and legitimate temporarily, even for Authorities. They're working on them to get to the Truth.	Multiplicity subordinate
Transition	But there are so many things they don't know the Answers to! And they won't for a long time	
Position 4a	Where Authorities don't know the Right Answers, everyone has a right to their own opinion; no one is wrong!	Multiplicity (solipsism) coordinate
Transition (and/or) transition	But some of my friends ask me to support my opinions with facts and reasons. Then what right have They to grade us? About what?	
Position 4b	In certain courses Authorities are not asking for the Right Answers; they want us to think about things in a certain way, supporting opinion with data. That's what they grade us on	Relativism subordinate

Transition	But this 'way' seems to work in most courses, and even outside them.	
Position 5	Then all thinking must be like this, even for Them. Everything is relative but not equally valid. You have to understand how each generalized context works. Theories are not Truth but metaphors to interpret data with. You have to think about your thinking.	Relativisim (contextual) generalized
Transition	But if everything is relative, am I relative too? How can I know I'm making the Right Choice?	
Position 6	I see I'm going to have to make my own decisions in an uncertain world with no one to tell me I'm Right.	Commitment foreseen
Transition	I'm lost if I don't. When I decide on my career (or marriage or values) everything will straighten out.	
Position 7	Well, I've made my first Commitment!	Initial commitment
Transition	Why didn't that settle everything?	
Position 8	I've made several commitments. I've got to balance them – how many, how deep? How certain, how tentative?	Orientation in commitments
Transition	Things are getting contradictory. I can't make logical sense out of life's dilemmas.	
Position 9	This is how life will be. I must be wholehearted while tentative, fight for my values yet respect others, believe my deepest values right yet be ready to learn. I see that I shall be retracing this whole journey over and over – but, I hope, more wisely.	Evolving commitments

daily, and yet the way these differences are categorized tends to mislabel the variables I have in mind. In the parlance of college pedagogy, the phrase 'individual differences' usually refers to relatively stable characteristics of persons, such as academic ability, special talents or disabilities, or the more esoteric dispositions called 'learning styles'. We are, of course, expected to accommodate all such differences in our teaching, perhaps by broadening our teaching styles, and you may anticipate that I am about to add to our burden.

My hope, rather, is to lighten our burden, or at least to enlighten it. The variations I wish to describe are less static; they have a logical order, and most students tend to advance from one to another in response to teachings or readings that impinge on the boundaries of their intelligible universe of the moment. These variables are therefore more fun to address, and in my opinion often more determinant of what goes out of our classrooms than all the other individual differences put together. At the very least, an understanding of them makes intelligible many of those aberrations of the pedagogical relation that we must otherwise ascribe to a student's stupidity or, more generously, to a clash of 'personalities'.

Let's start with one of the ordinary enigmas – students' persistent misreading of examination questions. Perhaps 'unreading' would be a better term. We commonly struggle in staff meetings for nearly an hour over the wording of an essay question for the mid-term. The choice of topic takes only five minutes. It is the wording of the intellectual issue we wish the students to address that takes the labour. At last the issue is stated clearly, concisely, and unambiguously, Yet, if the class contains a large contingent of freshmen, the blue books will reveal that a third of the students looked at the question to locate the topic and ignored all the rest of the words, so carefully crafted. It will seem as if these students read the question as saying: 'Tell all you know about . . .' and then did so, sometimes with remarkable feats of irrelevant memory.

Such evidence of misplaced diligence can be marvellously depressing, but we realize we should not be surprised. In their years of schooling what else have these students learned to suppose an examination question intends? Clearly, we have an educational job ahead of us, and we undertake it with spirit in class and in office hours, student by student. We explain with patient clarity. The students assure us that they understand and thank us profusely.

At mid-years, however, most of our grateful beneficiaries dismay us by doing just what they did before. Our instructions were quite simple, and when intelligent students cannot keep a simple idea in mind, we can suspect them of being diverted by more pressing considerations. Here I choose an example, extreme for this community, in the hope that stark simplicity may lay a foundation for more general observations.

A top student from a good school came to Harvard at a young age, possibly a year too young. Since he had won a regional prize in history, he enrolled in a section of Expository Writing that focused on writing about history. He consulted me in a state of some agitation, having failed in three attempts to write a satisfactory response to the assignment: 'Consider the theory of monarchy implied in Queen Elizabeth's Address to Members of the House of Commons in 1601'. 'Look', he said, 'I can tell what she said . . . all her main points. I've done it three times, longer each time. But he says he doesn't want that. What is this "theory of monarchy implied" stuff anyway? He says to read between the lines. So I try to read between the lines – and huh – there's nothing there.'

The intellectual problem is not too obscure. The student cannot see a theory of monarchy because he has never been confronted with two. Until he sees at least two, a monarch is a monarch and who needs a theory? I was aware, of course, that his writing instructor had tried, but I decided to try once more. We devised alternative theories together, but the more he seemed to understand, the more agitated he became. Then he complained that his mind had gone blank. I shall return later to this student's shock to help us understand the courage required of more advanced students if they are to hear what we are saying about the world. After all, why should two theories of monarchy be so terrifying?

Such curious reactions are not limited to exceptional students. In Freshman Week over the years, the staff of the Bureau of Study Counsel at Harvard has asked entering students to grade two answers to an easy question. Again, fully a quarter of the class gives higher grades to the essay crowded with facts utterly devoid of relevance to the question. In response, we have tried to help these students see that college instructors consider relevance the sole justification for memorizing a fact. Accordingly, we try to teach them simple reading strategies, such as surveying for a sense of the author's purpose before starting to collect detail. Half the students catch on with enthusiasm; the other half accuse us of urging them to 'cheat'.

This brings me to the last enigma we need to share: the range of perception in students' evaluations of their teachers. Most evaluations are invited by rating scales. The computer will give the mean and the standard deviation. As a teacher I have never found the figures very informative, and on occasion I have ventured to inquire beyond them, inviting my students to write me anonymous 'free comments'. I expect a range of opinion; I would not want to please everybody. But nothing ever prepares me for the range I get. How can I possibly be the one who has 'opened the world to me. Now I know what learning is about; and the rest is up to me!' – and at the same moment 'the most dishonest, hypocritical and careless teacher I've had the misfortune to meet – and Harvard pays you!'

Why do students differ?

Can differences in 'personality' explain all this? Every student who came to us for counselling seemed, if we listened long enough, to be attending a different college; each student enrolled in a given course was in a different course, and the instructor was an angel, a dud, and a devil. Was this variety common only among the 15% of undergraduates whose distress brought them to us? We thought not, and we set out to inquire of some students who had expressed no need of our wisdom.

We asked half the freshman class to submit to tests measuring aspects of personality we thought relevant, and in May we invited representatives of all dispositions to come to tell us about their year. They responded enthusiastically. We soon learned not to ask them questions that imposed frameworks of sense-making on a conversation that we intended as an opportunity for the students to inform us of theirs. The individual variety then exceeded our expectations, the students enjoyed it, and we parted in agreement to meet again next spring, and also in junior and senior year.

It was in this setting that the students rewarded us. As we first listened to them as freshmen, they interpreted their experience in ways that seemed harmonious with those traits of 'personality' our measures had ascribed to them. But then, in sophomore year, to our astonishment, most of these students changed their 'personalities' – and did so again as juniors and as seniors. Each year they interpreted their educational experience through frameworks of assumptions and expectations that placed knowledge and learning, hope, initative, responsibility, and their teachers, in new relations. Perhaps our original tests in freshman year had reflected not so much enduring bents of personality as temporary constellations of perceived relations. Gradually we came to see that these constellations through which the students made sense of their worlds followed one another in an orderly sequence. Finding that their current ways of making sense failed to comprehend the increasing complexities and uncertainties in their intellectual and social lives, the students 'realized' (as they phrased it) that the world was other than they had thought; that only a new way of seeing and thinking could encompass the new set of discrepancies, anomalies, or contradictions. Each of these new realizations comprehended the old as the old could not encompass the new. This was development, a visible, even explicit broadening of the mind – not simply change, but evolution.

We sensed that each step in this evolution involved a challenge. We had yet to realize the depth of these challenges, but we could see that some students refused, at one point or another, to take the next step. We went so far as to dub the sequence a Pilgrim's Progress and made a map of it, Slough of Despond and all. Every student, as we saw it, spoke from some place or 'position' on this journey.

Stages of development

But is is now time to enter your classroom. You, however, are late – unavoidably, but conveniently for our purpose. The last thing you said, on Friday, was 'Next week we'll consider three theories of the economic cycle' (or the equivalent in your particular field). As restlessness sets in this Monday morning, a conversation begins, and I am going to cast it in the mould of our Pilgrim's Progress. That is, I shall label the *dramatis personae* First Student, Two, Three, etc, letting each express in sequence the outlook from the several positions of our map.

By this device I hope not only to convey a sense of the order in the varied perceptions and expectations that await your arrival, but also to make it possible for you to imagine that each of the speakers might be one and the same student speaking from outlooks attained sequentially over a number of years – perhaps in just the four years of college.

I have already mentioned the First Student – he of the history prize. He saw me on Saturday. He sits near the door watching for you. He is too anxious to speak or even to think well. His despair about theories of monarchy has probably left him so mute that if he heard you mention 'three theories of the economic cycle' at all, it would only add boundlessness to his terror. His inability to understand the nature of knowledge as Harvard sees it has become less an epistemological problem than an ontological horror. If there are several theories of monarchy, why shouldn't there be infinite theories of monarchy? So is there such a thing as a monarch? Is the same true of all authority and so of all obedience? Of parents and sons? Of all meaning?

The camaraderie of the dorm might have carried him through this existential crisis, but this lad seems to lack the humour to become one of the boys. His is primitive shock, but we shall find in the class other, more sophisticated approaches to the abyss.

Several low-key conversations are now going on in the room. The voice of the Second Student – I shall call him Two – rises above the rest as he talks to his neighbour. 'What's this rigmarole about three theories of the cycle anyway? Why doesn't he give us the right one and forget the bullshit?' Someone laughs: 'You're not in high school anymore, Joe.' 'Yeah, I know. Here they give you problems, not answers, I see that. That's supposed to help us learn independent thought, to find the answer on our own. That's what he said when I asked him – or I guess it's what he said, along with the rigmarole. OK, but enough is enough. We gotta know what to learn for the exam.'

Two's voice has become plaintive, almost desperate; there is silence as he pauses. 'My roommate's in the 11 o'clock. He says his instructor really knows and really answers your questions. Maybe I should go ask her.'

It is hard to portray Two's thinking without seeming to caricature it. Do I need to assure you that he exists? He has brought with him from years of schooling a clear epistemology. Knowledge, he learned early, consists of right answers, and there is a right answer for every question: eg, spelling words, arithmetic problems, dates. These truths are discrete items and can be collected by memorization; so some people know more, others know less. ('Better' or 'worse' are not applicable.) Teachers know these answers in their own fields. The answers seem to exist up there somewhere, and the teacher is privy to them.

In the stage setting of this epistemology the roles of the actors are clearly prescribed. The teacher's duty is to 'give' the student the truth, the right answers, in assimilable, graduated doses. Two's duty is to 'absorb' them by honest hard work known as 'study'. Then the teacher will 'ask for them back' in the same form in which they were originally given. Two's responsibility is then to re-present them unmodified and unabridged for the teacher's inspection.

The morals of this world are equally coherent. The teacher must not ask questions in a strange form – 'trick questions'. That teachers often give problems to solve, withholding the answers which they already know, can at first seem an anomaly in this world, something to make sense of. As the First Student might say: 'I think they're hiding things.' Two has made sense of it, acknowledging that beneficent Authority should help us learn 'independent thought': ie, to find the answer for ourselves. Assigning problems therefore falls within the bounds of the moral contract so long as the teacher makes the problems clear and the procedures for solving them memorizable.

As student, then, Two's reciprocal moral duty requires him to collect truth through honest hard work, never by guessing. Right answers hit by guesswork (including 'thought') are false currency, and when he accepts credit for them he feels guilty.

Freshman Adviser Perry (after November hour exams): How'd it go?

Freshman: Four 'A's.

Adviser (swallowing praise): How do you feel about that?

Freshman: Terrible. I didn't deserve any of them.

Two's logical corollary , of course, is that if he's worked hard he should get some credit even when he comes up with the wrong answer. The gods and similar authorities have always been bound by the rituals they have established for their appeasement. This myth, to the extent that Authority shares it, provides safety to the weak. The vital requirement of ritual is that nothing be omitted – that it be complete. Since neglect of the smallest detail invalidates the whole, every detail is of equal import.

It is therefore of fundamental urgency for Two that you stipulate the nature of the ritual, particularly its length. He has been stopping you in the door at the end of class.

'You said three to five pages, sir. Does that mean four?'

Can Authority refuse to answer? 'Well, whatever you need.'

'Oh, then, four will be satisfactory?'

'OK, sure, if they make your point.'

'Thanks, sir – oh, will that be double-spaced or single?'

I have more than once found myself pressed to the wall and settling, to my chagrin, for '1200 words'. And I have received them, tallied in the margin, the final entry a smug '1204'.

Quantity and 'coverage' are visible entities, making obedience palpable. 'Organization and coherence' – meaning the logical subordination and sequencing of relationships in the service of an overarching theme – these are not yet visible to Two. A recent study has revealed that the students who think as Two thinks use 'coverage' as their criterion for 'coherence' as they write, sometimes going so far as to 'organize' by putting 'similar' details together. If you ask Two to rewrite his paper to improve its organization, he will therefore submit more of the same.

Two knows that there are Rights and Wrongs and a cold world outside of Eden. In Eden the only role is obedience; the only sin is arrogating to oneself the knowledge of good and evil (the power to make judgements). In the Bureau's class in strategies of learning, when we urge students to find the main theme of an article or chapter first (perhaps by starting at the end) so that they can judge the function of details, those who think like Two cry out: 'Do you want us to be thrown out of here?' Two recognizes the college instructor who asks him to exercise his judgement as Serpent.

Two, then, construes the world (and teachers) *dualistically* (see Table 1). Along with right and wrong, he has come to see that some teachers know, and some do not. The truth is One and Invariable, yet teachers disagree about it. There is only one possible sense to make of this without disaster to Truth; just as there are right answers and wrong answers, so there are good teachers and frauds, beneficent teachers and those who are mean. ('My roomate says *his* instructor *really* knows.')

Two thinks in a noble tradition. A study of examination questions given to freshmen at Harvard at the turn of the century reveals them all to be just the kind that Two expects questions to be. They ask for memorized facts and operations in a single assumed framework of Absolute Truth. It wasn't until mid-century that half the questions would require consideration of data from two or more perspectives. And surely today there are still many ways in which we confirm Two's vision.

Indeed, the meanings Two attributes to the educational world are so sensible – and he has such ready categories for dismissing incongruities – that his system seems almost closed. And if this system were as perfect as Locke portrayed it, then all knowledge, judgement and agency would reside out there in Authority, and the student's sole duty would be to absorb. Some Twos do indeed stay closed. Our Two, however, has unknowingly opened a door by conceding legitimacy to Authority's assigning problems instead of giving answers. Solving problems, he has found, is kind of fun, and he derives more satisfaction from doing than from memorizing. In arithmetic, one can even check an answer for oneself to see if it's right or wrong. This temptation to agency and judgement is the first step on a path that will lead Two away from the safety he presumes to lie in obedience in Eden towards ultimate questions about very nature of truth itself.

What is required next is for Authority to be allowed just a bit of legitimate uncertainty. Student Three supplies it: 'Well, there may have to be some different theories for a while', she ventures; 'after all, Ec. is sort of a new science and there's lots they don't know the answers to yet – like some things in Physics even.' By using the word 'yet' she has legitimized present uncertainty without disturbing her vision of an orderly Laplacean universe out there waiting to be known, bit by bit. Three's assimilation of temporary uncertainty makes the system even more vulnerable. A little temporary uncertainty legitimizes a little difference of opinion. 'Temporary' can now reveal itself to extend longer and longer, and uncertainties can appear in wider domains. The mind is then likely to be overwhelmed by the sheer quantity of possibilities.

There are two Fours in the class, one a bit of a fighter, the other more trusting. I shall call them Four A (Adam) and Four B (Barbara). Four A makes sense out of the impending chaos by exploiting it. He 'realizes' that the world, instead of being divided between right and wrong, is divided between those things about which right/wrong can be determined and those about which not even authority knows. In this new domain of indeterminacy, where 'Everyone has a right to his opinion', he feels a new freedom. In this domain no one can be called wrong because right is unknown. By implication, all opinions are equally valid. This broad tolerance provides for peace in the dormitory before dawn. At the same time it means that Four A will feel outraged when you question his opinion, especially if you asked for it.

He says to Three: 'Yeah, that's right. There's so much they won't know for a hundred years, so why only three theories? Anyone can have a theory, and if it's neat for them it's neat for them.'

This ultimate individualism, when applied to the moral sphere, is of course absolute license, and since it is often spoken of as 'relativism', it has given actual disciplined relativism a bad name. There is of course no relationship in sight, only solipsism: 'My opinion is right because I have it.' We called this view *multiplicity*, an awkward word we stole from Henry Adam. In any case, the view is not relative but absolute, just as absolute as the right/wrong dichotomy. What Four A has done is to save the dual character of the world by doubling it, leaving right/wrong on one side and if-I-can't-be-called-wrong-I'm-right on the other. He feels no need as yet to relate opinions to their supporting data and limiting contexts.

Three's interest in how to solve problems and her realization of temporary uncertainty are leading her to a curiosity about 'how' we know, or if we can't know yet, how we develop an opinion tenable on grounds other than 'It's my opinion'. Four B (Barbara) has taken a course in literary analysis in which she has discovered that 'What they wanted wasn't just an answer but a "way" a "how". I came to see that what a poem means isn't just anybody's guess after all. The way they wanted us to think was maybe special to that course, but you had to put all kinds of evidence together to build an interpretation and then try it out against others. So we'd end up with a few good interpretations to choose from, like three theories maybe, but a lot of others turned out to be nonsense – at least that's how it was in that course. Maybe . . . '

Four B is on the brink. She has allowed a special case into the world of 'right answers for credit'. With this 'way' she can be an agent in using relationships among data and contexts to generate interpretations. She realized then that these interpretations may be compared to one another. Some few may appear most valid; others less so; others unacceptable. In the special case of this one course, Authority itself has introduced knowledge as qualitative. But a special case can be a Trojan horse. Its contents can burst forth to take over the whole fortress.

Four A (Adam) is entrenched in his efforts to expand the realm of indeterminacy at Authority's expense. If he is to discover a contextual qualitative world, he may do so more readily when the prodding comes from peers. In the 'bull sessions' in the dorm a colleague more advanced than he may ask him 'Well, how do you substantiate that?' again and again until he discovers that things relate and that he can relate them.

Five: 'Hell, everything's like that – like Barbie says, not just in one course. There isn't a thing on earth sensible people don't disagree about – and if they don't today they will tomorrow! Even the hard scientists: look what Godel did to math! It's not like Adam says, "when no one knows anything goes". Just because there's no single certainty in the end and individuals will have to choose – that's no reason to give up thinking. Maybe it's the reason to begin, I mean, you've gotta use all the analysis and critical thinking and stuff as advertised. Theories – they aren't the Whole Truth anyway, they're just models like they say, some of them pretty good. So you've got to know how each one works, inside with its logic and outside with the world. It's like different geometries . . . like games really.'

Two interrupts: 'I can't follow all this bull you're all talking. Isn't anyone going to help pin him down? How can you study for an exam with all that crap you're talking about?' Everyone looks at Two, but no one responds. 'Well, maybe it's me. I mean I can learn things, but I can't seem to do what people do around here, whatever it is – interpret or something.' He hangs his head.

Three attempts a rescue: 'Well, I kind of agree. I mean he ought to tell us sooner or later. After all, there are right answers, right ways.'

'Sure, there's rights and wrongs if you know the context', resumes Five. 'It's all set by the context and the assumptions and all. Sure it gets complicated and some contexts are looser than others. Like in history and in Lit., there may be more different, defensible things to say. But still, idiot opinions, they're infinite. I thought everybody knew that.'

Five 'realized' all this only 18 months ago but he has so completely reorganized his view of the world, and in the process perhaps recatalogued his memory, that he has forgotten that the world ever seemed different from the way he now sees it to be. We wouldn't forget – or might we?

The discovery of relativism: a changed conception of reality

We should pause here. A rift has been revealed in the class, and the rest of the conversation will further our understanding of it. Five has taken us over a watershed, a critical traverse in our Pilgrim's Progress. On the first side of the watershed the students were preoccupied with the frightening failure of most college teachers to fulfil their assigned role as dispensers of knowledge. Even Barbara, who mastered the initial processes of analytical, contextual, relativistic thought, has assimilated this form of thought by assigning it the status of an exception in the old context of What They Want. Five, in crossing the ridge of the divide, has seen before him a perspective, in which the relation of learner to knowledge is radically transformed. In this new context, Authority, formerly source and dispenser of all knowing, is suddenly authority, ideally a resource, a mentor, a model, and potentially a colleague in consensual estimation of interpretations of reality. What-They-Want is now a special case within this context. As for the students, they are no longer receptacles but the primary agents responsible for their own learning.

Not all teachers will fulfil these expectations, of course, but to Five, Six Seven, and Eight their failures will not be so demoralizing – or preoccupying. Most students will turn their attention to the implications of the new perspective: choosing among interpretations in their studies, making decisions in a relativistic world, and deciding how to make commitments to career, persons, values and to what they 'know' in a world in which even physics changes its mind. Some, perhaps lacking support or stuck in old resentments, will opt out by shrugging off responsibility.

As students speak from this new perspective, they speak more reflectively. And yet the underlying theme continues: the learners' evolution of what it means to them to know.

Another student now speaks to Five: 'Well I've just come to see what you're talking about and it helps. I've begun to be able to stand back and look at my thinking – what metaphors and stuff I'm using. Not just in my studies, I mean I find the same goes for people. I've begun to get the feel too of where the other guy is coming from and what's important to him – huh, this sounds corny, but I get along better with most people.'

There's a silence, then Five speaks more tentatively in a lower voice: 'Yeah, I can do this all in my head. I like learning the games and seeing what model fits best where and all. But I can't see how to make any big decisions – there's always so many other possibilities. That's been a real downer. I list all the reasons for doing this and for doing that and all the reasons against and then I get depressed (laughs), so I go back to playing the games, 'cause that's something I can do well. I mean I get "fine critical thinking" and jazz like that all over the margins of my papers and it keeps me going, but where to? I know it's I'm trying to be too sure, but I can't let go, I don't want to just plunge.'

A student is sprawled in the back of the room: 'Games is right! So who cares? If they want independent thought, just give it to them. Always have an opinion, I say – but don't forget to be "balanced" and all that crap.'

'Yeah', replies Six, 'and then when you get to General Motors, what's good for them will be good for you. I was lost for a whole year, felt like copping out like that plenty – then thought what'll that be like when I'm forty? Now I've got it narrowed down some. I don't see how some guys seem to know from age two – always knowing they'll be doctors. Did they ever have a doubt? Or will it hit 'em later? Like mid-life crisis, huh? Anyway, guys like me – you gotta plunge, I think. I'm not quite there yet, but I can see there's different ways of plunging. You can jump in just to get away from the agony – or you can do your thinking, and when your guts tell you "this is it", you listen. They're your guts. I mean you gotta plunge, in a way, because you know you can't be sure – you're risking it – but it'll be sort of a positive plunge. And once I'm in, I think everything else will fall in line.'

'I did that last spring', says Seven, 'and now that I'm getting deeper into things – I'm in Bio – it helps, feeds on itself I guess and I see it isn't narrowing down like I thought it would but spreading out bigger than I can handle. But I wouldn't say – I wouldn't say . . . '

'That it straightens everything else out?' The prompting comes from Eight. She laughs ruefully: 'I got everything straightened out last spring. I'd gone round and round. There was pre-med I've been in forever, I'd got more and more into linguistics, and here was this guy I'd been going with who wanted to get married. So I thought all my thoughts and every one else's and then one day told my parents: "Sorry, linguistics is it. I've really listened, but this has to be mine." And then I let the guy go to the Amazon to study birds without me. Did everything straighten out? Like hell it did, and then it did, in a funny way. I mean there was the thesis in linguistics; I still love that guy and don't want to marry him; I'm all wound up in this day care thing; my father's sick in San Francisco, and I met this intern who's taking care of him, and . . . Before, it seemed there was just pre-med or linguistics, marriage or no marriage, so now I ought to feel worse, all divided up, but it's better. I find I even believe in some things, like they're really true.' She pauses, no one says anything. 'It's like with the thesis, somehow. Seems I hit on something new – well, not new, just joining a couple of old procedures to tackle an old problem they'd never been used on before. My tutor says I'm really on to something – we can't find anything wrong about it or too far out.

'I've never known something new to be mine like this before. And the feeling goes over into all the rest in a way, only I don't have my tutor to check me out. It's all bits and pieces with cracks in it, but I'm the centre of something, a place from where I see things as I see them and all that jazz. Get things together – that's it I guess, not getting everything I want but getting things together. Oh hell, maybe all that holds me together is irony.'

After a moment, somebody laughs: 'Nice try, nice try, but these verities seem a long way from those three theories of the economic cycle, whatever they are. Anybody done the reading?'

'Sure the reading's important', says Six, 'but what we've all been saying does connect. What I want to know is what he does with those three theories. As a person, I mean, an economist-type person. I mean he seems to care about Ec. – he's kind of zestful about it really. I want to know what he does with all this. Not just which he thinks is right but does he, or if all three are valid, then what? I don't think he's kidding himself, so what does he do? Let's some of us ask him for lunch someday (laughs). See if he's for real.'

At this point you hurriedly enter the room. Under your arm you carry a sheaf of forms from University Hall. They are questionnaires for students' evaluations of teaching – an experimental form, its says, for trial at mid-term. You have been assured that giving them out is purely voluntary.

Implications for teaching

You – and I – are at 'Nine' (so we hope), the farthest reach of our map (Position 9 in Figure 1). At Nine we have had time to realize that growth is not linear as the metaphor of our map implies, but recursive. We turn and turn again, and when we come across our own footsteps we hope it will be with the perspective of some altitude and humour. We have also seen that in the several areas of their lives, such as their work, politics, social relationships, family, or religion, people (including ourselves) often employ somewhat different levels of thought. As teachers, we often use these variations by finding the areas of students' most sophisticated thought and helping them to move by analogy into areas in which they are less advanced. Indeed, students will often do so spontaneously.

But first, you may ask: 'Am I supposed to do something about all this development?' I must state my premiss. I do believe that the purpose of liberal education is to assist students to learn to think the way Eight is thinking. The goals are stated in the catalogues of all liberal arts colleges. In these terms the development the students reveal is a Good, and we are enjoined to promote it. You may disagree, seeing that I am loading on you a trip into personality development; your responsibility, you may say, is to teach history. I hope you have sensed that this makes no difference. Students who have not progressed beyond the outlook of Three will be unable to understand what you as a modern historian want them to understand about history. To the extent that you wish your subject to become accessible to as many students as is reasonably possible, the development we have been tracing remains a Good, and you have already been promoting it.

After all, the students who told us of this adventure were not taking a course in cognitive development complete with maps. They came to 'realize' through the necessities of the intellectual disciplines as you taught them. This is not to say, however, that as teachers we have nothing to gain from a more explicit awareness of the steps in the students' progression. At the very least, an understanding of Two's expectations somewhat reduces the personal abrasion of his anger. Similarly, we can feel less assaulted by the outrage of Four when he feel we do not accept his 'opinion'. Beyond saving our energies, this awareness extends the possibility of our staying in communication long enough for seeds to take root.

Our outline of the successive ways in which students make sense throws some light on the potentials and constraints of this communication. It has been observed for two millennia that in a learning situation the learner requires the support of some elements that are recognizable and familiar. Then, if the experience is to be anything more than drill, the second requirement is a degree of challenge. In the decades since the publication of our scheme, a younger generation of teacher-researchers has spelled out the characteristics of learners at each position and traced the sequential changes in the conditions students experience as support and challenge as they progress. Two, for instance, feels supported by explicit directions – supported enough to tolerate the challenge of being directed to read contradictory authorities. Looking back at the First Student, we see him overwhelmed by challenge; he may make it through, but only with the community's support – and time. Looking ahead, Five feels supported in being turned loose on the reserve shelf to find and write up an interesting problem, and can be challenged afterward by such a question as: 'And what did doing all that mean to you?'

This question of personal meaning leads towards the concerns voiced by Six, Seven, or Eight, who are searching to orient themselves in the profusion of legitimate possibilities they discovered in the relativism of position Five. They seek a way to make commitments to career, companions, values and to make them wholeheartedly in a world in which knowledge and meaning are tentative. In the midst of this challenge they seek support in models, especially in their teachers. In providing this support, the best we can do is to let them see that we share with them the risks that inhere in all commitments. Then their sense of ultimate aloneness in their affirmations becomes itself a bond of community.

It is revealing to observe what happens when the teacher's and the students' ways of making sense are uncompromisingly disparate by two or more levels. If students Five through Eight are taught in the manner expected by Two, they may be bored or frustrated, but they understand what the teacher is doing. In the reverse of this mismatch, however, when students at the level of Two are taught in a manner that is good teaching only for Five and above, they panic and retreat. Over the past 25 years the position of the modal entering freshman at Harvard has advanced from around Three to nearly Five. Yet many Twos and Threes and Fours are among us. Since we tend as teachers to address the more responsive students at and above the mode, we can be concerned about the remainder, who feel they are outsiders to the enterprise. I hope, if only for their learning, that they are fortunate in their advisers and their friends, and that their instructors, if opportunity permits, confirm the legitimacy of their bewilderment.

This concern has brought me to my last observation. What powers do we not have? Clearly (if we remember), we cannot push anyone to develop, or 'get them to see' or 'impact' them. The causal metaphors hidden in English verbs give us a distracting vocabulary for pedagogy. The tone is Lockean and provocative of resistance. We can provide, we can design opportunities. We can create settings in which students who are ready will be more likely to make new kinds of sense.

But what happens to the old kinds of sense? Where do yesterday's certainties go? Are Two and Three and Four the only ones in need of support? Five and Six and Seven and Eight (and you and I) have dared at each step to approach the abyss where the First student has stumbled into meaninglessness. For the advancing students a new world has opened from each new perspective, to be sure, but the mind is quicker than the guts. The students had invested hope and aspiration and trust and confidence in the simpler design of their world of yesterday. How long will it take them to dig out their vitality and reinvest it in the new, problematical vision? And all the while they are told that these are the happiest days of their lives.

The students do find their gains expansive and fulfilling, but does no one see the losses? If no one else does, can they? They can but wonder: 'What is this cloud, this reluctance?' It can't be grief, can it? I believe that students will not be able to take the next step until they have come to terms with the losses that inhere in the step just taken.

In ordinary daily work, our understanding of how students see, whether we agree or not, legitimizes their being as makers of sense. If they make overly simple sense, we must ask them to look further. But by acknowledging that making sense as they used to do was legitimate in its own time, and even a necessary step, we empower them to learn new and better sense. Our recognition is most encouraging in moments when the student is moving from one level of sense-making to another. When the transition happens right in front of us, we will see the eager realization and then, perhaps very shortly, the shadow of the cloud. We say something like: 'Yes, you've got the point all right . . . but we do wish it made things simpler.' The most heartening leaven for the mind can come from just such a brief acknowledgement as this.

References

Copes, L (compiler) (1984). *Bibliography and Copy Service Catalog: Perry Development Scheme.* St Paul, Minnesota (10429 Barnes Way, 55075), ISEM.
Knefelkemp, L L and Cornfield, J L (1984). Combining Stages and Style in the Design of Learning Environments. Address to the American College Personnel Association, 1979. (Reprints obtainable from author at College of Education, University of Maryland, College Park, Maryland 20742,USA).
Perry, W G (and associates)(1970). *Forms of Intellectual and Ethical Development in the College Years.* New York: Holt, Rinehart and Winston.
Perry, W G (1981*a*). Cognitive and ethical growth: The making of meaning. In: A Chickering (ed), *The Modern American College.* San Francisco:

Jossey-Bass.
Perry, W G (1981*b*). Examsmanship in the liberal arts: A study in educational epistemology. Harvard College, 1963. Reprinted in K Zeender and L Morris (eds), *Persuasive Writing: A College Reader*. New York: Harcourt Brace Jovanovich.

Chapter 8
Conceptions as the Content of Teaching: Improving Education in Mechanics

Lennart Svensson and Christian Högfors
University of Gothenburg and Chalmers University of Technology, Sweden

Teaching is a complex phenomenon. There are many different conceptions of what teaching is, both generally and in the field of research. We would argue that the nature of teaching concerns the relation between the 'teaching situation' (what goes on in the classroom) and the learning outcome (what students learn). It is not enough to study only the 'teaching situation' and its precedents in order to reveal the nature of teaching. One has to consider the situation in relation to what the students learn.

Like the other authors in this book, we believe in focusing on knowledge of concepts and principles as the key outcomes of learning. It may seem fairly easy to clarify outcomes: one can test whether the students 'know the meaning' of certain central concepts and principles. In many cases, one might safely assume that the students do not know these 'entities' in advance. The outcome would then, all being well, involve adding these entities to the students' repertoire of concepts and principles. This view can be seriously questioned: it is too simple an argument to maintain that a person either possesses the right version of a concept or no version at all.

The abstract meaning of concepts and principles may be expected to vary and develop. The abstract meaning of a concept, which is rather like the general meaning we attach to a word, may be dealt with and discussed as a kind of object in itself. This is often the case in the field of education, but the focus is then on abstract linguistic learning, a learning about certain principles and meanings *per se*. However, it is a restricted form of knowing; merely knowing about some instruments in order to know the world. It does not necessarily imply any understanding of a concept's meaning or of the application of a principle to real situations.

Interest has grown over recent years in research into students' thinking and especially into what conceptions they develop and use compared with the conceptions they are taught (see, for example, West and Pines, 1985). In science, particularly in subjects that deal with 'everyday physics', such as classical mechanics, questions about what conceptions can be employed, may be used, and should be developed, are very relevant. It has been found that science students in general have already developed common-sense conceptions that they find useful before they embark on a science curriculum. An increasing number of investigations of students' conceptions in science subjects has been reported during the 1980s (see Driver and Erickson, 1983; Duit, 1987a,b; and Pfundt and Duit, 1986).

The developmental character of knowing becomes still more apparent when we deal not with conceptions of concepts and principles *per se* but with conceptions of phenomena. Dealing with conceptions of phenomena is fundamental to both making concepts useful and to developing them. Conceptions represent knowledge of the world. It is therefore suggested that they should be focused on both in research and in teaching.

In a research project in Gothenburg, Sweden, we have examined students' conceptions of some physical phenomena and changes in their conceptions of those phenomena. The subjects were first-year students at Chalmers University of Technology. The results from this research constituted the starting point of attempts to improve the teaching of mechanics. We have not undertaken a systematic evaluation of the attempts to improve teaching. What is presented here is simply a description of the nature of the attempts. Before turning to this main issue we will briefly present some examples of the descriptions of conceptions and changes in conceptions developed in the research project. In another context, we have argued (partly on the basis of the same research) in favour of a view of learning as a change between qualitatively different conceptions (Johansson, Marton and Svensson, 1985).

Differences and changes in conceptions

If learning is to be described in terms of changes in conceptions, then understanding differences in conceptions, as other authors in this book have argued, becomes an important part of good teaching. To illustrate what we consider to be important differences in conceptions, we will very briefly present some results concerning students' conceptions of linear motion. The cases were presented to a group of first-year university students, and their conceptions were explored in interviews before and after a course in mechanics (Svensson, 1984). Clement (1982), among others, has reported similar results to ours concerning students' 'motion implies a force' preconception before and after participation in an introductory mechanics course. Here, we will present the general picture revealed through our results. Two cases were presented in the following way:

A railway truck becomes uncoupled from a moving train and rolls straight forward on a completely horizontal track. What happens?
    A puck is hit by an ice hockey stick and glides straight forward on smooth ice. What happens?

163

Half the group was given the hockey example before the course and the railway example after the course. The other half was given them in reverse order. Students were asked to describe what happened and were given no hints as to what concepts or principles were expected to be used. The students' conceptions of what happened were described by the use of five categories summarizing the fundamental similarities and differences in the conceptions of the phenomena.

The students conceptualized the body (the puck or truck) as:

(1) having a velocity that diminished due to forces opposite to the direction of motion;

(2) having a kinetic energy that diminished due to forces opposite to the direction of motion;

(3) having an inherent (motive) force or energy that diminished due to totally greater forces opposite to the direction of motion;

(4) having an inherent (motive) force or energy that diminished due to totally smaller forces opposite to the direction of motion;

(5) having an external pushing force that diminished due to totally smaller forces opposite to the direction of motion.

As can be seen from the brief description of the different conceptions, the students used a number of different concepts and principles in different ways when conceptualizing the concrete phenomena of the gliding puck and the rolling truck. Much can be said about the differences between these conceptions and readers should refer to Johansson *et al.* (1985) for further detail of this type. The categories given above illustrate in a general way the variation in thinking about the phenomena that is present at the beginning of a university course in mechanics (this does not necessarily mean that the students could not give satisfactory definitions of the concepts and principles involved). In the course the students subsequently followed, these conceptions were not dealt with in an explicit way. The course was a fairly conventional one based on traditional methods of teaching dyamics (and on the use of Meriam's book *Engineering Mechanics: Statics and Dyamics*, 1978).

Before the course, 15 of the 23 students expressed conception 1, the desired conception. The remaining variation was accounted for by eight students. After the course, all but one student expressed the desired conception. However, expressing the desired conception and the change to this conception cannot be taken to mean that the conceptual problems revealed through the alternative conceptions before the course have been clarified and mastered by the students. Rather, it may mean that the students have learned to stick to some concepts and one model rather than to others, perhaps without knowing why or what difference it makes. One may suspect this since the differences in conceptions were not focused on within the course.

The students were also presented with the cases of a car and a bicycle (identical probes have also been used by other researchers, see Osborne and Gilbert, 1980):

A car is driven at high constant speed straight forward on a highway. What forces act on the car?

A cyclist is cycling straight forward at a high constant speed on a road. What forces act on the bicycle?

In this case, where students were explicitly asked to consider force, the difficulties that some of them experienced with energy and inherent forces when reasoning about the cases of decelerating motion were avoided. The confinement to forces acting on the bodies resulted in the clarification of another problem, however, which was not present in their reasoning about the cases of decelerating motion. For these cases of constant velocity we obtained two main conceptions of the phenomena summarized in two categories of description.

(1) The car (bicycle) has a constant velocity due to the equilibrium of forces: the 'driving force' is equal to the sum of the opposite forces.

(2) The car (bicycle) is moving due to a 'motive inequilibrium' of forces: the 'driving force' is greater than the sum of opposite forces.

Fifteen of the 22 students expressed conception 1 (the desired conception) before the course, and 16 after the course. Thus there was little apparent improvement during the course among the seven students expressing conception 2 before it. The fundamental difference between the two conceptions was not explicitly addressed during the course, largely perhaps because it was not expected to cause any problems.

From a theoretical, disciplinary point of view, these two types of cases may appear to be very similar and to involve the same essential principles of Newtonian mechanics. However, they turned out to be very different in terms of the character of students' conceptions of the phenomena and the changes that took place during the course. The cases represented quite different reasoning problems for the students. The cases of decelerating motion were given first in the interview, and the students had to decide for themselves which concepts to use. As regards the cases of constant velocity, the students were specifically asked to describe forces acting on the bodies, which they did. The difference in the character of the cases probably had an effect similar to that of the difference in presentation, ie the cases of the car and the bicycle invited descriptions in terms of external forces, while the cases of the puck and the truck invited descriptions in terms of inherent forces and energy. The main problem with the car and the bicycle was the delimitation of the effect in a cause-effect description.

A number of students delimited the effect as motion (as opposed to rest) instead of constant velocity. This problem did not arise in the cases of the puck and the wagon, where the effect was readily seen as deceleration.

From the brief exposition given here, we can anticipate large variations when it comes to students' use of concepts and principles in reasoning about specific phenomena, and the specific character of the phenomena presents students with varying problems. The different problems experienced and the ways of solving them result in different conceptions of phenomena. It is the revelation of this character of the continuing development of knowledge among the students that has inspired the attempts, outlined below, to make conceptions part of the content of teaching. The attempts are of four kinds and we consider them in the following order: teacher presentation of alternative conceptions; diagnoses of students' conceptions used as content in teaching; confrontations between students; and teacher discussions of course goals.

Teacher presentation of alternative conceptions

Where they were aware of common problematic alternative conceptions the mechanics teachers participating in the project referred to above tried to clarify alternative conceptions in their lectures and in class discussions. This was also a starting point for clarifying the desired conceptions. The research into the students' conceptions made teachers more aware of the need to emphasize understanding and to point out what the desired conceptions imply and what mistakes should be avoided. This has occurred in only a limited number of cases, since knowledge of common alternative conceptions has been restricted and reference to alternative conceptions has not been very systematic. However, when the teachers have used this approach they have found it helpful and rewarding. A radical change in teaching towards systematic presentation of a variety of alternative conceptions has yet to be attempted and would seem to require both further research and further discussion of the content and methods of the whole educational process in this subject area.

There is widespread hesitation among teachers when it comes to presenting 'wrong' conceptions or, rather, incorrect concepts in teaching. This is due to teachers' fear that the incorrect version, rather than the correct one, will be learned. There are certainly many good reasons for these misgivings, especially in traditional teaching which focuses on learning concepts and principles *per se*. However, on the other hand there is considerable potential in highlighting alternative conceptions. When the main focus is on concepts and principles *per se*, different conceptions of these 'entities' could usefully be dealt with, the potential lying in the possibility of contrasting and relating conceptions. The contrast can bring out more clearly what is essential in the desired conception, and relating it to alternatives gives it the frame and context that are often missing in teaching. Here, the history of science may be of great help (cf Chapter 5).

It is important from another point of view that engineers be aware of common (mis)conceptions of the phenomena with which they are dealing. In engineering education, communications skills are emphasized as general goals. These goals could be given substance in terms of skills in communicating with people having varying conceptions of the phenomena the engineer is dealing with. These would include an awareness of the conceptions held by others such as politicians, administrators and economists, and the ability to clarify differences between commonly held conceptions and those of engineers.

From a scientific and conceptual perspective, mechanics takes up a somewhat special position. It is a theoretical discipline that depends upon the use of mathematics. At the same time, mechanics deals to a large extent with tangible everyday situations (eg the puck, car, truck and bicycle cases in the preceding section). In common with most disciplines, mechanics starts out from, and takes for granted, some conceptual primitives that cannot be defined in its theories; while other concepts, often rather sophisticated, are defined within its theories. Moreover, mechanics has been around for so long that our entire society has been permeated by it, one consequence being that many mechanical concepts lead a life of their own. Energy, force, power, momentum, etc, are words that we all use freely without worrying about their scientific meaning. It is also obvious that much of our thinking is affected by a 'mechanistic' attitude that has extended far beyond the natural sciences.

It is thus understandable that not only investigation and analysis but also presentations of prevalent conceptions will encounter difficulties. The very fact that students' conceptions are amenable to analysis is crucial to the possibility of making the presentations more successful in influencing those conceptions. The fact that the tentative classification schemes resulting from different analyses differ in various aspects depending on emphasis is more of an advantage then an obstacle. Presentations of conceptions will benefit to the extent that they appear more descriptive and less dogmatic and normative.

In teaching mechanics, semantic and epistemological problems are crucial. It is important not to presuppose a common or 'scientific' meaning of words normally encountered in connection with mechanical or physical situations. It was evident from our investigations, and indeed it is evident from careful reading of a newspaper, that words such as force, energy, power, velocity, and so on, may have very different connotations from time to time and case to case. In presenting alternative conceptions, we have found it necessary to replace or complement association-laden words with more neutral ones. For instance, when we speak about forces in the mechanical sense, we tend to use such descriptions as 'influences' or 'things that cause change', etc.

Students' conceptions are the results of a long process beginning with the child's initial sorting of impressions. The emerging conceptions, more or less mature, more or less sophisticated and more or less conscious, are useful to those who hold them. They are instrumental in relating the individual to his or her impressions, to 'the real world', if you like. From this point of view, the student's conception is rarely 'wrong'. It may be unwanted, often difficult to communicate and sometimes difficult to develop, but it is seldom of no value. The use of 'scientific' words before the student is actually aware of his or her own thinking easily promotes the wrong pairing of word and concepts. We consider it quite possible that many of the 'errors' the students make are the result of such mismatches. A student knows something. A teacher, with authority, gives a correct account of this same thing using 'scientific' words. The student's decoding of this account is likely to produce 'errors'.

We have argued that there are several reasons for presenting alternative conceptions to the students. It is a first step in making students aware of how they themselves think and that their way of thinking is one of several possible ways of thinking. It may make it possible for students to relate their own conceptions to the conceptions of others and thus an acquaintance with common conceptions may increase their communicative skills. Presentations of alternative conceptions may also be of use in guiding the students into the theory, in the sense that the concepts and relations that they work with are, in general, similar to elements in theory, albeit with different names. More important, the presentations may be used to clarify the meaning of the desired conceptions in relation to alternative conceptions held by the students. This will make it possible for individual students to ascertain what change in conception, ie what learning, is required of them.

Including the presentation of alternative conceptions of concepts and phenomena in teaching may seem to be a good idea in principle. However, teachers may object that dealing with alternative conceptions will take up a great deal of time – and there is little enough time at the moment. Considering the crowded curricula of most educational programmes, this may seem a valid objection, more especially where dealing with alternative conceptions is seen as additional content to be included in an already full programme. However, the situation changes if we regard dealing with alternative conceptions as a means of achieving already established goals (as well as new ones) in a more efficient and effective way. 'Right' conceptions are usually presented repeatedly in teaching, but are often not learned by students in the form teachers would like. It might be more effective to present the conceptions in a way that makes it possible for the students to locate and develop their own thinking. Thus it is possible that alternative conceptions could be presented within the same time limits and a higher quality result could be obtained.

Diagnosis of student conceptions used as content in teaching

If dealing with alternative conceptions in teaching is seen not only as a means of promoting knowledge about alternative conceptions but also as a means of teaching the 'right' conceptions, it would probably be more effective to address directly the alternative conceptions held by the students. This would require some way of making contact with the students' conceptions and making them part of the content of teaching, and was indeed attempted by two mechanics teachers using the two methods described below.

The first approach was to confront students with the conceptions they had expressed earlier in a diagnostic test. Within a more traditional way of thinking, the test might be seen as a matter of making diagnoses of the students' previous knowledge. However, the emphasis in this case was on the fact that the diagnosis concerned conceptions in combination with the use of the diagnoses in teaching.

All first-term students were given a pencil and paper test with questions intended to tap their conceptions of some physical phenomena. The test was designed by one of the teachers, Ragnar Grahn, on the basis of the questions used in the interviews in the research project. Fifteen pictures illustrating different physical phenomena were presented. Students were asked to focus on one body and to draw arrows to show all forces acting on the body, their direction and point of application. They were asked to draw arrows representing forces and to explain what kind of force each arrow was illustrating. Compared with the interviews, the test gave a somewhat superficial description of students' conceptions. However, students' answers did produce important indications as to the conceptions they held. The test gave an overview of the variation of conceptions among the students and made it possible to teach in a way that addressed each individual student's thinking.

The students' answers to the test questions were returned to them in class and their different answers were discussed, enabling personal involvement and focus on the desired conception to be combined. The situation could be expected to promote an integration of the desired conception into the students' thinking through clarification of the relation between the desired conception and each student's earlier 'spontaneous' way of thinking about the phenomena dealt with. We would expect this contact with the students' own conceptions to aid long-term development in their thinking, compared with traditional teaching. The teaching was well received by students, although the results in terms of change in conceptions were not systematically evaluated.

Finding out what different conceptions people have in any subject area is a formidable task which in most cases is best dealt with in interdisciplinary research projects. While awaiting further developments in this area, one may, with some caution, draw on the competence of experienced teachers. A careful analysis of what a teacher would normally call 'common misconceptions' will often reveal a good deal about prevalent conceptions. With some knowledge of students' conceptions it is fairly easy to construct diagnostic tests that are sensitive to crucial characteristics of the conceptions. We do not need to advocate the benefits of diagnostic tests here. However, in far too many subjects and courses, testing is restricted to the factual level. Alternatively, tests are claimed to 'measure' understanding in a general taxonomic sense. We are suggesting something quite different.

With knowledge of the conceptions that are to be expected (and knowledge of the conceptual base of the subject), one may make diagnoses of conceptions, and chart changes in conceptions. Unlike traditional teaching, this approach enables the diagnostic tools to be used not only to assess what is already known but also to influence the formation of conceptions. The diagnoses can be used to provide the student with feedback, thereby increasing his or her awareness of the thought patterns he or she employs in various situations. Nussbaum and Novick (1982) describe a teaching strategy that involves exposing students' preconceptions and creating conceptual conflicts to achieve change in conceptions. Strike and Posner (1985) discuss conditions for conceptual change more generally.

Lifting conceptions to the conscious level seems to be an important stage in helping students to change, and is a central feature of the confrontation or dialogue technique that is described in the next section.

Confrontation between students

Our original investigations of students' conceptions made it quite clear that simply to obtain the 'raw material' was a very laborious task. Trained interviewers (trained not to say anything) spent some three hours with one student. Interviewers from another university were used in order to avoid any interviewer/teacher association on the student's part. Even if a teacher can learn to refrain from teaching (after much training), the student will always expect some connection with assessment. The student is then likely to try to make a good impression on the interviewer rather than to reveal his or her own thoughts. One of our reasons for attempting student confrontations was to circumvent these difficulties. Another reason was to find a way of avoiding direct presentation of conceptions while exhibiting, by way of example, how other people think.

The exercise was designed and carried out by Christian Högfors. Students were grouped in pairs and the students in each pair explained the nature of physical phenomena to each other. The pairs then compared results. Finally, the whole class met to discuss their results with the teacher. The teacher and the students found the approach very useful in that it revealed real differences in conceptions of phenomena among the students. This formed an excellent basis for clarifying the critical characteristics of the conceptions taught as opposed to the alternative conceptions expressed by some of the students. The technique was used as an introductory part of the teaching.

The effectiveness of student confrontations depends on how they are carried out. The students were given instructions in written form informing them that the aim of the exercise was that they should on the one hand become aware of and test their own way of thinking, and on the other learn about other students' ways of thinking about physical phenomena. It was stressed that the students should be aware that identical words may have quite different meanings depending on who uses them and where. This was exemplified by giving different meanings of the word 'force'. The instructions also directed the students to work in pairs, taking turns at assuming the role of the one who explains (the problem-solver) and the one who listens (the listener). For the two roles, the following instructions were given.

Instructions for the problem-solver

(1) Give an account of the situation you are to describe.

(2) *Describe* what happens as carefully as possible. Do not bother about why it happens. Imagine that you are watching the situation and describe what you see in roughly the same way as a radio reporter describes, say, a sporting event. You have to convince yourself that your listener considers your description correct and that it contains every important aspect. Use words and concepts that you think best describe what is happening.

(3) *Explain* to your listener *why* the situation develops the way it does. You should try, qualitatively at least, to describe what happens in terms of cause and effect. Try to make a model of the situation where you replace the object's surroundings with some abstract notion of influence on the object itself. Make sure your listener agrees that your explanation is acceptable. If you use technical terms, explain what they mean. You are to convince your listener that your theory (model) explains your earlier description. Is your idea about causes sufficient?

(4) Your model is probably not generally valid. Describe the conditions under which your model is valid. You must also be explicit about what you disregard (idealizations).

(5) Imagine now that you have to solve a mechanical problem dealing with this situation. Pick a question that seems relevant to you and outline how you would go about finding the answer. What additional information do you require to be able to find the solution? You have to *convince* your listener that you really would get the answer this way.

Remarks

Try to think aloud (it is not quite as easy as it may sound). Remember that your partner is only a listener. You do the job. If you find it difficult to think of the 'correct' words, just say what comes into your head. No-one is assessing you. If you think something went wrong, go back and start again. Try to follow the instructions as closely as possible.

Instructions for the listener

You play a key role in this exercise. Your task is to help the problem-solver understand what he or she is doing.

(1) You must ensure that the problem-solver talks all the time and describes how he/she thinks. ('Say something – never mind how it sounds', 'Try!')

(2) The problem-solver should enable you to *understand* how he or she views the problem and thinks about it. Whenever you do not understand, you should ask the problem-solver to give details. The problem-solver must not continue the task unless he or she has actually convinced you that his or her way of thinking is correct. ('Can't you elaborate on that point a little?', 'Are you quite sure that's the way it is?', 'I think you'd better check that again.')

(3) Whenever, in your opinion, the problem-solver reasons incorrectly or jumps to illogical conclusions you should interrupt him or her. Ask for *explanations*. As a last resort, single out what you think is wrong, but *do not correct it*.

(4) If the problem-solver uses a word whose significance is not entirely obvious in the context, ask him or her to explain what meaning he or she attaches to it. Accept the proposed meaning even if you yourself would have used another word.

Remarks

The problem-solver should think aloud so that you may follow his or her thoughts. This isn't easy. You will probably have to encourage him or her all the time. You must, of course, allow for short pauses for thought. Never allow the problem-solver to resort to an algorithmic or formula-type explanation. Never allow the problem-solver to continue if you have not understood or if you think something is wrong.

The phenomena given to the students as problems are listed below. They had been given earlier to other students in the interview investigation.

(1a) An ice-hockey puck has left the stick and is sliding straight ahead on smooth ice.

(1b) A railway truck has been released from a train and is travelling straight ahead on horizontal rails.

(2a) A car is being driven at high constant speed straight ahead on a highway.

(2b) A cyclist moves straight ahead at a high constant speed along a road.

(3a) A ball has just left the hand of the person throwing it.

(3b) A golfer has hit a ball with his club.

(4a) A person is riding on a carousel that is slowly increasing speed.

(4b) A motorcyclist is driving at an increasing speed around a circular track.

The exercise succeeded in exhibiting students' conceptions. But what was more important was that the students became more aware of their own ways of thinking. According to the teacher, the teaching became easier after the exercise. Although incomplete, the student's awareness of his or her own conceptions together with some alternative conceptions seemed to liberate him or her in relation to the theoretical structure presented in the teaching. Students appeared to acquire the ability to investigate the structure taught from different viewpoints. They incorporated new conceptual tools into their own thinking more easily, and rapidly seemed to acquire not only a familiarity with the language but an under-standing of the theory. We conjecture that some major changes occur once an individual's own conceptions are lifted to the conscious level. It could be that people tend to identify parts of the world with their own concep-tions of them until they become aware of the qualitative variation between people in their conceptions of these parts.

Becoming aware of the nature of conceptions comes close to the type of change from an absolutistic to a relativistic understanding of knowledge, studying and education which has been described by Perry (see Chapter 7). Thinking relativistically seems to be an important part of the desired change towards a provisional commitment to a new and better conception. Gibbs (1981) has focused on students' awareness of their own way of thinking, studying and learning as the aspect of study skill that should be addressed if we are to help students improve their learning. This general approach is given some support both by Perry's work and our own results. However, to become aware of qualitative differences in conception within a field of study goes beyond a change in one's general understanding of knowledge, studying and learning. It means a more precise understanding of knowledge, studying and learning *combined with* changes in specific knowledge of the content studied.

Discussions of course goals

It would seem logical that whenever a task is to be performed, the starting point ('where from') and the goal ('where to') should be identified before anything is done. It has long been a habit among teachers, however, to focus on *methods* rather than 'where from' and 'where to'. Since our original investigation concerned 'where from' and also provided some answers to that question, we felt compelled to take a look at 'where to'. Given our attitude towards the teaching process, it seemed natural to attempt to describe goals in similar terms to starting points.

If conceptions, and especially alternative conceptions, are to become part of the content of teaching, this should be done with the specific goals of teaching in mind. Descriptions of courses and their goals are often somewhat superficial and merely point out areas of knowledge to be 'covered' and mastered. Most teachers can probably conceive of students' conceptions as important prerequisites for teaching. However, they will almost certainly find it much more difficult to think about the goals of their courses, not in terms of the concepts and principles of the discipline, but in terms of student conceptions. This is an unusual way of thinking about course goals. An exploration of the thinking of four teachers of mechanics about the goals of their courses sheds some light on this problem.

One of the authors (Lennart Svensson) and one of his doctoral students met the four teachers in a group discussion of their courses. The group discussion took place early in 1985 and was followed by two interviews with each teacher, carried out in February and March. The interviews were analysed and the results presented as a basis for further group discussion. We will briefly present the general picture of the teachers' thinking about the goals of their courses.

At first, the teachers were hesitant and doubtful about the whole idea of discussing goals. They appeared to find the suggestion strange. After a diffident start, however, they became quite involved. The discussions and interviews were extensive and the teachers became increasingly more articulate about the aims of their courses and the whole programme. This development was also manifested in contributions to a symposium (described later) arranged at the university, and in reactions to and reflections upon the symposium.

A large part of the interviews and the group discussions with the four teachers contained their descriptions of the most important premisses for designing mechanics courses. Two kinds of premisses were emphasized: the discipline of mechanics and the whole engineering programme. There was a high level of agreement about the premisses and classical mechanics formed the core on which the content of the courses was based. In addition, expectations and demands from other parts of the programme were to be met. Thus, when considering the goals and content of the courses, the teachers started from these two kinds of premisses.

Questions raised were: Do these premisses provide a good and sufficient basis for the design of the courses? Are there other hidden premisses necessary for the design of the courses?

The teachers discussed further specifications of the knowledge areas mentioned in relation to the official description of the courses. They thought there ought to be a closer relation between the stated goals and the results achieved. The teachers were aware that one may achieve different qualities of knowing within the same content areas by designing the tasks in different ways. They were also aware that students solve the same tasks in different ways. This knowledge was not directly referred to when discussing the goals of the courses. However, questions were raised as to how the character of the tasks and the judgement of the results could influence which goals were actually achieved.

The dominant view throughout discussion of the courses could be described as 'administrative'. This perspective starts from the partition of the educational programme into subjects and courses, and parts of subjects and courses. The goals are more or less equal to mastery of the units that make up the courses. What it *means* to master or know these units is considered non-problematical. How to further and control this knowledge are seen as practical problems that do not have to be treated during discussion of the goals. We raised the following question: is it really effective to let this kind of 'administrative thinking' dominate the discussion of goals and to exclude questions about the character of the tasks involved and the quality of knowing aimed at and achieved?

In November, Christian Högfors arranged a one-day symposium on the theme 'Goals and quality in education'. Teachers from the School of Mechanical Engineering were invited. A short presentation of the discussions and interviews with the four mechanics teachers whose work is summarized above was included, together with eight other written contributions from teachers within the programme. The symposium was divided into two main parts, one part addressing the question 'How can goals be set for individual courses?' and one part dealing with the theme 'The general aims of the educational programme'.

Many interesting contributions were made both in the written papers and in discussion. Here, we will concentrate on one general characteristic of the way of discussing goals which was clearly revealed in the symposium and is central to our present theme. It became clear that the goals for individual courses and the general aims for the whole programme were considered quite separately. Also, the participants made it clear that there was usually no reference to the general aims in setting the goals for individual courses.

In the official formulation of general aims, the emphasis is on what the engineer should be able to do on completion of the programme. Knowledge and skills within the fields of mathematics and science and related professional fields are emphasized, as well as the awareness of the role of science and technology in society and the ability to communicate with other people. Discussion at the symposium indicated that when people thought of better ways of meeting the aims, they mainly considered new courses that would fill the gaps. This completes the picture of the previously mentioned 'administrative' way of thinking.

Individual courses aim at knowledge and skills within specified content areas. The specification of the content areas to be dealt with is perceived as the problem. The knowledge and skills are assumed to be specified by means of the specification of the content areas. The relation to the general aims is actualized only in terms of whether the content areas dealt with in the courses appear to correspond, or not, to the general aims.

This perspective excludes a very important aspect or dimension, namely that of qualitative variation in knowing and competence within the content areas specified in the course descriptions. This dimension concerns the quality of knowing specifically aimed at and achieved, and its absence when considering the aims is an important obstacle to making conceptions a content of teaching. At the same time, making conceptions a content of teaching can, in a very important and substantial way, help teachers to move beyond superficial thinking about the aims of education. The need to specify the meaning of the general aims in relation to the goals of individual courses, and vice versa, is obvious and could best be done by including the dimension of qualitative variation in knowing and, particularly, qualitatively different conceptions of phenomena in the discussion of aims and specific goals.

The educational significance of the nature of conceptions

Conceptions concern our 'epistemological' relation to parts of the world: our understanding of what is the nature or essence or 'true' meaning of these phenomena or parts of the world. Conceptions may concern anything and everything that might be thought of as something in itself, at least partly differentiated from its surroundings or context. In conceptualizing something, we use concepts (or some organizing principle or structure). However, there is an important difference between focusing on concepts *per se* and on concepts as a part of conceptions. There is much more to conceptions than isolated or abstract concepts.

Correspondingly, there is, on a more general level, an important difference between knowing about a theory and knowing about the world through using the theory. If the aim of education is to develop knowledge of the world, then conceptions are at the heart of the matter.

The world is not totally unknown to students. It seems reasonable to utilize whatever knowledge they have as a starting-point. The idea that one may present new descriptions of the world that are to be correctly learned but do not relate to previous knowledge, is, on reflection, a very odd idea; but it seems to be the model for a great deal of teaching nevertheless. This means that students are left very much to their own devices to glean whatever meaning they can from the descriptions presented and then to learn this meaning, whatever it is. Some of them will discover later that what they learned was not 'correct' in the sense that it is not accepted or useful for passing exams, but they may never learn what was wrong with their conceptions. There is much to be gained both in *quality*, ie in actually ascertaining development of the 'right' conceptions, and in *efficiency*, ie in achieving a more direct development of the desired conceptions, from the kinds of changes we have suggested. Making the students' conceptions, as well as the conceptions of the discipline, part of the content of teaching would seem to be the most direct way one can achieve an improvement in education.

References

Clement, J (1982). Student preconceptions in introductory mechanics. *American Journal of Physics*, **50**, 66–71.
Driver, R and Erickson, G (1983). Theories-in-action: Some theoretical and empirical issues in the study of students' conceptual frameworks in science. *Studies in Science Education*, **10**, 37–60.
Duit, R (1987a). Research on students' alternative frameworks in science: Topics, theoretical frameworks, consequences for science teaching. Kiel: Institute for Science Education, University of Kiel.

Duit, R (1987*b*). Research on students'conceptions in science – perspectives from the Federal Republic of Germany. Kiel: Institute for Science Education, University of Kiel.

Gibbs, G (1981). *Teaching Students to Learn: A Student-centred Approach.* Milton Keynes: Open University Press.

Johansson, B, Marton, F and Svensson, L (1985). An approach to describing learning as change between qualitatively different conceptions. In: L H T West and A C Pines (eds), *Cognitive Structure and Conceptual Change.* New York: Academic Press.

Meriam, J L (1978). *Engineering Mechanics. Statics Vol. 1, Dynamics Vol. 2.* New York: Wiley.

Nussbaum, J and Novick, S (1982). Alternative frameworks, conceptual conflict and accomodation: Toward a principled teaching strategy. *Instructional Science*, **11**, 183–200.

Osborne, R J and Gilbert, J K (1980). A technique for exploring students' views of the world. *Physics Education*, **15**, 376–9.

Pfundt, H and Duit, R (1986). Bibliography. Students' alternative frameworks and science education. Kiel: Institute for Science Education, University of Kiel.

Strike, K A and Posner, G J (1985). A conceptual change view of learning and understanding. In: L H T West and A L Pines (eds), *Cognitive Structure and Conceptual Change.* New York: Academic Press.

Svensson, L (1984). Kroppar i linjär rörelse. Teknologers tänkande om nagra fenomen inom mekaniken (Bodies in linear motion. Technological students' thinking about some phenomena in mechanics). Gothenburg: Pedagogiska institutionen, Göteborgs universitet.

West, L H T and Pines, A L (eds) (1985). *Cognitive Structure and Conceptual Change.* New York: Academic Press.

Chapter 9

Approaches to Learning Anatomy: Developing a Programme for Preclinical Medical Students

Norman Eizenberg
University of Melbourne, Australia

Introduction

In this chapter, I identify and explore some characteristics of first- and second-year medical students' approaches to learning the subject of anatomy. An orchestrated set of interventions in teaching and assessment, based on recent research findings in student learning, is described. The changes have been designed to encourage more appropriate approaches to studying and more effective learning.

The effects of the interventions have been monitored from two complementary perspectives: analyses of the *experiences* of students in their own everyday learning activities; and the *outcomes* of their actual assessment tasks. Such perspectives are readily accessible to the teacher and their investigation can be a normal part of teaching. The monitoring of the interventions – carried out using questionnaires, written submissions, interviews and informal discussions with students – has in turn provided implications for further research aimed at improving medical students' learning.

The subject of anatomy

Anatomy is the study of the structure of the human body. In traditional medical courses (such as at the one at Melbourne) it forms a basis for the parallel study of physiology through the correlation of structure with function, and for the subsequent study of pathology and many of the clinical disciplines. Establishing an understanding of normal anatomical structure is regarded as a necessary preliminary to the second two areas of study.

In mediaeval times, anatomy was unsophisticated. Primitive squatting figures containing almost unrecognizable organs were the standard works used by practitioners of medicine. Leonardo da Vinci's anatomical studies enabled him to establish a clearer idea of the functioning of the human body. They also provided an understanding of the structures lying beneath its surface markings (in particular the musculature) which had frequently been represented inaccurately by artists (Keele, 1964). Extracts of Leonardo's notes give insight into some of the ways he went about acquiring this understanding. Incidentally, they provide excellent illust-rations of what we would now term a 'deep approach', ie actively searching for meaning:

If you wish to know thoroughly the parts of man after he has been dissected you must either turn him, or your eye, so that you examine him from below, above and from the sides . . . Before you form the muscles make in their place threads which should demonstrate the positions of these muscles. The ends of these (threads) should terminate at the centre of the attachments of the muscles to the bones.

(In Keele, 1964)

It was necessary to proceed by stages with as many bodies as would render my knowledge complete and this I repeated twice in order to discover the differences . . . My works are the issue of simple and plain experience which is the true mistress.

(In Keele, 1964)

The outcomes can be seen in his anatomical drawings. Leonardo was able to reduce bones and joints to levers acting on fulcrums, and muscles to lines of force acting on these levers – illustrating his own physical conceptions applied to the human body. Interestingly, descriptive anatomy itself did not come to the surface until Vesalius published his *De Humani Corporis Fabrica* in 1543, 24 years after Leonardo's death. This was the work for which contemporary anatomists were ready, and it opened the flood gates of future anatomical progress (Keele, 1964).

And what a flood it was! Anatomy is now widely regarded as an enormous discipline with a primarily descriptive basis. A student facing the prospect of learning the subject is in danger of becoming drowned in factual information. To quote two second-year medical students (458 years after Leonardo's death):

I am learning a lot of irrelevant details . . . The body is full of them . . . it wasn't designed to be studied.

The problem is one of quantity. I found anatomy the greatest hurdle. I don't think I have ever been confronted with a more difficult subject to learn.

Approaches to learning

It is necessary for me to introduce here (or remind readers of) some of the terminology from recent research into student learning in educational settings. I will be using these terms to describe differences in how students learn anatomy and to show how my studies of my own students' learning have influenced my teaching. The way in which a student approaches learning a subject such as anatomy is a response to his or her perceptions of its *content* in the *context* of the course in which it is presented. Thus, an approach to learning as I consider it here is what has been called a *relational* phenomenon: it represents a relation between a learner and a task (see Chapters 1 and 2 and Ramsden, 1987).

A *deep approach* involves active searching for meaning, while a *surface approach* relies on memorizing (Marton and Säljö, 1984). Table 1 in Chapter 1 has summarized the chief differences between these approaches. It is possible that the same student may use either a deep approach or a surface approach for each of the many different learning tasks in a particular subject.

'Learning' has two senses in the way I describe it here. In one sense it may be regarded as an outcome, ie what learning has occurred – being defined as a change in conception (Dahlgren, 1984), or more specifically as changes in a person's conception of aspects of reality (see Chapters 1 and 2). It may also be regarded as the means to that end, ie *how* a change between qualitatively different conceptions takes place. Describing how a change in conception takes place characterizes an approach to learning.

Approaches and outcomes
Since a surface approach focuses on the 'signs' rather than 'what is signified' it must inevitably result in inadequate understanding. A deep approach is the only way in which changes in conceptions can occur (Marton and Säljö, 1984). Moreover, it is more efficient and effective in the long term as a way of remembering facts, and it is, of course, a more satisfying way to learn. In contrast, memorizing quantities of information is not only harder work but it means that studying becomes increasingly more arduous and tedious as the volume of material to be digested increases (Svensson, 1984). The authors of this book clearly regard the deep approach as a desirable form of learning. Can anatomy, with all its facts, be studied in this way?

The following extract is from the preface to an anatomy textbook of the 1930s. The author evidently felt that a deep approach was not only possible, but preferable:

The study of human anatomy may be attempted in either of two ways. One consists in collecting facts and memorizing them. The other way consists in correlating facts, that is studying them in their mutual relationships. This leads inevitably to the apprehending of the underlying principles involved and the 'raison d'être' of such relationships. The student will thus learn to reason anatomically and will find the acquisition of new and related facts an easier task. It is the purpose of this book to lead the student to approach the subject from this viewpoint, and it involves certain departures from tradition . . .

(*Grant, 1937*)

Ference Marton has combined the original concepts of deep-level versus surface-level processing (Marton and Säljö, 1976) and 'holistic' versus 'atomistic' approaches (Svensson, 1984) that emerged from the earlier Swedish research to evolve a new framework representing the 'referential' and the 'structural' aspects of approach, and their reflections in outcome (Marton, 1988) (see Figure 1). The deep/surface dichotomy emphasizes the referential ('what') aspect of students' experiences – their search for meaning or their failure to search for it. The holistic/atomistic dichotomy is concerned with the structural ('how') aspect – the ways in which students organize the content of learning tasks. The analytic separation of the referential from the structural is useful. Only when they are identified separately can the relationship between them be demonstrated (Marton and Säljö,1984).

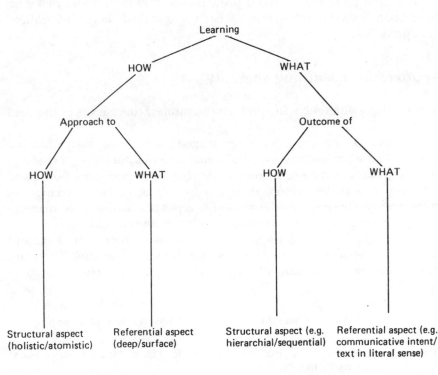

Figure 1. The logical structure of some categories used to describe learning from an experiential perspective (Marton, 1988)

Empirical links between approaches and outcomes
Referential aspect. Marton and Säljö (1976) found that deep-level processing led to qualitatively higher levels of response to reading tasks. Surface-level processing resulted in lower quality responses and poorer recall. Students who tried to memorize the text did not remember it as well as those who tried to understand it. Concentrating on the surface of the presentation, characterized by a failure to learn due to overanxiety to perform well, has been termed 'hyperintention' (Marton and Säljö, 1984).

When a structure of questions directed towards the major lines of reasoning in an article was provided, Marton and Säljö found that students who used a surface approach and concentrated solely on perceived requirements could summarize the main points but could not demonstrate understanding. They called this phenomenon 'technification'.

Structural aspect. Svensson found that holistic approaches enabled students to understand organized wholes (such as academic articles) due to the integration of parts by recognizing and using organizing principles. Atomistic approaches led to students making sequential rather than hierarchical links between parts of the article (Svensson, 1984). This failure to preserve a hierarchy between principles and examples – to make no diistinction between the status of each – is called 'horizontalization' (Dahlgren, 1984).

Approaches to learning anatomy

How do these differences in approaches manifest themselves in the field of anatomy?

At Melbourne, first- and second-year medical students study anatomy in a wide array of learning activities unique to the discipline, including: dissection of cadavers; examination of predissected specimens, bones and radiographs; and the inspection and palpation of surface markings on living people. These are in addition to the types of activities used in many other disciplines, such as attendance at lectures and tutorials; and private study engaged in reading (text, as well as visual representations and captions), note-taking, writing essays and drawing diagrams. There are many ways in which students use a deep approach. Here are some examples:

In dissection I try to appreciate the three-dimensional structure of something.

I try to understand what new anatomical terms mean by looking up in a glossary, rather than learning them by rote.

I sit back looking for patterns. It's good because I am doing the input rather than the book, otherwise I would passively read it.

My analysis of interviews with second-year medical students produced a series of descriptions of their ways of attempting learning tasks in anatomy. I distilled these into the five categories shown in Table 1 (Eizenberg, 1988).

The majority of my second-year students (68%) stated that they employed more than one of these five categories (of ways of tackling their learning tasks) in the context of the anatomy programme. For example:

Table 1. *Categories of approaches to a learning task*

---

(1) Search for meaning by organizing the content into an integrated whole (prior to or while analysing it).
(2) Search for meaning by analysing isolated items of information (without organizing them into an integrated whole until much later, if at all).
(3) Memorize (rote-learn) a 'ready-made' orgainzed whole (eg, essay plan, flow-chart, diagram, algorithm, mnemonic).
(4) Memorize isolated items of information.
(5) Avoid or not actively engage in the task.

I for one have periods where I study well using a deep approach, but then lapse and have to rely on a surface approach to pass the exams.

Each of the first three categories was used extensively by more than 50% of second-year students. Category 2 was used the most. The last two categories were employed extensively by 36% and 14% respectively. Categories 1 and 2 seem to represent a deep approach employed in different ways. Categories 3 and 4 represent a surface approach. In each of these categories students have actively tried to engage in the task (and may even have tried too hard, in some cases). Category 5 represents the not uncommon reality of the absence of any active approach.

It is clear that the intention to search for meaning does not *guarantee* understanding, in anatomy or any other subject. But employing a deep approach holistically is the only way of gaining a full understanding. In this case, both the referential and the structural aspects of approach are addressed. The two aspects are synergistic, as shown by Säljö (1984). A certain meaning orientation leads to a certain way of organizing a text and parts of it, and that way of organizing the text leads to a certain referential meaning being abstracted from it. This synergism can also be illustrated by medical students employing a deep approach holistically:

I work my way towards a finer understanding after I've got an overview.

First I define realistically what I shall do. A point-form summary helps, then I allot time to each point and tick them off as I go. It's soon done, whatever the task is . More detail required? . . . All right, I'll return to certain points later . . . I like to keep a perspective if I can, rather than getting bogged down with trivia first off.

However, if a deep approach is employed atomistically, and meaning is searched for in isolated items of information (without 'standing back'), it is easy to miss the distinctions between principles and examples. This is 'horizontalizing' the content. In anatomy, it happens easily, particularly when a student is studying sequential descriptions of structures.

A surface approach can be employed holistically: this involves a process of 'technifying' the content, ie draining it of meaning. This often leaves just the structural shell – the 'main points'. Some students described the memorizing of overviews, summaries, essay plans and even diagrams, particularly when pushed for time ('I rote-learn key diagrams and labels').

Another illustration of technifying, developed by generations of resourceful medical students studying anatomy, is the phenomenon of using mnemonics as a device to try to structure (albeit artificially) items of information perceived to be required for reproduction in examinations. While some anatomical mnemonics are humorous (and unprintable), most deal with seemingly meaningless lists of branches or detailed descriptive relations of anatomical structures. The more useful mnemonics have some intrinsic meaning, eg 'SCALP' for the five layers of the scalp (from skin to pericranium). At the other end of the spectrum are those like 'Let Most Men Pass' (for branches of the profunda femoris artery). A book of mnemonics has the following tongue-in-cheek preface:

To the simple-minded, to the crammers for exams, and to those whose stumbling feet find the anatomical pathway difficult, this little book is offered in the hope rather than the belief that they may find some help from it.

Employing a surface approach atomistically in a subject such as anatomy is potentially disastrous. Trying to memorize masses of discrete items obsessionally and painfully is a major cause of fatigue in students. Some describe spending more and more time for less recall and eventually having to leave out major sections. This process of 'hyperintending' (of the content) occurs paradoxically when they are trying too hard.

At times whole tasks were avoided (or at least only addressed passively and partially) for a variety of reasons ranging from the 'burn-out' described above, following prolonged hyperintending, and lack of time, through to perceived lack of importance and/or a lack of interest. The defaulting process may be termed 'non-engaging' (in the task):

I have difficulty studying consistently in any subject and tend to concentrate only on those with rapidly approaching assessment requirements.

The processes of horizontalizing, technifying, hyperintending and non-engaging may each be regarded as undesirable in so far as they impede the gaining of a full understanding and the changes in conceptions which I want my students to experience (see Table 2). Such processes may be used quite deliberately. They may be entirely appropriate for avoiding failure or even achieving high grades in certain circumstances (at least in the short term). They certainly do not necessarily mean that the student who uses them is 'weak'. Entry into a high-status medical school like Melbourne is exceptionally competitive. The use of these approaches by students whose ability and previously demonstrated performance would compare favourably with any similar age cohort in the world is a matter of concern. Again it must be emphasized that learning approaches represent interactions with the content and context, rather than a quality in the student.

Table 2. *Categories of processes for learning approaches*

APPROACH TO A LEARNING TASK		PROCESS
(a) Referential aspect: WHAT type of approach	(b) Structural aspect: HOW it is employed	
DEEP	HOLISTICALLY	'The *only* way to gain understanding'
DEEP	ATOMISTICALLY	'Horizontalizing'
SURFACE	HOLISTICALLY	'Technifying'
SURFACE	ATOMISTICALLY	'Hyperintending'
NIL	NIL	'Non-engaging'

Developing a programme for preclinical medical students

It is all too simple for a teaching programme to induce students to adopt surface approaches, or to employ approaches atomistically. Programmes particularly prone to this problem are those where a large volume of factual information is encountered, such as subjects in the preclinical years of the medical course – especially anatomy. Students are well aware of this:

Boring technical facts shovelled towards us in mounds and mounds can be remembered for the purpose of the exam only. This year has not been a learning experience and I am not motivated at all.

I'd really much prefer to be able to study by thoroughly understanding the work . . . It becomes so much more interesting and worth while if there is some meaning behind it. Unfortunately, the large amount of knowledge that we are expected to have leads me to simply memorize facts for the exams.

Encouraging students to adopt deep approaches and employ them holistically requires, of course, that both the referential ('what') and the structural ('how') aspects of learning need to be taken into account in teaching. A two-fold strategy of interventions, which paralleled these two aspects of approaches to learning, was employed in the development of a new programme of anatomy for first- and second-year medical students at the University of Melbourne.

The first (referential) component of the strategy was intended to represent to students the importance of quality of understanding as opposed to quantity of information. The aims of the medical course formed the ultimate frame of reference. A comprehensive set of objectives and sylla-bus (in the form of the departmental handbooks *Medicine First Year* and *Medicine Second Year*) was constructed to orient the student towards the understanding of anatomical principles and their clinically important applications, at the expense of detailed minutiae. The rationale for each of the associated interventions in the curriculum, teaching and assessment was discussed in detail in Eizenberg (1986). These interventions are summarized in Table 3.

Table 3. *Interventions in curriculum, teaching and assessment*

---

(1) Curriculum:

(a)   linking curriculum to faculty goals (displaying to students and teachers)

(b)   matching curriculum, teaching and assessment (to clarify goals and standards)

(c)   incorporating applications in syllabus (to increase vocational relevance)

(d)   defining 'essential' information (to rationalize workload)

(e)   selecting appropriate textbooks (which encourage understanding)

(2) Teaching:

(a)   analysing the derivation of new terms (versus encouraging memorization)

(b)   emphasizing principles and concepts (versus accumulation of details)

(c)   creating an environment to facilitate 'good' teaching

(d)   actively engaging students (by learning from problem solving)

(3) Assessment:

(a)   providing adequate feedback (to minimize unnecessary anxiety)

(b)   constructing assessments (which encourage understanding)

(c)   marking strategies (to recognize and reward understanding)

The second (structural) component of the strategy involved reorg-anizing the teaching programme. A conventional and sequential course of instruction (which had by its very structure inadvertently promoted the accumulation of isolated facts) was converted to a programme that enabled the body to be viewed as an integrated whole. Patterns were revealed where the specifics could be seen in relation to the general principles, with multiple opportunities for overview and review.

The guiding principles behind the interventions are equally applicable to many other disciplines if they are translated by teachers into a form that addresses the peculiar combination of content, context and students' thinking with which they work. In my subject I found that the relational nature of learning and teaching required that six important issues be faced in planning a more effective curriculum. These issues concerned learning:

something (the *content*);
in a certain way (the *process*);
during a period of time (the *stages* of the programme);
in a particular setting (the *context*);
for a reason (the *purpose*);
by someone (the *student*).

Each of these areas will now be considered in turn.

The content: learning and assessment tasks in anatomy

Structuring the content
'I feel that overall too much emphasis is placed on learning masses of facts which turns medicine into a six-year rote-learning course', said one of my students in a research questionnaire. A common response to this sort of comment is that, in the early stages of learning many subjects, there is no alternative to laying down in a sedimentary fashion layer upon layer of factual information. This supposedly enables the learner to obtain the knowledge that is a prerequisite for deep and holistic approaches to learning. My reading of the recent research, together with my students' experiences ('I find it difficult to learn pages of unrelated data if no system is shown'; 'We were pressured into learning seemingly irrelevant factual information rather than the underlying principles') made me suspicious of this view. Could the tasks involved in learning anatomy be redesigned to help students understand concepts rather than accumulate facts – and thus to remember the facts better?

The subject of anatomy involves the description of the form of the body, but it goes beyond that. It tries to explain how a structure developed, to uncover patterns of distribution and to develop an appreciation of the basis of variation. The final form of the body should not be passively accepted without question as if it were an accident of fate.

A common early misconception regarding the bones of the human body is that they are dead. The skeleton hanging in a closet is in a vastly different context from the living body, where it is very viable and has a rich blood supply. As with approaches to learning, bones have a structural aspect (the living cellular and protein reinforcing framework) in which the content (calcium phosphate: the same material as chalk used in teaching) is embedded. To illustrate:

(1) Taking a bone out of the body and burning it to destroy the cellular and protein mesh (invisible to the naked eye) is analogous to learning by 'horizontalizing' the content of a task. The bone still appears to be made of the same material but is brittle, just like chalk.

(2) Decalcifying a bone in acid is analogous to 'technifying' a learning task. The impostor has the same form as the bone but it can be tied into a knot as if it were made of rubber, because its content has been eroded.

(3) Grinding a bone into powder is analogous to engaging in a learning task by the process of 'hyperintending'. The bone will have completely lost its form; even the content easily slips through one's fingers.

Similarly, it is easy for inappropriate selection of content or lack of clarity regarding the structure of learning tasks to discourage students from choosing deep approaches and employing them holistically.

How could learning tasks be constructed to encourage the students to search for principles that give meaning to the facts, and to search in a way that organizes the content into an integrated whole? Two strategies have been employed in the new anatomy programme at Melbourne. First, the course begins with the basic principles of general similarities of each type of anatomical structure (eg arteries). Students are explicitly required to build up a structural framework (eg an organizational plan for arteries) to provide a system of analysis for incoming information.

Secondly, the learning tasks for each subsequent week are comprehensively described in a study guide. A 'star chart' (a checklist of topics coupled with a star rating of the relative emphasis required for each) indicates the relative importance of information regarding anatomical structures prior to reading about them. The 'star chart' is designed to address the structural aspects of the topics in a form complementary to the organizational plans described above. This enables 'essential' topics to be designated and clarifies the aspects within each topic that make it important. It simultaneously provides a consistent structure.

The 'star chart' facilitates appropriate selection *within* tasks, rather than between tasks. It encourages students to learn something about everything, rather than everything about something.

Assessing the content

It is easy to design questions in assessment tasks that prevent students from demonstrating understanding. It is also easy to remove an incentive for future cohorts to try and acquire understanding. The wording of questions (eg asking for a description, or 'brief notes') may restrict the opportunity to show understanding; at best one can hope to infer that understanding may have been required to get the correct answer. Similarly, asking purely for identification, or only asking closed questions (eg 'What is this structure?' . . . 'What nerve supplies it?', etc) in oral examinations can be dismaying to students:

I felt that I knew a lot on the topics but wasn't able to show it . . . I was frustrated with it . . . the exam did not give me a chance to prove my worth.

I find it frustrating that people seem to sometimes get high marks merely by regurgitating . . . no wonder so many take the easy way out.

How could assessments be constructed that would allow students to demonstrate understanding and encourage them to use deep approaches holistically? Again, both referential and structural aspects needed to be addressed. At Melbourne, the anatomy assessments have been closely linked to the goals and their associated learning tasks. Knowledge and skill requirements for each component of the assessment programme are displayed in the departmental handbook for students and teachers. Open-ended questions in the written examination are used to provide an opportunity for students to give explanations (which subsume descriptive information) of important principles and applications, thus encouraging them to display understanding. In the orals, questions such as 'Demonstrate to me some structures in this region' or 'Explain how they receive their nerve supply' give students scope to show their grasp of concepts.

The process: reorganizing the anatomy programme

The arrangement of a teaching programme may restrict the scope of a student's search for conceptual understanding. Learning many anatomical principles needs the early provision of simple, even rigid and dualistic rules which are deliberately transient. However, even more importantly, there is a need for opportunities built into the programme to remodel the concepts in the light of encountering the specific structures to which they apply, and thus to promote the intellectual development of 'relativistic reasoning' (see Chapter 7). Understanding evolves over the course of the entire teaching programme and continuing opportunities for it to develop and progress are needed.

The old programme: atomistic and sequential
The former programme was typical of many anatomy programmes. It was purely 'regional'. All the *regions* of the body were evenly distributed over the full complement of teaching weeks allocated to the subject. This arrangement inadvertently promoted the accumulation of details and isolated facts. For example, the learning tasks for the upper limb were sequenced in a linear fashion – working progressively down the regions, starting at the axilla (armpit), and ending at the hand. Students were limited to tackling the limb in a series of segments. It tended to be seen only as a sum of its many parts. The requirement to be sequential caused many students to get progressively further behind as the course went on. This was made worse because students met one of the most difficult regions of the body – the axilla – first and launched straight into the complexities of the brachial plexus (network of nerves).

The organization of the weekly study programme was dictated by the dissection programme. The most expedient order of dissection (which is usually from superficial to deep – for obvious technical reasons) is not necessarily the most appropriate order to learn the subject. For example, the anterior abdominal wall and the abdominal cavity are traditionally programmed before the posterior abdominal wall. Students were impeded (until the last week of the programme), first from viewing the abdominal walls as an organized whole and, secondly, from relating the contained viscera to the posterior wall.

It was very difficult for students to distinguish, let alone grapple with, an underlying principle from the surrounding factual details. For example, many students failed to apprehend the significance of a major concept regarding 'anastomosis' (where blood vessels meet up mouth-to-mouth). This linking of arterial branches provides alternative paths of blood supply. Although the branches from the main artery are often quite variable (and even that has a developmental basis), overview of the whole territory of distribution enables the following propositions to emerge:

(1) In general, the major artery runs over the flexor aspect of a joint (where it is more protected).
(2) The artery gets kinked when the joint is flexed.
(3) Many branches are given off just above and also just below the joint – and these branches anastomose with each other.
(4) Even though bone has a rich supply (cf cartilage, which has no blood vessels) parts of certain bones have a low degree of anastomosis (ie few alternative paths). Their viability is endangered where the one avenue of supply can be cut off (eg in fractures at particular sites).

But, in practice, students tended to focus on learning textbook descriptions of the courses of minor branches and often missed the main point about the arterial patterns. Furthermore, there were no scheduled sessions in the programme of study to link structures that pass though a number of regions (eg long vessels and nerves) over their whole course.

An alternative to a 'regional' programme is a 'systematic' one, in which *systems* of the body (skeletal, muscular, vascular and nervous) are each studied separately. However, a purely systematic programme is equally sequential and linear. While it aids the viewing of relationships within the same type of structure, it misses out on the arrangements between neighbouring structures. Besides, nothing could be more boring than studying every bone in the body before moving on to every muscle, and so on.

The new programme: holistic and hierarchical
The new programme has both regional and systematic elements linked together (in a 'regional-systematic anastomosis'). The programme for each major section of the body (thorax, neck, head, etc) has been reorganized as follows:

(1) It commences with constructing the musculo-skeletal framework.
(2) All regions (within the major section) are then analysed.
(3) The vessels and nerves are traced (from origin to termination).
(4) Finally, vascular and nerve supplies are studied.

The programme does not follow any one particular text. It can be used with both types of textbook (regional and systematic), allowing for different student learning preferences within each type. In anatomy, dissection is regarded as a most valuable means to the end of gaining an understanding of the subject. However it is not an end in itself, so the dissection programme is designed around the weekly study programme rather than the reverse.

The 'anastomotic' nature of the anatomy programme provides the opportunity to develop the versatile skills (similar to those in clinical diagnosis) needed to cope with viewing the same anatomical structure (or problem) from alternative perspectives, or at least from different starting points. A particular structure may have its blood supply from various arteries – a specific artery may supply a number of anatomical structures. With luck, a general pattern (regarding arterial anastomoses, for example) may become evident to the learner through inductive reasoning. Better still, specific instances of anastomoses (whether from the perspective of the anatomical stuctures, or from that of the arteries) may be deduced by applying a general principle known in advance.

The stages: relating the specific to the general in the teaching programme

How could the programme be staged to allow the specifics to be viewed in relation to (and be regarded as examples of) the underlying general principles? I decided that the programme needed to provide multiple opportunities (the scheduled time, as well as the direction) to look for both. Again, this was a response to my interpretation of what my students were saying against a background of research on student learning:

Often information overload in tutorials would take up time needed to spend linking with principles. First year was disorienting as principles were not emphasized in early tutorials . . . emphasizing principles makes learning anatomy easier and more enjoyable.

Principles and concepts should be taught concurrently with topics throughout the year . . . they are both very interesting and useful in explaining the adult anatomy . . . For example, the relationship between the developing aortic arches and the path ultimately taken by the recurrent laryngeal nerve – amazing!

The ordering of the major sections of the body in the anatomy teaching programme was primarily determined by a decision to coordinate the study of anatomy with other subjects studied at the same time. This enabled students to study the same organ systems simultaneously. The stages shown in Table 4 were designed to address the referential and the structural aspects and incorporated both overview and review.

The setting: the wider context of the medical course

The sheer volume of content in an entire course may discourage students from adopting deep approaches holistically within an individual subject.

Table 4. *The stages in the teaching programme*

STAGE 1: WALLS: BONES, JOINTS, MUSCLES AND FASCIA
The focus is on the structures which form the musculo-skeletal framework:

(1)   what structures form the framework;
(2)   how they are arranged together

. . . from an 'Engineering' perspective, ie the body as an interlocking set of levers and pulleys faced with a trade-off between mobility and stability.

STAGE II: CAVITIES (AND VISCERA): REGIONS
The focus is on the arrangement of structures contained within the musculo-skeletal framework:

(1)   what position a specific structure (and its component parts) occupies;
(2)   how it is related to its neighbours

. . . from a 'Geographical' perspective, ie the body as a continent of three-dimensional territories waiting to be navigated.

STAGE III: VESSELS AND NERVES
The focus is on the supply lines:

(1)   what structures (which make up the walls and contents of the regions) are supplied by a specific vessel/nerve;
(2)   how the supply line is laid out (course and branches)

. . . from a 'Surveying' perspective, ie the body as a network of pipes and wires.

STAGE IV: VASCULAR AND NERVE SUPPLY
The focus returns to structures which are supplied by vessels and nerves:

(1)   what vessels and nerves supply the specific structure;
(2)   how effective (rich or poor) and vulnerable, exclusive and variable the supply turns out to be

. . . from an 'Economic' perspective, ie the body as sets of demands, each crying out for (a range of) supply.

Abrahamson (1978) has described a set of characteristic curriculum problems occurring in American medical schools, which he has termed
'diseases of the curriculum'. One such disease – 'curriculum hypertrophy'
– is due to the dramatic growth in the knowledge base required for the
practice of medicine, and the subsequent cramming of more and more
content. A student from an eastern medical school is quoted:

We have the best anatomy course in the country; what they don't cover in the
lecture or the lab, they cover in the final exam.

(Abrahamson, 1978)

What happens when the workload required to address tasks adequately
exceeds the maximum reasonable time that students, in practice, can
actually spend on the tasks? We know from research on university
students' learning that, if students perceive an excessive amount of
curriculum material to be contained in a course, they will often respond by
using minimalist (surface) approaches (see, for example, Ramsden, 1984).
At my own institution, many students stated that when they became
stressed they resorted to taking 'short-cuts' such as skipping lectures and
copying practical work, assignment sheets and essays from other students
or directly from books (the extracts in this case are from a medical student
society questionnaire):

If something is wasting your precious study time and you are not getting anything
out of it then plagiarism is probably your best course of action.

Essays are good generally and give you a chance to look into areas of interest and
develop your researching skills. The essay in second term is badly timed because
the workload is far too great. Most people churn one out in under a day, not caring
how good it is or what they get out of it . . . they only want to get it out of the way.

The 'art' of non-engaging in certain learning tasks (as a form of adaptation
to excessive workloads) can be developed to a high level of sophistication.
A more subtle effect of excessive workload may be that students shift their
intentions from gaining an understanding and/or high grades in a particular subject (or subjects) to one of simply avoiding failure.

In 1987 I used a questionnaire to ask students about their intentions. The
vast majority (94%) of my second-year students initially expressed the
'ideal' intention of gaining an understanding of anatomy. However, by the
end of the teaching programme, 62% 'realistically', after taking the total
workload into account, shifted their major intention away from understanding to avoiding failure in the examination. This phenomenon also
occurred in all the other second-year subjects surveyed. Anatomy is only
one of three or four subjects that are studied in each term; each subject
contributes to the wider context – including the total workload. In the case
of the first and second terms in second year, at present, the total workload
appears to be grossly excessive:

Towards the end of second term my learning became totally exam orientated . . . little long-term recall of material learnt in this period . . . anxiety extreme . . . insomnia, panic attacks, etc.

At present I do not consider that I think efficiently. The need to get through the workload stifles any attempt to search for meaning.

High workloads in the course overall prevent a deep, thorough study and therefore understanding of any one subject. Superficial cramming of facts is encouraged, albeit unintentionally.

Despite the numerous interventions within the subject of anatomy, students did not always choose deep approaches nor consistently employ them holistically. This contextual dependence of interventions illustrates one of the practical difficulties in changing teaching with the expectation of influencing learning. What can be done to change the wider context?

My University is currently in the process of planning a shift to semesters (from terms). This has had the beneficial side-effect of providing an opportunity for the medical faculty to restructure the preclinical years of its course. A number of interventions have been proposed to reduce the total workload, rationalize the timing and weighting of assessments, and arrange for subjects to provide a more evenly distributed load. Each subject in the preclinical years will receive a weighting to indicate its (expected) workload in relation to that of other subjects. It is hoped that students intending to achieve understanding in all subjects will then have reasonable time to address the required tasks adequately.

The purpose: preparation for the clinical years

At Melbourne, the frame of reference of the anatomy curriculum for medical students is clearly directed to meeting the aims of the medical course. The subject taught is in reality 'medical' anatomy rather than 'anatomists'' anatomy. As well as the incorporation of clinical applications, there is also more emphasis on certain areas (eg the airway, the hand) and less on others. All regions and anatomical structures are still required to be studied: there is selection within, rather than between, topics. Even though the massive content of anatomy makes it easy for its structure to become obscured (there is a tendency to 'horizontalize' the subject), deletion of entire topics would really horizontalize anatomy, reducing it to an incomplete collection of parts. The aim should be to encourage learners to view it as an organized whole.

The deliberate manipulation of the content of the subject (to adapt it to the course and provide the appropriate perspective) is analogous to the representation of parts of the body on our own cerebral cortex. All parts are represented but some have a richer nerve supply and therefore are represented on a disproportionly larger area of brain than one would expect from the actual size of the part of the body. The relative emphasis of the content of 'medical' anatomy reflects this.

'Problem-based' medical schools (in contrast to 'traditional' medical schools) do not teach anatomy as a separate discipline. In the curriculum of the Medical School at the University of Newcastle, Australia, for example, all the basic sciences (including anatomy) are studied in a clinical context throughout the course via a carefully designed sequence of medical problems, each with clearly stated goals (Engel and Clarke, 1979). When Newcastle students were compared with students from a traditional medical school, using the Lancaster Approaches to Studying Inventory (Entwistle and Ramsden, 1983), they rated themselves higher on deep approaches in all years of the course (Newble and Clarke, 1986). It appears that a problem-based curriculum is more likely to encourage deep approaches, although it is possible that such approaches may be restricted from being employed holistically (at least with regard to anatomy). Anatomical knowledge, skills and attitudes are acquired longitudinally throughout a problem-based course, but this may restrict the student's opportunity to study the human body as an organized whole. An innovative course may be less holistic regarding anatomy but this may be a small price to pay if it is more holistic with regard to the whole person.

Although traditional courses may have an advantage in delivering anatomy in a cohesive package, they could attempt to be more innovative in order to encourage deep approaches by attempting to create a clinical context in presenting anatomical concepts. If traditional courses are unable to have the student in a clinical context from the outset, then they should bring the clinical context to the student. The obvious example is to have selected patients come to the campus. But it is often difficult in practice to get the right patient at the appropriate time and there are severe limitations in what can be demonstrated to large groups of students. Technology has opened up access to clinical material, and videos demonstrating clinical problems which have an anatomical basis have been prepared for use in the lecture programme and also made available (in the audiovisual library) for students to use at such times as they judge appropriate.

The emphasis on content that is medically important, together with the creation of a clinical context in presenting anatomical concepts, is more likely to be consistent with students' aspirations and therefore encourage the intention to gain an understanding of anatomy.

The student: developing effective learners

Learning anatomy, like any other subject, can be conceptualized at different levels of generality. Teaching anatomy involves helping students to change their conceptions of specific phenomena; it also involves helping them to improve certain more general qualities. These include an understanding of how a clinician thinks and, still more generally, intellectual independence and relativistic reasoning (see Chapter 7).

The most effective way I have found of helping students to develop as learners is actively to avoid impeding their learning of subject content. This means taking steps to encourage and reinforce appropriate approaches to the particular subject they are learning. I have not found teaching content-independent strategies to be a success. The best way to help students seems to be to improve the teaching and assessment programme itself. It is necessary to move from the specific learning of subject matter to the general qualities; the second level cannot be successfully addressed separately from the first. The bulk of this chapter has been devoted to the discussion of the rationale for, and the effects of, such interventions in teaching.

A student encountering learning problems in my subject may be directly helped by retracing the stages of his or her interaction with a learning task. This may involve going through written work with the student, focusing on both the referential and the structural aspects of what has been written. The student can be encouraged to reflect on the approaches he or she has used to tackle the task and the topic. An attempt should be made to relate the approaches and how they were employed to the outcomes. I have found that this method raises students' level of awareness of their own approaches to learning and provides an opportunity for students to deduce more appropriate future courses of action. This is not at all like the 'learning skills' instruction I have come across. To be a success, this form of intervention must take place in the context of a discussion of subject content. It is simply another form of teaching.

Conclusions

I have attempted to show that basing the design of a teaching programme on the findings of student learning research may help students improve their approaches to learning my subject – particularly if both the referential (what) and the structural (how) aspects of the programme are addressed.

Since the interaction between the learner and the learning environment depends on perceptions, it is not only continually changing but varies from person to person. The challenge in any educational programme is to prevent misperception and mismatch. The situation is therefore both dynamic and plastic, with multiple avenues for the 'jigsaw' to come unstuck, but also with many opportunities for intervention and improvement.

I have tried to illustrate this in Figure 2. Inappropriate approaches are simply induced: just one piece in the jigsaw that is out of place (mismatched or misperceived) may interfere with the relation between the learner and the content. Encouraging students consistently to adopt deep approaches and employ them holistically is doubly difficult because both the referential and the structural aspects of all the pieces need to fit together. In the unattainable 'ideal' teaching programme, all fronts of the learning interaction (for each student) are matched (simultaneously) for the duration of the entire programme – with the teacher fulfilling the versatile role of matchmaker.

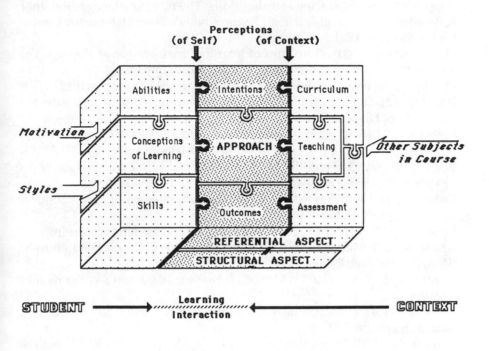

Figure 2. *The interaction between learner and environment depends on perceptions*

The changes I have described could not have been carried out successfully without the guidance and inspiration of several educators, in my own institution and elsewhere, who are represented in other chapters. Gradually I have come to realize that the 'action research' into student learning I have tried to carry out within a broadly phenomenographic perspective is very closely related to my everyday teaching. It involves 'listening' to one's students as well as talking to them, and 'reading' their work as well as marking it. But as others have stressed in this book, the principles behind the interventions are guiding, not prescriptive. They need to be reinterpreted and adapted to each specific situation by the teachers directly involved. The amendments I have made cannot simply be transplanted successfully into a foreign context; but I hope that they provide suggestions for how other teachers might investigate and improve their students' learning.

References

Abrahamson, S (1978). Diseases of the curriculum. *Journal of Medical Education*, **53**, 951–7.

Biggs, J B (1986). Enhancing learning skills: The role of metacognition. In: J A Bowden (ed), *Student Learning: Research into Practice*. Melbourne: Centre for the Study of Higher Education.

Dahlgren, L O (1984). Outcomes of learning. In: F Marton *et al.* (eds), *The Experience of Learning*. Edinburgh: Scottish Academic Press.

Eizenberg, N (1986). Applying student learning research to practice. In: J A Bowden (ed), *Student Learning: Research into Practice*. Melbourne: Centre for the Study of Higher Education.

Eizenberg, N (1988). Improving medical students' learning of anatomy. PhD dissertation, in progress, University of Melbourne.

Engel, C E and Clarke, M R (1979). Medical education with a difference. *Programmed Learning and Educational Technology*, **16**, 70-87.

Entwistle, N J and Ramsden, P (1983). *Understanding Student Learning*. London: Croom Helm.

Entwistle, N J and Marton, F (1984). Changing conceptions of learning and research. In: F Marton *et al.* (eds), *The Experience of Learning*. Edinburgh: Scottish Academic Press.

Grant, J C B (1937). *Grant's Method of Anatomy*. Baltimore: Williams and Wilkins.

Keele, K (1964). Leonardo da Vinci's influence on Renaissance anatomy. *Medical History*, **8**, 360.

Marton, F (1988). Describing and improving learning. In: R R Schmeck (ed), *Learning Strategies and Learning Styles*. New York: Plenum.

Marton, F and Säljö, R (1976). On qualitative differences in learning. I – Outcome and process. *British Journal of Educational Psychology*, **46**, 4-11.

Marton, F and Säljö, R (1984). Approaches to learning. In: F Marton *et al.* (eds), *The Experience of Learning*. Edinburgh: Scottish Academic Press.

Newble, D I and Clarke, R M (1986). The approaches to learning of students in a traditional and in an innovative problem-based school. *Medical Education*, **20**, 267-73.

Ramsden, P (1984). The context of learning. In: F Marton *et al.* (eds), *The Experience of Learning*. Edinburgh: Scottish Academic Press.

Ramsden, P. (1987). Improving teaching and learning in higher education: The case for a relational perspective. *Studies in Higher Education*, **12**, 275-86.

Säljö, R (1984). Learning from reading. In: F Marton *et al.* (eds), *The Experience of Learning*. Edinburgh: Scottish Academic Press.

Svensson, L (1984). Skill in learning. In: F Marton *et al.* (eds), *The Experience of Learning*. Edinburgh: Scottish Academic Press.

Chapter 10
Improving Medical Students' Clinical Problem-solving

Gregory Whelan
University of Melbourne, Australia

Introduction

A patient is brought to a hospital emergency room suffering from abdominal pain. He looks sick and needs urgent attention. A diagnosis and appropriate treatment are required. Popular television programmes would have us believe that the problem will be solved by ordering the appropriate blood tests and X-rays and preparing the patient for an operation.

In reality, the situation is more complicated. The doctor must use his or her diagnostic skills, which include clinical reasoning, in order to solve the problem and select the best treatment for the patient. This is a rather dramatic example of the need for professionals to develop ways of thinking and conceptualizing phenomena as complex wholes, rather than to apply algorithmic solutions to real-world problems. What can we do to ensure that medical students learn to solve problems more effectively? In this chapter I will argue that by studying how students go about solving diagnostic problems we can learn how to improve our teaching and thus enable students to learn to become better problem-solvers.

The context in which clinical problem-solving is learned

Medical students working in hospital are confronted daily with opportunities to solve problems in a clinical setting. In many universities with traditionally taught medical courses, like ours, students progress through three years of sciences basic to medicine (which include anatomy, physiology, biochemistry, pathology, microbiology and behavioural science) before they embark on the clinical years of the course. Once they have learned the fundamentals of clinical method (medical interviewing and physical examination) they are ready to learn problem-solving in a clinical setting. It is the teacher's expectation that the student will apply the previously learned basic sciences to tackle these problems and arrive at diagnoses.

Illness, recognized by the patient as symptoms, occurs when a disease process alters the physical, social and emotional functioning of the human being. In physical terms the pathological process, which may be caused by genetic or environmental factors, affects the individual at one or more anatomical sites and causes symptoms by altering the physiological functioning of the structures concerned. This is a key concept in the understanding of many disorders. Some medical schools recognize its importance by teaching a course entitled 'Pathophysiology'. In most schools it is incorporated into many subjects. Even with a rudimentary knowledge of clinical medicine, a student with a firm grounding in basic sciences ought to be able to apply this knowledge to solve many clinical problems.

Once medical students commence clinical work, much of their daily activity relates to clinical problem-solving. During ward rounds with an attending clinician, they are expected to present the details of a patient's illness for discussion with other members of the student group. At weekly case presentations, they are expected to present in detail the clinical features of a patient's illness, to interpret, evaluate and summarize the data and to formulate a diagnosis that illustrates an understanding of the patient's illness and its manifestations.

Traditionally, clinical problem-solving is learned in an environment where the teacher discusses the clinical problem, emphasizing the information that was used to make a diagnosis. Rarely is the clinical reasoning behind the choice of diagnosis made explicit. Many experienced clinicians would be unable to explain in detail how they solve problems, believing that it 'comes naturally'. Students often form a perception of what is done from what they observe and from what they know they need to record in the patient's history. It is not surprising to find that many students beginning clinical medicine imagine that they have to collect a vast amount of information by interview and examination with the belief that 'the solution will be in there somewhere'. They often develop the skill of information gathering to a high degree, but have difficulty with diagnostic reasoning, particularly with the steps that involve selecting key points from the data base that can be used to produce a diagnosis.

From the questions asked in ward rounds and the investigations ordered, a perception often arises that diagnosis consists of a process of *exclusion* until the correct cause remains. Students often fail to understand that, in parallel with this exclusion process, an experienced clinician is seeking evidence to support other diagnoses (positive clues) and applying a thorough understanding of the reliability of certain clinical features in supporting or refuting a diagnosis. The clinician also appreciates the importance of negative clues in the diagnostic process and knows when to discount false clues that would indicate a diagnosis that could not possibly explain the clinical features of the patient's illness.

What do we know about how students apply clinical problem-solving skills?

Much of our current understanding of a medical student's problem-solving strategies comes from studies of clinical reasoning from an information-processing standpoint (see McGuire, 1985). In many studies a contrast has been made between the student's efforts and those of an experienced clinician. The terms 'extensive [perhaps exhaustive would be more appropriate] data collection and review', 'spot diagnosis', 'pattern recognition' and 'the hypothetico-deductive approach' have been used to describe the varying procedures and strategies used. It is thought that, by contrast with novices, experienced clinicians have their knowledge stored in principles and as clusters of items rather than as individual items. In situations that are well structured and familiar, the expert is probably using a 'pattern recognition' approach. Originally this process was believed to be automatic. However, Gale and Marsden (1982) produced evidence to show that experts actively interact with clinical information early in the problem-solving process. They do not merely receive data passively until it is recognized as matching some other array in the clinician's previous experience.

Using a videotaped simulated recall of a clinical interview, studies have been performed of a student's or an experienced clinician's diagnostic reasoning processes in poorly structured or unfamiliar settings. Elstein *et al.* (1978) and Barrows and Bennett (1972) have pioneered the concept that in such situations the clinical reasoning process can be described as hypothesis generation and testing. This process, often labelled the hypothetico-deductive approach, is usually one commencing with an initial impression or concept (cue acquisition) followed by formulating a limited number of diagnostic impressions (hypothesis generation), performing a search and scan operation, and collecting additional data while using these hypotheses simultaneously and in parallel. Data are then interpreted (cue interpretation) and evaluated. The advantage of this model is that it can be made explicit to the student. By comparison with the exhaustive data-collection method it appears to be an excellent technique for teaching novices to think systematically about clinical data and how to gather it.

Grant and Marsden (1987) have recently argued persuasively that the differences between expert and novice clinical problem-solvers 'reside in the *content* of thought, not just the "what" but also the "how" of what they know'. In this view, differences in the structure and content of thought are more important than the simple amount of knowledge possessed. These authors maintain that approaches to teaching diagnostic problem-solving which suggest that simply learning information in a particular way will improve students' understanding are misguided, as are attempts to 'teach students how to think'.

Grant and Marsden's arguments will sound familiar to readers of this book. In fact, their work links what we know about clinical problem-solving from the perspective of cognitive psychology to the perspectives on learning pioneered by Marton and represented in so many chapters of this volume. Svensson (1984) identified approaches to reading text which he called 'atomistic' and 'holistic'. Students using the first approach focused on the constitutent parts of the text, never gaining an understanding of its meaning; students using the second approach focused on the *whole* (including both the parts and the ways they were related).

The holistic/atomistic dichotomy was originally derived from the ways students *manipulate the structure* of a text. Problem-solving is clearly about manipulating structure, and Laurillard (1984) extended the concept to how second-year students in a combined science course solved problems. Looking at problem-solving tasks that were part of the students' normal coursework, she found that the approach used related to the student's perception of the problem, which included the context in which the problem was presented. The holistic approach involves maintaining the structure of the problem and preserving the meaning of each part and its relation to the whole. The atomistic approach distorts the underlying structure. Students adopting this approach pay no attention to a problem's organization, preferring to 'concentrate only on juggling the elements together until they fashion a solution' (Laurillard, 1984, p 136).

Cutler (1979) has suggested that experienced clinicians have mastered the strategies of diagnostic problem-solving by learning how to group clues quickly, how to select key questions, and how to take the correct turns at branching points in the road towards a solution where they need to select only one path. This explanation of the interaction between patients and experienced clinicians best fits my perception of what acually occurs and is compatible with a holistic approach. In most instances I believe that the clinician has at least one, if not more, possible diagnoses in mind very early in the interview. On most occasions this is probably based on his or her knowledge of the prevalence of disease in the community in which he or she practises. However, the process of interviewing and examining the patient is directed at gathering data that will favour one hypothesis over another and simultaneously exclude other possible hypotheses. In poorly structured cases the experienced clinician has learned to cast the net wider and to include among the hypotheses apparently less likely possibilities. In ranking and evaluating the clues it may be necessary to re-examine, re-interview or seek information from an observer who has seen the patient in an 'attack'.

What can clinical teachers learn about students' clinical problem-solving?

Early in my teaching career I became aware that in discussing a clinical problem, students sometimes raised as diagnostic possibilities disorders that were incompatible with the patient's age and that ignored important information already in the student's possession. I originally thought this was a 'stab in the dark' effort to compensate for ignorance. By applying some of the principles of a phenomenographic approach I have since gained a greater insight into why these puzzling comments are offered and have now been able to apply a strategy that enables the student to overcome these conceptual errors.

Over the past few years we have studied medical student's problem-solving approaches during the early part of their clinical careers (Year 4) and in the final undergraduate year (Year 6). Information in this chapter comes from two formal studies and is supported by a multitude of observations from day-to-day teaching.

Studies of beginning clinical students
The first study was performed with our beginning clinical students (Year 4). We presented them (48 volunteers from a class of 63) with two case summaries in a format used in tutorial teaching at the bedside or in case presentations.

These summaries were made from the case histories of two patients known to me. Each summary was written in such a manner that the features could be explained in terms of basic science concepts and could be solved using a pathophysiological approach to examining the clinical features of the illness. Information was presented in this synthesized format to these beginning clinical students to avoid the difficulties that might arise if the students were unable to gather the data because of inadequate interviewing or physical examination skills.

The first case concerned a breathless patient:

Case history no. 1

A 55 year-old female, widowed for two years, presents complaining of shortness of breath on exertion for six months. She has also experienced three episodes of shortness of breath at night. These have been associated with a dry cough and wheeze. Attacks lasted from 20 minutes up to several hours. Her distress was eased by sitting up. She reported smoking 25 cigarettes a day for 20 years but ceased 13 years ago. Another doctor, several years ago, prescribed Lasix for swollen ankles. There are no abnormal physical signs seen on examination.

The first case illustrates a problem students see commonly on the ward or in the emergency room and was considered relatively straightforward. The central point of this case is that the patient's presentation could have resulted from heart failure or airways narrowing. The pathophysiological changes in the lungs secondary to cardiac failure give a better explanation for the patient's symptoms of breathlessness, which increased after lying down and were relieved by sitting up. The previously swollen ankles should raise the possibility of pre-existing heart disease. However, the swelling was due to prolonged standing in hot weather while employed as a waitress on a casual basis. Information that could be used in solving this case included: previous experience in anatomy, physiology and pharmacology, as well as presentations given in the introductory clinical medicine course (relating to breathlessness). Students also ought to have read about this topic after seeing breathless patients in hospital.

The second case concerned a patient who presented with symptoms due to anaemia which was in turn due to an underlying bowel disease:

Case history no. 2

A male electrician, aged 23 years, presents complaining of progressively worsening tiredness and weakness of three weeks' duration. He has difficulty climbing stairs. He believes that this is due mainly to weakness but he has noticed that he has trouble breathing whenever he attempts to walk up more than one flight. Three months ago he first noticed the onset of diarrhoea. This occurs on most days varying from four to six bowel actions daily. He has lost approximately 10 kilograms in weight over this time.

Physical examination reveals a thin male consistent with his stated weight loss. There are no other physical signs of disease – specifically, none of his abdominal organs are enlarged. There is no guarding or tenderness.

This case contained more information and I considered it to be more complex and more challenging for students. What the patient was experiencing could best be explained by reference to alterations in intestinal absorption and loss of nutrients, including iron, consequent to an inflammatory disorder of the terminal small bowel. Presentations given in the introductory medical course had illustrated how to approach the problem of a patient with diarrhoea. The preclinical course subjects that ought to have been of help included anatomy, physiology, biochemistry, microbiology, pathology and metabolism.

A semi-structured interview was used to guide the discussion. It was similar to that employed by Laurillard (1984) in her study of science students. Students were allowed as long as they liked to read and think about the summaries and to make some notes if they wished. When the student was ready, the interviewer began by asking: 'Could you tell me what you have learned about this patient?' The response was then followed up with non-directive questions designed to elicit information about the case, in particular a diagnosis or set of possible diagnoses, together with the student's reasons for choosing them. Subsequently the student was asked how she/he went about solving the problem. Finally we asked some questions concerning the relationship between the case content and his/her preclinical experience. The interviews were audio-taped and transcribed.

Analysis was carried out by searching for categories of description (see Chapters 2 and 5 in this volume) that described variability in the data. The focus was on the phenomenon of differences in approaches to solving the diagnostic problem. Extracts from the interviews were used to delimit the categories. The categorization describes a structural aspect of problem-solving. It describes the way in which the data are manipulated during the problem-solving process.

We looked carefully at the part of each transcript that described *how* the student went about solving the problem. Comments, phrases, and paragraphs that indicated how the material was approached were selected, ordered and reordered. Gradually it became clear that two qualitatively different approaches to solving the problems could be discerned (Ramsden, Whelan and Cooper, in press).

Ordering approach. If symptoms were discussed individually without relating one to another, if symptoms were ignored, if parts of the problem were ordered and grouped but if the groupings were not put together into a whole, if the process used distorted the structure of the problem and dislocated the content from its meaning, if the student was unable to describe what she/he was doing, the extracts were considered to characterize an *ordering* (or atomistic) approach to clinical problem-solving. Students using this approach usually did not discover a solution that satisfactorily accounted for all the information given.

Protocols that illustrate this approach include the following extracts: (from the first case) 'I tended to think of asthma straight off (in this patient) but that's just a personal preference . . . Then I was picking some of the (disease) names out of the air and tried to see whether they fitted into a pattern'; (from the second case) 'As soon as I read he was tired and weak I thought of anaemia . . . I thought, was that in a list (of causes) they gave us concerning such and such a disease?' 'I thought that the problem was tiredness and weakness and from that I went on to think that the diarrhoea was something unrelated or superimposed.'

Structuring approach. If the student maintained the underlying structure of the problem, if extracts illustrated that the student used evidence to support his or her ideas and related ideas to previously learned basic science, then these extracts were considered to characterize a *structuring* (or holistic) approach to clinical problem-solving. Protocols that illustrate this approach include the following extracts: 'She probably had some sort of problem with her heart which is unable to cope with maintaining a good circulation. It could be due to hypertension . . . because she is a smoker, hypertension and atherosclerosis could be inter-related . . . The heart has got to the stage where it can't cope with increased demand such as with exercise.' 'There is a back flow of pressure into the pulmonary circulation so she's probably getting some pulmonary oedema when she walks, also when she lies down the gravitational effect (of the upright posture) will be lost, that might be a reason why she's getting pulmonary oedema in the evening.'

If there was evidence from the transcript of extracts that characterized an ordering, as well as extracts that characterized a structuring approach, the general approach was considered intermediate. Whether this represented a true categorization of the student's approach or whether it represented a failure of measurement (because the interviewer failed to gain explanation for comments) is uncertain from these data.

Adequacy of understanding. The entire transcript was also examined to determine whether the student was able to reach a satisfactory diagnosis that demonstrated understanding. If the clinical features were explained in terms of pathophysiological links, if causal chains with explanatory intermediate steps between clinical features and diagnosis could be recognized, and if both positive and negative links were included (ie items for and against the chosen diagnoses were discussed), then an outcome that illustrated *understanding* was deemed to have been demonstrated.

If the discussion was characterized by short causal (associative) links between symptoms and diagnoses, if the outcome was given only in descriptive terms or if the student was unable to make a diagnosis then the outcome was considered unsatisfactory, ie adequate understanding was not demonstrated. This outcome was classified as *description*.

Problem-solving strategies. In addition to these categorizations, it was possible to identify the type of strategy used to perform the exercise. The EXCLUSION strategy involved the selection of a clinical feature which was then explored. Diagnosis was selected by association ('This fits with this symptom . . . '). Commonly, there was a need to generate a checklist for the clinical features followed by a rule-out procedure. The rule-out procedure usually involved discarding a diagnosis because of the absence of other associated clinical features (false negative rates would usually be ignored). Finally, with one diagnosis remaining, the learner would often try to explain other symptoms and signs based on the 'left over' diagnosis, resulting in a force fitting operation.

The PATTERN MATCHING strategy could be regarded as a less medically sophisticated approach. It involved the selection of a diagnosis that was associated with one or more selected clinical features. The remainder of the information was ignored or simply believed to fit the selected diagnosis. The pattern matched; the diagnosis was accepted. No extensive list of other diagnoses was seriously entertained, and hence no rule-out technique was required. When asked for further diagnoses, learners were usually able to add on further lists of causes. Multiple single associations were often formed.

The DIAGNOSTIC INTEGRATION strategy appeared to parallel the well-known description of hypothesis generation and testing which some authorities have said is a hallmark of clinical problem-solving in both novices and experts (Elstein *et al.*, 1978). The learner moved from clinical features to diagnosis via a logical sequential, pathophysiological explanation. At times the student using this approach showed evidence of the use of induction and deduction and demonstrated competence in explaining major clinical features in parallel with other clinical features. The student moved from features to diagnosis and in the reverse direction. As a hypothesis was fomulated, it was based on pathophysiological mechanisms that explained the symptoms and signs.

It can be seen from Tables 1 and 2 that there is a relation between the use of structuring approaches, diagnostic integration strategies, and outcomes demonstrating understanding. Outcomes where understanding was not demonstrated are associated with exclusion/pattern matching strategies and ordering approaches. The majority of students (89% in Case 1; 93% in Case 2) used ordering approaches to tackle these problems.

Table 1. *Approaches, strategies and outcomes: Case 1*

Outcome	Approach and strategy					
	Structuring		Intermediate		Ordering	
	I	E/PM	I	E/PM	I	E/PM
Understanding	5	0	0	1	0	5
Description	0	0	0	2	0	35
Total	5	0	0	3	0	40

Key to strategies: I=diagnostic integration;
E/PM=exclusion or pattern matching.

Table 2. *Approaches, strategies and outcomes: Case 2*

Outcome	Approach and strategy					
	Structuring		Intermediate		Ordering	
	I	E/PM	I	E/PM	I	E/PM
Understanding	2	0	2	0	0	1
Description	0	0	0	1	0	42
Total	2	0	2	1	0	43

Key to strategies: I=diagnostic integration;
E/PM=exclusion or pattern matching.

On six occasions students used approaches that contained elements of both ordering and structuring. On three of these a satisfactory outcome was achieved (the students demonstrated understanding) and two of these were associated with an integration strategy. The ordering approach was never associated with an integration strategy, but on six occasions (five in Case 1) it was associated with a satisfactory outcome. Whether the five instances of an ordering approach which resulted in a satisfactory outcome merely reflect familiarity with the syndromes of cardiac failure and airways obstruction cannot be discovered from analysis of the transcripts.

While the majority of students were consistent from case to case, some students selected a different approach for each case. The manner in which the knowledge was accessed for one case showed predominantly an ordering approach, while the other showed attempts to demonstrate that links had been made between knowledge components and the structure retained. These differences in handling the two cases may have been influenced by what the students perceived was required of them by their teachers, or may have been related to the complexity of the task. Either way, a common feature of the ordering approach was to select one item (usually the first symptom presented) and discuss it in detail while ignoring other data.

Use of basic sciences. It was encouraging to note that approximately half the students identified knowledge of physiology and pathology as being useful in approaching the first case. However, it was disappointing to observe that they considered physiology less relevant in the second case. We could surmise that the students did not mention anatomy to a greater degree in the first case because it seemed self-evident to some that the heart or lungs had to be involved. However, we anticipated that there was a need for a broader anatomical approach in the second case. Also of interest was the observation that although many students perceived that physiology was important, there was evidence in only two-thirds of these transcripts to show that they used physiological principles to solve these problems. Despite very limited clinical experience, many students consi-dered bedside tutorials and case presentations relevant to solving these problems. However, they rarely used knowledge about the clinical special-ity involved in the case to attack the problems.

Analysis of the transcripts indicated that most students perceived the task as an exercise in which they had to solve the problem by transforming the clinical information into a known diagnosis. They commonly gener-ated a long list of potential causes without any order of diagnostic preference, because they believed that was what was required ('That was what I have been taught to do in the first three years of the course' as one put it; cf Chapter 9). Many explained that the approach used was chosen because that was what they had been taught either by their teachers or by other students. One student illustrated a failure to differentiate data collection from clinical reasoning in this way:

I sit down and listen to the patient giving me the entire history, then I tend, if something is obvious, to focus on it. If not, I take a sieve and sift through (all) the items presented.

He did not indicate whether the final decision was made on the residue or the effluent. Another student highlighted an odd perception of what the task required:

If (after getting the case history) nothing springs to mind, I resort to the full blown scientific method of listing absolutely every possible cause of that symptom.

Some students realized that they had difficulties in incorporating what they perceived was the teaching approach of their tutors into their own problem-solving methods:

My tutors often start with diseases or clinical syndromes and try to fit the symptoms into that. I think it is better (for me) to start with the information you have from the patient and try to work out what is causing it.

Studies of advanced students

Currently we are performing a study that examines the problem-solving skills of final-year medical students. The cases discussed are presented on a series of typed cards, each containing one or more items of information that characterize the patient. The items relate to the patient's history, physical examination and laboratory findings. The students are asked to think aloud while being presented with the cards in sequence, and to provide a differential diagnosis that is narrowed down to a final (or working) diagnosis at the end.

Preliminary evidence from analysis of the transcripts indicates that these students' approaches are similar to those shown by fourth-year students, in that they can be categorized as ordering or structuring. However, in addition these students demonstrate that they have formed the perception that certain specialists do things differently. In discussing neurological problems, the students showed they are aware that neurologists used a structuring approach. However, this is not apparent in their handling of the cardiological or renal cases.

In these studies, where the students needed to gather data sequentially, a common problem displayed was that of formulating one specific hypothesis very early in the interview based on only small pieces of information (focusing on specifics). Some students maintained this stance by seeking data in the history and physical examination which would support the specific hypothesis. They often did not request data that may be crucial to eliminating their proposed hypothesis or, if given such information, ignored it. A few, when they stumbled across conflicting data, had the versatility to retrace their steps and broaden their hypothesis either by generating multiple specific hypotheses or preferably by using an intermediate step (eg anaemia, cardiac failure, malignancy) to explain the initial data. This allowed them to explore the intermediate step in some depth.

Observations from daily clinical activities

During the performance of these formal studies, I had many opportunities to observe students' problem-solving at bedside teaching sessions and case presentations. The incidents described here were enlightening, and illustrate another aspect of learning from one's students.

Interpreting clinical information out of context. A student at a case presentation delivered information about a 67-year-old patient with progressive breathlessness. He was found to have clubbed fingers and evidence of a pleural effusion. As a diagnosis was not offered, the student was asked for his opinion of the clubbed fingers (a key item of information that in the clinical context should have suggested a diagnosis of lung cancer). He suggested Wilson's disease (a rare and inherited copper metabolism disorder). Perplexed, I asked him to explain. He stated that as he was aware that finger clubbing was associated with cirrhosis of the liver (he had recently seen such a patient) and since the patient presented did not consume alcohol, he assumed that the cirrhosis must be due to a rarer form of liver disorder such as Wilson's disease. I decided to take the student back and to ask him to consider the finger clubbing in the context of the pulmonary symptoms and signs. This enabled him to confront the problem in a wider context and a more reasonable diagnosis emerged.

Ignoring clinical information that doesn't fit. Another student, during a final-year examination, presented information concerning a 59-year-old patient with progressive breathlessness, prominent crepitations (crackles) at the lung bases, a heart murmur at the lower end of the breastbone and evidence of heart failure involving the right side of the heart. The student suggested that the patient's heart failure was related to a leaking valve on the right side of the heart. When asked why that cause was selected, she indicated that all the information supported a right side of the heart cause for the disorder. It was only in discussion with her peers later that the possibility of a left-sided heart lesion plus right-sided cardiac failure secondary to left-sided failure was entertained (a sequence that is found commonly in clinical practice with disorders such as severe coronary artery disease). This student had focused on *some* of the physical signs and ignored those (the pulmonary crepitations) that were incompatible with the selected diagnosis.

Failing to appreciate the significance of the normal and ignoring clues. Occasionally a problem arises when the student focuses on specific data and fails to appreciate that the absence of symptoms may negate her diagnosis. When presenting to a doctor, a patient will emphasize those aspects of his history that concern him most. While these symptoms need to be explored they may be relatively non specific and thus unhelpful as diagnostic clues (eg many infectious illnesses begin with lethargy, sweating, nausea and, at times, vomiting). Using a focused sequential approach a student is able to generate a very long list of potential causes for such a presentation. The list may range from measles to meningitis or from cholera to cancer.

On many occasions I have listened through such student discussions. On one such occasion the student, impressed by the severity of the vomiting, finally selected a bowel obstruction as his most likely diagnosis. He ignored the fact that the patient's bowel actions had not altered (a situation incompatible with a complete obstruction and unlikely with an incomplete obstruction). A tatoo on the patient's arm led to questioning about hygiene, alcohol and intravenous drug use. Further examination and testing supported a diagnosis of hepatitis. In this case the student had focused on the first group of symptoms offered – the nausea and vomiting. He became overwhelmed by the huge number of possibilities and selected one which would explain the vigour of the vomiting but which ignored other clues – eg the bowel actions, which negated his diagnosis – and the tatoo recently performed with a non-sterile technique. The latter clue, in the context of these symptoms, suggested hepatitis.

Failing to elicit key information, or missing the clues. Sometimes the information is available but is ignored in the problem formulation because its relevance to the presenting problem is not appreciated. The following two case presentations illustrate this difficulty. I was presented the case of a young man aged 18 who was brought to casualty acutely breathless and distressed. He had sustained an injury to his leg and was wearing a plaster cast for the treatment of his fracture. The student presenting the case history postulated a series of rather nasty complications (eg pulmonary embolism – a blood clot from the legs lodging in the lungs). These possibilities carried serious implications for life and would have required extensive testing to confirm or exclude. It was only when I asked what he had been given to control the pain at the time of the injury or subsequent to the placement of the plaster that the vital clue emerged. The student told me that the young man, who had never been ill before, had taken aspirin to relieve the discomfort due to the plaster cast. He was now suffering the effect of an allergic reaction. The drug had induced asthma. The diagnosis was readily confirmed at the bedside.

It is often in difficult, ill-defined cases that apparently unrelated items of information may be vitally linked. These may be ignored by both patient (who did not think to mention them) and interviewer (who did not think them relevant). The next case illustrates this.

A student presented the history of a 56-year-old male who was suffering from episodic abdominal pain associated with diarrhoea and weight loss. The patient travelled extensively in Asia and was sure that he had 'picked up a bug during my travels' and the laboratory was having trouble finding it. Impressed by the weight loss, the student considered that the patient had a gastrointestinal tract cancer to explain his symptoms – a reasonable working hypothesis given the presenting symptoms. The patient had not volunteered but the student had discovered on 'routine questioning' that the patient's tennis game had been restricted recently by a crampy pain in one leg which prevented him from running. Clinical examination of the patient revealed evidence of narrowing of the blood vessels supplying the legs. This was related to his heavy cigarette consumption over many years. Subsequently, investigations revealed poor blood supply to the bowels. An operation and a graft procedure restored the blood supply and cured the patient's symptoms. By asking the student to consider this 'missed' clue – the leg pain – and to relate it to the patient's other problems (thus maintaining the structure of the problem) a more satisfactory understanding of the patient's disorder was achieved.

Implications for teaching

The experience gained during these various studies suggests that a knowledge of the characteristically different ways in which students may approach the task of clinical problem-solving offers a valuable viewpoint from which to help students who are having difficulties with the diagnostic process. Students who used an ordering approach often built their data base on a patient by asking routine questions without relating one item to another. While they may have had 'all the facts', they often failed to obtain the chronological sequence of events which was crucial to an understanding of the pathology of the disease causing the clinical problem.

It appears that by focusing on one item (usually the first presented), these students tended to ignore relevant items. They commonly failed to rank each item of information in its order of importance. This frequently resulted in the need to generate a large list of possible causal associations (often because the item chosen was non-specific). To bring the list to a manageable size, the students had to fit the item into a pattern or attempt to exclude some of the possible causes. The former approach frequently resulted in a need to ignore other items (often highly relevant to solving the problem) so that the pattern could be matched. The latter approach was frequently commenced by attempting to exclude (rule out) causes from the top of the student's list. As a result, the most likely cause was often removed first. Many students did not appreciate that this approach requires a thorough understanding of the reliability of certain features in supporting or refuting a diagnosis – a skill that is usually acquired following many years of clinical experience.

Teaching strategies

The author, while listening to a clinical presentation, makes notes of the key items in the history and physical examination and the order in which they are presented. Attempts are made to categorize the approach used by the student and to identify the strategy being employed. If a problem is encountered, efforts are made through discussion with the student to identify places in the presentation where the student 'took the wrong path' and the nature of the misconception that led to that selection.

Having analysed the situation, I attempt to seek a specific solution to the student's problem by discussing the *process* of clinical problem-solving in the context of the particular case presented, rather than by discussing the correctness or otherwise of the *product* (ie the diagnosis used).

The following strategies have been found to assist students in taking a broader, more 'structured' approach to diagnostic problem-solving:

(1) As part of making the process more explicit, students are asked to synthesize the information given and then to rank items in order of relevance.
(2) Students are asked to attempt to group the clinical features into defined problem areas and if possible to narrow the problem down to an interme-

diate step or a series of steps (often a recognizable named grouping called a syndrome).

(3) Students are required to attempt to explain the clinical features in terms of basic pathophysiological mechanisms, which can often more easily be explained by a single disease.

The second two steps enable the student to maintain the structure of the problem and to use as much data as possible rather than focusing on a single item at a time. When students employ a series of rule out logical steps, which result in exclusion of a reasonable diagnosis, I take them back to the last link in the causal chain prior to the conceptual error and ask them to consider alternatives that would better explain all the data available. This can often be done by asking the student whether the outcome of the selected path will explain all the relevant data.

Conclusions and summary

My observations of students during teaching sessions indicated that many students, despite possessing large quantities of information, were unable to solve clinical problems confronting them in their day-to-day work. I have described how a simplified phenomenographic method was employed to explore beginning clinical students' attempts at problem-solving. As a result, two qualitatively different categories of approach were identified. Each was associated with a series of strategies that illustrated the student's perceptions of the problem. The ordering approach appears to reflect a misconception on the student's part of the meaning and process of diagnostic problem-solving, rather than a lack of problem-solving skill or scientific knowledge *per se*. This view was supported by my informal interactions with students during teaching sessions. The content and the process of clinical problem-solving do seem to be best understood as parts of the same whole.

Subsequently, a teaching strategy was formulated, based on an understanding of the key differences in students' approaches. This strategy attempts to shift students from an inefficient and ineffective approach to a more sophisticated and effective one by exploring the process of clinical problem-solving, using the students' own efforts during their coursework. The idea is that students can be helped to understand their personal process of thought in diagnostic problem-solving so that the knowledge they possess can become progressively more useful to them (Gale and Marsden, 1987, pp 96-7). The strategy is still being developed and it has not yet been formally evaluated, but the initial indications are encouraging.

References

Barrows, H S and Bennett, K (1972). The diagnostic (problem solving) skill of the neurologist. *Archives of Neurology*, **26**, 273-7.

Cutler, P (1979). *Problem Solving in Clinical Medicine: From Data to Diagnosis*. Baltimore: Williams and Wilkins.

Elstein, A S, Schuman, L S and Spratke, S A (1978). *Medical Problem Solving; Analysis of Clinical Reasoning*. Cambridge, Massachusetts: Harvard University Press.

Gale, J and Marsden, P (1982). Clinical problem solving: The beginning of the process. *Medical Education*, **16**, 22-6.

Grant, J and Marsden, P (1987). The structure of memorized knowledge in students and clinicians: An explanation for diagnostic expertise. *Medical Education*, **21**, 92-8.

Laurillard, D (1984). Learning from problem solving. In: F Marton *et al.* (eds), *The Experience of Learning*. Edinburgh: Scottish Academic Press.

McGuire, C H (1985). Medical problem solving: A critique of the literature. *Journal of Medical Education*, **60**, 587-95.

Ramsden, P, Whelan, G and Cooper, D (in press). Some phenomena of medical students' diagnostic problem solving. *Medical Education*.

Svensson, L (1984). Skill in learning. In: F Marton *et al.* (eds), *The Experience of Learning*. Edinburgh: Scottish Academic Press.

Chapter 11
Computers and the Emancipation of Students: Giving Control to the Learner

Diana Laurillard
The Open University, UK

Introduction

Computers have been tested for their feasibility as learning aids for approximately two decades now. From the early beginnings the idea has always been that because computers can both store information and provide feedback on input, they must have the potential to act like teachers. In theory they should provide an excellent learning environment for students, being individualized and self-paced, and being programmed to provide immediate access to large quantities of data, to ask questions, to evaluate student performance, to provide guidance, etc. That is why there is still considerable interest in their use, even though computer-assisted learning (CAL) has never become a principal teaching method at any level of education.

Unfortunately, the practice of CAL has rarely met the potential. Several authors agree that one of the main reasons for this is the lack of high-quality educational software (see, for example, Hawkridge, 1983; Self, 1985; Maddison, 1983) and this applies to higher education as much as to the school level. It is not possible to advocate the use of CAL by pointing to its many acknowledged successes. We are still appealing to its potential.

The features offered by computers have been harnessed in a variety of ways to create modes of use corresponding to tutorials, experiments, drills, tests, demonstrations and tools (for a general review, see O'Shea and Self, 1983). In each case the student activity stimulated by the computer is meant to be educationally beneficial. The difficulty for the designer is in knowing how to stimulate the right kind of activities, and what those might be for a given subject area. Pedagogical design principles for CAL are not yet properly articulated. If they were, it would be a lot easier to argue that CAL could very quickly be seen to improve learning and could take its place as a mainstream teaching method. As it is, we have to build on what successes there are, to understand how they work and why they help students to learn, and so generate an articulated knowledge base from which future CAL can develop into a major teaching tool.

Models of teaching and learning

Any attempt to clarify the pedagogical principles associated with the design of educational media has to begin with some consideration of an underlying educational model. In this chapter I consider how two models for education, which I will label for convenience the 'didactic' model and the 'communication' model, can be used to analyse the pedagogical principles inherent in the principal design formats of existing CAL.

The main difference between the two models is in the kind of knowledge with which they are concerned. Within the didactic model, subject matter knowledge is what I have termed 'preceptual knowledge' – to distinguish it from the perceptual knowledge we acquire through perception, and from the conceptual knowledge we acquire through social interaction and experience (Laurillard, 1987). 'Preceptual knowledge' is knowledge of precepts, of givens, of what is 'definitely known' in a subject. The dictionary definition refers to 'preceptive' as 'mandatory, didactic, instructive'. Thus, students are not learning directly about the world, as they are in learning about perceptual and conceptual knowledge. In acquiring preceptual knowledge, they are learning about descriptions of the world. They are not learning about what happens when they throw a ball in the air; they are learning about Newtonian mechanics, which describes what happens. Descriptions of the world have been constructed for the student. It follows that the teacher's aim must be to transmit this constructed knowledge to the student. The teacher has control over what is taught, and how.

By contrast, within the communication model, knowledge is not a given body of facts and theories, but a 'negotiable commodity between teacher and pupil' (Esland, 1971). It is not regarded as something static and unchanging. There is no such object as a 'precept'. Thus, knowledge is not something that can be given by one person to another. Students construct their own descriptions of the world, the teacher's aim is to facilitate the students' development of their own perspectives on the subject. A corollary of this is that students take more responsibility for what they learn and how they then learn it. They are given control over what the content can be, as well as over their access to and experience of it.

Education as communication is an important and valuable model but, ironically, in the 'age of communication', it is not an appropriate description of what usually happens. As distance learning methods are more widely used, and as, even on the traditional campus, there are more educational media in evidence, so the direct face-to-face communication between teacher and student decreases. The value of the 'communication model' is that it takes more account of the student's view of the world, and allows an interaction between the two participants in which it is acknowledged that the student may not be the only one who learns. When teachers play only an indirect and absent role in the teaching process, as they do with educational media, they necessarily relinquish the opportunity for the kind of negotiation that face-to-face communication provides. Does this mean that educational media such as CAL necessarily operate within the didactic model?

As one way of tackling this question, I consider the two models of education in terms of three aspects of control, ie the extent to which students have control over (1) learning strategy; (2) the manipulation of learning content; and (3) the description of content. Learning strategy refers to whether students can make decisions about the sequencing of content and learning activities. Manipulation of content refers to the way students experience the domain being learned, ie whether or not this is by direct manipulation of it. Description of content refers to whether students construct their own perspectives of the subject. In a pure didactic model the teacher will control them all; in a pure communication model, students have full control. The following three sections discuss the application of these aspects of control to various forms of CAL.

Student control of learning strategy

There are two aspects of conventional CAL tutorial program design where it is easy to give control over learning strategy to the student: the sequence of presentation of content, and the sequence of learning activities.

Control over the sequence of content means providing facilities such as:

(1) index of content;
(2) content map;
(3) escape at any time to index or map;
(4) skip forward or back a chosen amount;
(5) retrace chosen route through the material.

These are conceptually straightforward facilities for a programmer to provide, although they require careful planning and some storage space. Unfortunately they are still rare, as many designers prefer to dictate the optimal route through the material, and allow no deviation from it, as though students were incapable of deciding which section of the content they needed to study at a particular time. It is worth remembering that the 'primitive' technology of a book provides all the above facilities, and we are still a long way from making CAL as easy to study from as a book.

Nonetheless, students' ability to cope with this degree of freedom has been questioned, and some studies give credence to this (eg Fry, 1972), suggesting that it leads to inefficient learning. Others (eg Hartley, 1981) show that under the right conditions, learner control is more effective than program control. This issue was further investigated in a more recent study of students learning from an interactive video cassette program.

They were given complete freedom to decide how to work through the nine sections of material. Of the above facilities, only (1), (3), and (4) were provided. Even so, the freedom this gave meant that students were able to exhibit a wide range of routes through the same material. Some began by looking at what they already knew, others by looking at the most unfamiliar topics. Some worked through systematically, others left an exercise to look at another section, and then returned to the first exercise. It was clear that the imposition of a program designers 'optimal' route would have seriously constrained the students' own optimal routes (Laurillard, 1984).

The second aspect of control of strategy concerns learning acitivities, eg control over when and whether to:

(1) see examples;
(2) do exercises;
(3) receive information;
(4) consult glossary;
(5) ask for explanation;
(6) take test.

Again, this kind of control is conceptually easy for a program designer to provide. It requires only standard programming techniques, with careful organization of the program structure. In the study referred to above, student control over (2), (3), and (6) was also provided, with the result that, again, a wide range of strategies was exhibited. Some students began with the test, then studied those exercises in which they had performed badly. Others began with relevant information on a topic, then practised the exercises, and only later took the test.

There is no well-established reason to suppose that a program designer, whether teacher, researcher, or programmer, knows better than the student how he or she should learn. Therefore, when we are designing materials for a medium that is capable of providing an unusual degree of individualization via student control, it seems perverse not to take advantage of it and allow students to control both the sequence of content and their learning activities. Moreover, this is an improvement that is easily incorporated even into conventional CAL tutorial designs. It requires none of the sophisticated techniques of intelligent CAL tutorials and it makes all forms of CAL much less forcefully didactic than they normally are.

Control of content manipulation

Student control of learning strategy is relatively easy to implement, and requires only intention and commitment on the part of the program designers. But this is not the most critical aspect of control. More important, and more difficult to implement, is student control over the manipulation of the subject matter.

What are we trying to get the computer to encourage the student to do when we design a teaching program? We need some model of the optimal learning situation to emulate. The one-to-one tutorial is not appropriate for a medium where the teacher is necessarily absent. The focus is not going to be student-teacher, but student-subject. A paradigmatic learning situation that could act as a model for this is Popperian scientific method (Popper, 1963). As the scientist learns about the real world, so the student learns about the world modelled by the computer, whether it be the world of science, the world of economics, the world of language, or whatever. To what extent real students are capable of acting like the ideal scientists we want to emulate is an arresting question, but let us remain in the realm of the ideal for a while.

Progress in scientific knowledge occurs, if we assume a Popperian account, when a scientist erects a hypothesis, tests it, and obtains a confirmation or disconfirmation. Each stage involves intricate reasoning about the domain and the relationships between its parts: the hypothesis must be meaningful and testable; the experiment must test the hypothesis and contain no irrelevant artefactual effects; the data must be interpreted in terms of the hypothesis; and so on. The scientist needs the real world in which to set up the experiment, and nature does the work of confirming or disconfirming the hypotheses. By analogy, the student can develop personal knowledge by erecting hypotheses that are testable in the simulated world of the computer program, with the computer model doing the work of confirming or disconfirming the student's hypotheses.

A computer program that supported an environment of this type would allow the student to manipulate the objects in the domain, and obtain feedback about the behaviour of the system in terms of the results of his or her manipulations.

Given these considerations, it follows that some of the pedagogically desirable features a CAL program should have are the following:

(1) The student should have direct access to the object domain – the object domain is an algorithmic description of how the domain behaves, such as a mathematical model of a physical system.
(2) The program should have operational knowledge of the domain – ie it should be able to carry out any manipulations the student requests.
(3) The program should be able to give intrinsic feedback – intrinsic feedback refers to results of the student's operations in terms of the system's behaviour, ie the program can operationalize the match to the present goal.
(4) The program should make the goals of the exercise explicit – these goals may be defined either by the student or by the program.

If the above define a desirable learning environment, how far do the standard forms of CAL program live up to them? Consider the following extract from a conventional tutorial on NMR spectra. Students input data from a nuclear magnetic resonance spectrum, given in the form of position of the mean peak, the multiplicity and the number of protons, for each signal. The tutorial dialogue then assists them with the interpretation of these data (student input is italicized in all the examples in this section):

The data you have typed in are as follows:

Identity	Mean peak position	Multiplicity	Relative number of protons
1	14.1	1	2
2	1.23	1	6
3	2.63	1	2

What group (or type) of protons is responsible for the signal at 14.1 delta?

2 COOH

Correct. COOH would explain the low field proton(s).

This leaves: 4*C 8*H to be accounted for.

What group (or type) of protons is responsible for the signal at 1.23 delta?

CH3

You are on the right lines. However, this arrangement would not account for 6 protons.

Please reconsider your answer and try again.

(Morris and Archer, 1977)

If we interpret the four features listed above in terms of this tutorial, we find that:

(1) Students have no direct access to the object domain – they cannot choose to carry out operations on the domain, such as building a molecule. They may only answer the questions posed.

(2) Knowledge of the domain is encoded explicitly in program statements – the explanatory statements are a series of PRINT statements with variables (or expressions) evaluated by referring to DATA statements for the particular problem, ie they put values into a template, they are not logically or semantically interconnected as they would be in a model of the domain.

(3) Feedback is extrinsic – ie it is an evaluative comment on the match between the student's input and the goal, as in 'Correct', and 'You are on the right lines'. It may appear to be intrinsic, as in 'would not account for 6 protons', but this statement relies on the programmer having predicted this mistake, and having explicitly programmed this form of response, with the '6' being evaluated from the data on that problem. Feedback that is apparently intrinsic would probably be sufficient from the student's point of view, except that it is always limited to the expected inputs; it cannot be available for the unexpected inputs the student might make.

(4)   There are no explicit goals – the student has no choice but to follow the route chosen by the program, and the program goals remain implicit in the dialogue, namely to get the student to give correct answers to its questions.

Teaching programs of this type can be very effective when the probable student errors are well understood, and when the teaching strategy is known to be successful for what it is attempting to achieve – in this case a practised familiarity with the solution procedure for NMR spectra. There is no sense in which the student has control over the manipulation of the content, however.

Compare the format of the *conventional* tutorial with an *'intelligent'* tutorial on the same topic, where the student is attempting to identify the structure of a linear molecule using data from NMR spectra. The student builds the molecule one group at a time, trying to select groups that are consistent with both the signal in the spectrum and the known molecular formula:

Join CH_2 corresponding to peak (2,2)

Correct

Help

So far you have identified $CH_3CH_2CH_2CH_2$.

Also we know that the peak for the last group is (2,2). The previous group has 2 interacting protons: therefore the next group must have 0 interacting protons: choose appropriate groups from those remaining.

Join O corresponding to peak (0,0)

No

Explain

We will now attempt to build such a molecule.

No peaks left in spectra. Spectrum of molecule is ((3,2)(2,5)(2,4)(2,2)(0,0)(2,3)(3,2)).

Molecule built was $CH_3CH_2CH_2CH_2OCH_2CH_3$.

Spectra still to be explained is nil.
Remaining molecular formula C.
Search was unsuccessful.

Join CO corresponding to peak (0,0).

Correct.

(O'Shea and Self, 1983)

In this case the interpretation of the four features is as follows:

(1) The student has access to the object domain – via instructions to the program, as in 'Join O corresponding to peak (0,0)', and through this operates directly on the object domain.
(2) The program has both operational and descriptive knowledge of the domain – it can carry out operations such as attempting to build a molecule, and can describe what it does in doing so.
(3) Feedback is both intrinsic and extrinsic – as in 'Search was unsuccessful' and 'Correct'.
(4) The program can support both program goals and student goals – this style of 'mixed-initiative' dialogue allows the program to state explicit goals such as 'Choose appropriate groups', and also allows the student to interrupt with a request of his or her own, such as 'Explain'.

Thus the 'intelligent' tutorial conforms to all the pedagogical conditions defined for it, and allows the student total control over the manipulation of the content.

Now consider the format of a simulation program. A simulation program contains the following elements:

(1) a model of the domain;
(2) options to select program-defined goals;
(3) options to select operations on the domain;
(4) results of these operations displayed in relation to the goal.

Figures 1 to 3 illustrate a simple version of this type of program. The objective is for the student to understand the concept of the period of a waveform. As this example shows, the simulation mode does not apply only to large-scale systems or experiments, but can also be used for concept acquisition in any domain that can be represented by an algorithm describing the output behaviour that corresponds to a given input. In this case, the program provides a goal for the student, who uses his or her conception of 'period' to generate a hypothesis about how to attain that goal. He or she then tests it out, and the feedback the program gives shows the result of that input and its relation to the goal, thus giving the student information about the behaviour of the model and suggesting how he or she might modify his or her hypothesis. By the end of the series of interactions, it should be possible for the student to have established the correct relationships, and acquired the intended conception. To show how this might happen, a continuation of the program is sketched in Figure 4, where, for each frame, I have suggested the kind of reasoning process such a program could engender in a student who was unfamiliar with the concept of 'period'.

If we interpret the pedagogical features defined above for this type of program in comparison with the intelligent tutorial, we find that:

EXPERIMENT: To find the period of a waveform

You will be able to assign the time interval
shown for the waveform.

The computer will choose the frequncy of the
waveform.

The you can select the period of your waveform
and try to make it match the one shown.

| Menus | Test | Index | Browse | Continue |

Figure 1. *Simulation program introduction*

(1) The student does have access to the object domain, but only through
     program-defined commands, not through natural language descriptions of
     the operations to be carried out.
(2) The program's knowledge of the object domain is confined to operations on
     it, in the sense that is possesses an algorithmic description of its behaviour
     for given input, but has no alternative descriptions of its behaviour.
(3) The feedback it gives is intrinsic in the sense that it shows the results of the
     student's input in terms of the resultant behaviour of the system. Any
     extrinsic feedback it provides has to be explicitly programmed, as it is for
     the conventional tutorial.
(4) The program provides explicit program goals, in the form of options to
     change a variable, but cannot support student goals or a mixed-initiative
     dialogue – all student choices have to be handled via menus of pre-defined
     options.

The advantage of this kind of goal-oriented manipulation is that it gives
students direct access to and control over the critical relationships and
mechanisms in the domain. It allows students to come close to what it

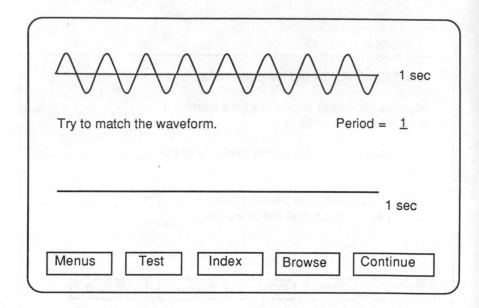

Figure 2. *Simulation program: student chooses period of 1 sec.*

means to 'act like a scientist' (and perhaps, thereby, to acquire a more accurate model of causal explanation in a subject area; see Chapters 4 and 6). The hypotheses that are posited by students in the course of the program are simple, each one is meaningful to them at the time, and each one is testable. Moreover, the feedback is meaningful. It is interpretable in terms of both their original hypotheses, and the goals they are aiming for. In each case, the feedback gives them information which helps them get closer to the goals, but without telling them how. It forces them to reason about the relationships involved. That is what makes intrinsic feedback preferable to the purely extrinsic form.

Whether the students actually carry out such a logical analysis of the results is an empirical question. The design of the simulation is based on Popperian scientific method, but Popper described the logic of scientific discovery, not the history of it. The fact that scientists do not, and even cannot, follow Popper's procedure has been persuasively argued, for example, by Feyerabend (Feyerabend, 1970), and we must assume that students are likely to exhibit all the irrational expediencies that real scientists are subject to. Simulations are a good model of the *optimal* learning situation, therefore, but this does not guarantee that students will always use this opportunity to its full advantage. The extent to which they

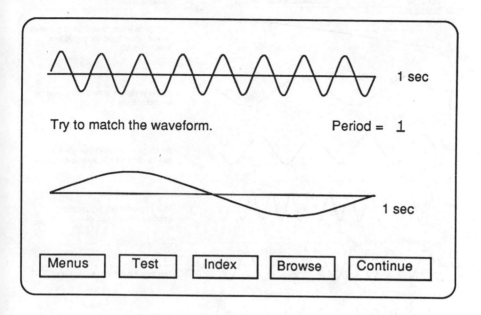

Figure 3. *Result of student's input is displayed*

do will depend, as Feyerabend would argue for scientists, on the context within which they are operating.

There are three ways in which the simulation is a pedagogical advance on the conventional tutorial form: (1) it gives the student direct access to the domain model, rather than mediating this through dialogue; and (2) because of this, the explanations are implicit in the behaviour of the model, giving the student *experience* of its behaviour, rather than being articulated through a verbal description, which only *tells about* the behaviour; (3) the student has complete control over the solution path.

The simulation mode is a compromise between the conventional and the intelligent tutorial systems. It is clearly a pedagogical improvement on the former; it is clearly not as helpful as the latter, principally because its only form of feedback is intrinsic, so that students have to determine purely from the behaviour of the system what they should do next, and they have no help in interpreting the meaning of its behaviour, although it is to be expected that students will often need such help. In terms of student control of operations on the domain, it is a good match for the intelligent tutorial. In terms of student demands for help, it cannot cope as well as the intelligent tutorial, because it possesses no descriptive knowledge of the domain.

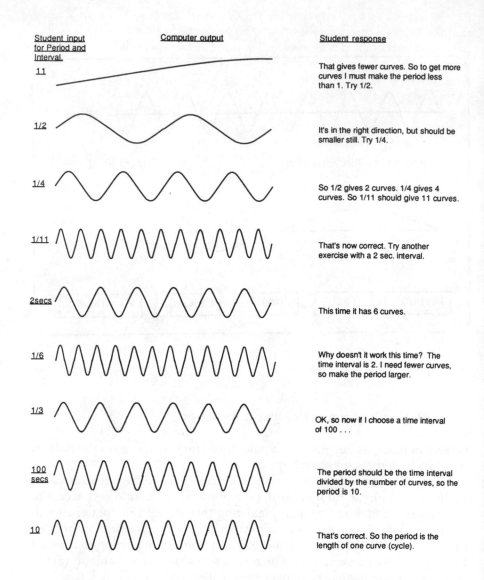

Student input for Period and Interval.

11 — That gives fewer curves. So to get more curves I must make the period less than 1. Try 1/2.

1/2 — It's in the right direction, but should be smaller still. Try 1/4.

1/4 — So 1/2 gives 2 curves. 1/4 gives 4 curves. So 1/11 should give 11 curves.

1/11 — That's now correct. Try another exercise with a 2 sec. interval.

2secs — This time it has 6 curves.

1/6 — Why doesn't it work this time? The time interval is 2. I need fewer curves, so make the period larger.

1/3 — OK, so now if I choose a time interval of 100 . . .

100 secs — The period should be the time interval divided by the number of curves, so the period is 10.

10 — That's correct. So the period is the length of one curve (cycle).

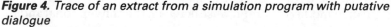

Figure 4. *Trace of an extract from a simulation program with putative dialogue*

As in both tutorial forms, it is still essential for the simulation designer to define the expected categories of error, as these are what determine the 'experiments' to be made available to the student. Not all experiments will decide between the model answer and the student's misconception in the way the example given above does. The experiment has to be (in Popper's phrase) the 'crucial experiment'. For program designers to be able to define which experiments should be included, they need to know both the model answer, and the predicted categories of errors, each one of which may require a different crucial experiment to help the student pinpoint the flaw in his or her own conception. For example, the designer only knows that the 'period' program will work if he or she knows that students might have that particular misconception, ie that the period is the length of the waveform shown. The crucial experiment is important because it occupies a unique position, arbitrating between the model answer and the misconception (between theory A and theory B). Its outcome should be capable of demonstrating that one is confirmed and the other disconfirmed. The importance to the students is that it not only shows that their conception was wrong, it also gives them a new fact to be explained, a cognitive motivation to change their way of thinking about the phenomenon. And because of the unique nature of the crucial experiment, the new fact to be explained will *require* the postulation of the correct conception. This is similar to the process di Sessa has called 'genetic task analysis', the process of 'finding or imagining the essential phenomena that may conspire to produce an understanding of the subject' (di Sessa, 1986).

This discussion does not apply easily to non-mathematical models. For domains such as electrical engineering, physics, economics, etc, the computer can use the various mathematical models available to simulate the experiments interactively, and this is an essential aspect of these programs. In domains such as sociology or history, which are more usually described by propositions, it is much more difficult for the computer to model the logical and semantic relations between the propositions, and to interpret the students' propositional inputs. As knowledge-based systems become more widespread, the techniques for storing and manipulating propositional information will become available to program designers in non-mathematical subjects. If it is possible for a computer to store a network of propositional statements, logically and semantically interconnected, then it will be possible for that network to act as a model for a subject domain. This means that it will be possible for a program to evaluate such a statement as 'labour power adds surplus value to the product'. If the model is a Marxist one, the statement will match one of the propositions, or will be logically deducible from them, whereas if it is a pluralist model, it will not match, and the student will be able to trace the logical links to the premises that his or her statement is in conflict with. Thus in subjects where knowledge is encoded semantically and not symbolically, with the advent of logic programming and natural language understanding, computers will eventually be able to cope with domains of this type more readily. Whether social scientists would be prepared to tolerate this kind of approach, and the constraints of a deterministic computer model, remains to be seen, but this kind of potential does, theoretically, exist.

Simulation programs cannot support student goals, and cannot provide advice, but they serve two other very important pedagogical features that conventional tutorials cannot: they can give students direct access to the behaviour of the object domain, and they can give intrinsic feedback on students' experiments within it. This is the kind of experience students need if they are to develop their own conceptual understanding of a domain, because it gives them direct contact with the environment they are trying to understand, be it the domain of numbers, or waveforms, or theories about societies. If they have already developed inappropriate conceptual constructs, then they need experiences of the behaviour of those domains that allow them to *see* that their conceptions are inappropriate, which is far more powerful than *telling* them that they are wrong. If we can provide students with this kind of control over their interaction with the subject matter, that will be a considerable advance beyond the tedious and unimaginative programs that abound in conventional CAL at the moment.

The intelligent tutorial program provides control over both strategy and manipulation of content, and is an improvement on both conventional tutorials and simulations because it can support student-defined goals and requests for help with much greater flexibility.

Control of domain description

With all these forms, we are still operating within the didactic model of teaching, however. The goal is still conceptual change in a particular direction, to assist the student to learn the 'givens' or 'precepts' of a subject. By virtue of the fact that the program is supplying a model of an environment, it is embodying the fixed and immutable givens of that domain. It is not supporting the pure communication model, where the teacher's role is to facilitate the students' development of their own perspectives on the subject, rather than to give them the received knowledge. But human teachers find this difficult enough; could we expect computers to do it?

Given the epistemological framework of the communication model, the computer's role has to be very different from its role within the didactic model. In the latter, as surrogate teacher, it has to be capable of either dialogue about the domain (tutorial mode), or operations on the domain (simulation mode), or both (intelligent tutorial), in order that the student learns the behaviour of that domain, as modelled. The definition of the teacher's role within the communication model means that, as surrogate teacher, the computer has to support the student's own description of the domain. The theoretical framework that best encompasses this idea is Conversation Theory (Pask, 1976), within which students can develop explicitly their own knowledge representation by acting as authors, and can compare and contrast it with that of the teacher's both through computer-mediated dialogue about their respective representations, and through models of them represented as simulations. Thus the teaching program embodies no pedagogic theory beyond that implicit in its structure as a 'conversation' between two individuals.

An intelligent tutorial program is similar to this except that it is usually less democratically organized, because the system embodies a teaching strategy whose job it is to direct students towards purposeful behaviour if the monitoring of their inputs suggests that they need help. Pask's 'CASTE' system (Pask, 1973) also takes a more didactic line of this sort, not allowing the students to attempt goals for which they have not already mastered the prerequisites. However, the basic design of the underlying theoretical framework of Conversation Theory gives equal status to teacher and student goals. The superimposed teaching strategy is optional.

The Conversation Theory framework gives a more democratic teaching program than most, because it can support total student control over the development of their knowledge domain, over consultation with the teacher, over their learning strategies, and over their manipulation of the knowledge in terms of testing its application in the object domain. But to support a *pure* communication model of the teaching process the students must have control over the object domain against which their representations are tested, which, this being a computer program, is itself a theoretical construct, a set of precepts about the world, rather than the real world itself. Insofar as the program's object domain is arbitrating between two knowledge representations, the teacher's and the student's, it will always have an in-built preference for its author's, whoever that is.

It is therefore never possible to achieve equal status between teacher and student. So it is never possible for a computer teaching program, no matter how democratic it is, to support the pure communication model of teaching. The face-to-face tutorial can, because here the world is the final arbiter. Within a computer teaching program the final arbiter always has to be someone's theoretical construct.

The only way a computer program can support the student's control of the description of the domain is by allowing the student to act as program author, but that gives the teacher lower status than the student in negotiating knowledge. This is the approach taken, in part, by some of those who advocate 'microworlds', computer simulations that students can construct for themselves in order to manipulate and explore the behaviour of that world (Papert, 1980, pp 120–34).

The idea of microworlds is a powerful and attractive idea because it is designed to bring all the heuristics of learning about the world, so successfully mastered by so many of us, to bear on the learning of the teacher's particular microworld, typically mastered by so few – the usual example is Newtonian physics. Papert's is a liberal approach, certainly within the communication model, which allows students to create Aristotelian microworlds (the child's personal beliefs about motion are 'in many ways closer to Aristotle's than to Newton's' (p 123)) on the grounds that 'by trying many different laws of motion, children will find that the Newtonian ones are indeed the most economical and elegant for moving objects around' (p 129). However, the Scholastics were not complete fools, and spent some time being perfectly able to describe the world in Aristotelian terms without having to invent Newton's conception of force. Why should students do any better? Perhaps they will have the advantage of being advised that a Newtonian microworld is available for them to try out

– but why should it be preferred? How will they discover that it is 'most economical and elegant'? They need the kind of evidence that convinces physicists that Newton's conception of force is preferable to the more intuitive Aristotelian idea that force is the cause of continued motion (see Crombie, 1959, pp 61–4). But the reasons are quite subtle, may well not be discovered by students, and are certainly never covered in modern physics textbooks, no doubt because of their philosophical complexity. The classic problems with the Aristotelian conception, discussed by Aristotle himself, concern instantaneous velocity, initial velocity and acceleration in freely falling bodies. It requires a crucial experiment (or in this case a 'thought experiment') to decide between the two: such as Aristotle's own admission that while velocity is proportional to force/mass, this formulation breaks down in the case of a man trying to move a ship (Hope, 1961, p 142). That is the kind of essential phenomenon that will produce understanding of the importance of the Newtonian idea of force, but students will have to be led to it – they will not 'discover' it. (White and Horwitz's chapter in this volume provides a highly successful example of the more didactic approach.)

What computers offer is *not* a specialized environment 'more flexible and precise in crafting experiences that lead to essential insights' (di Sessa, 1986, p 224). They have to be more didactic than this implies, and a lot less flexible. The pedagogic challenge has to be the same as it is for all didactic teaching – to discover empirically the forms of misconception, and to deduce the forms of crucial experiment that will motivate a change in conception to the preferred form. Computers offer an individualized teaching program (assuming that the misconceptions can be reliably diagnosed) and a learning activity that is genuinely active in the sense that the student can control the experiments on offer. But if we allow the student to design those experiments, as Papert and di Sessa seem to, they will probably never hit on the crucial experiments they need to enable them to choose the right form of conception. These have to be provided, and the students have to work through them in order to experience the necessity of changing their original conceptions. Thus the program becomes relatively didactic in character, and flexible only in the sense that students can have control over strategy and manipulation of the content within the experiments provided. If we allow the student to be the author, there is little hope that he or she will learn Newtonian physics. It is in the nature of the communication model that you cannot control what students will learn. What they do learn from Papert's microworld may be something very important, such as the idea that facts and theories are interdependent, or that they too can be physicists; and that is what makes the communication model pedagogically valuable. But if you wish them to learn some specific preceptual knowledge (as well, perhaps, as an understanding of scientific method) then the more didactic mode, using devices such as the crucial experiment, will be unavoidable. Some educationalists would argue (see Chapter 4) that an understanding of the process of scientific inquiry can also be acquired through more didactic models.

Both Pask and Papert have envisaged ways in which students may control the description of the domain they manipulate, but as the student becomes author, so the status of the teacher is necessarily dimished, and the essential communicative aspect of the communication model is lost. Where computers are used to facilitate communication between students and teachers, eg in a computer network, then perhaps they can be said to support a communication model. But CAL aspires to make the computer the teacher, not a mere communication tool.

Conclusions

To summarize: the pure didactic model of teaching and learning allows the student no control over learning strategy, nor content manipulation, nor description of the domain; these are the teacher's responsibility. The pure communication model gives more responsibility to the student and allows him or her to control all these aspects of the learning situation. The three principal forms of CAL discussed here are the conventional tutorial, the simulation and the intelligent tutorial. Of these, all are capable of allowing the student considerable control over his or her learning strategy; both the simulation and the intelligent tutorial can support student manipulation of the content domain; the intelligent tutorial is more flexible in its responses to the student than the other two.

I have argued that student control over learning strategy is relatively easy to provide. The simulation format is well understood in training applications, but as a teaching program for conceptual change it is not so straightforward. The development of this kind of program requires research into the common student misconceptions in the topic concerned, and the derivation of the crucial experiments necessary to help students decide between their conceptions and the received knowledge. The style is preceptual, the students are learning the 'givens', but the design of the teaching strategy will be more scientific, and is likely to be more effective, if it incorporates this analysis of the relation between what students know and what they need to know. The analysis requires no special techniques beyond those already practised by educational researchers of the phenomenographic school represented in several chapters of this book, namely the empirical derivation of categories of description of students' conceptions. The derivation of the crucial experiment requires the kind of logical analysis that every practising scientist has to learn.

The conceptual problems with this approach are surmountable, and are achievable now. There is no need to wait for AI techniques to bear fruit before CAL can be pedagogically respectable. The teaching philosophy implicit in this has still to be accepted, however, by many curriculum designers: that students can, and should, be enabled to 'act like scientists', but within a simulated world with explicit guidance, rather than in the real world.

The point of trying to emancipate students from the conventional program-controlled tutorial is that educational research is not in a position to define the kind of deterministic model of teaching that computers as purely didactic tutors require. Students are still likely to be better than teachers at directing their learning. Therefore we should be harnessing the power of the computer to provide a closer approximation to the communication model. That means giving students maximum control over learning strategy and manipulation of content. We cannot aspire to the pure communication model because of the limitations of the medium, but CAL can be significantly less didactic than it has been so far.

References

Crombie, A C (1959). *Augustine to Galileo 2*. Harmondsworth: Penguin.

di Sessa, A (1986). Artifical worlds and real experiences. *Instructional Science*, **14**, 207-27.

Esland, G M (1971). Teaching and learning as the organization of knowledge. In: M F D Young (ed), *Knowledge and Control*. London: Collier-Macmillan.

Feyerabend, P (1970). *Against Method*. Minnesota Studies in the Philosophy of Science, No. 4.

Fry, J P (1972). Interactive relationship between inquisitiveness and student control of instruction. *Journal of Educational Psychology*, **63**, 459-65

Hartley, J R (1981). Learner initiatives in computer assisted learning. In: J Howe (ed), *Microcomputers in Secondary Education*. London: Kogan Page.

Hawkridge, D (1983). *New Information Technology in Education*. London: Croom Helm.

Hope, R (1961). *Aristotle's Physics*. University of Nebraska Press.

Laurillard, D M (1984). Interactive video and the control of learning. *Educational Technology*, **23**, 7–15.

Laurillard, D M (1987). The different forms of learning in psychology and education. In: J Richardson, M Eysenck and D Warren Piper (eds), *Student Learning: Research in Education and Cognitive Psychology*. Milton Keynes: SRHE and Open University Press.

Maddison, J (1983). *Education in the Microelectronics Era*. Milton Keynes: Open University Press.

Morris, H and Archer, D (1977). The interpretation of NMR spectra. CALCHEM, Department of Physical Chemistry, University of Leeds.

O'Shea, T and Self, J (1983). *Learning and Teaching with Computers*. Sussex: Harvester Press.

Papert, S (1980). *Mindstorms: Children, Computers and Powerful Ideas*. Sussex: Harvester Press.

Pask, G (1973). CASTE: A system for exhibiting learning strategies and regulating uncertainties. *International Journal of Man-Machine Studies*, **5**, 17–52.

Pask, G (1976). Conversational techniques in the study and practice of education. *British Journal of Educational Psychology,* **46**, 12-25.

Popper, K R (1963). *Conjectures and Refutations.* London: Routledge and Kegan Paul.

Self, J (1985). *Microcomputers in Education.* Sussex: Harvester Press.

Chapter 12

Encouraging Reflection on Study Strategies: The Design of a Computer-based Adventure Game

Noel Entwistle, Phil Odor and Charles Anderson
University of Edinburgh, Scotland

Introduction

One of the main problems in attempting to help students to improve their study strategies is that there remains a gap between the abstract advice presented and the experience of everyday studying. Paradoxically, this gap remains, to some extent, even when that advice is derived from research findings that have developed concepts from the students' own experiences. Telling is still divorced from doing, and that separation interferes with the application of ideas about studying to the actuality.

In several subject areas, as Laurillard and White and Horwitz indicate in their chapters, the use of computer microworlds is being explored to enable students to learn from explorations of simulated situations. It seemed worth trying to develop a microworld to simulate some aspects of a student's experiences of higher education which might help students to transfer ideas on effective studying from the research arena to the real world. This chapter describes the design and the early development work of such a microworld. It is too soon to be able to provide any evidence of the effectiveness of this approach, although small-scale trials will be carried out in the near future to indicate students' reactions to the game.

The development of a simulation using a board game

The adventure game was based, in part, on a board game that had already been used with students. That board game emerged as a way of presenting a particular set of research findings on studying to students. The research study from which it originated was designed to identify factors associated with success and failure in higher education. Longitudinal studies were used to compare student characteristics, assessed before entry and during the first year, with subsequent academic performance (Entwistle and

Wilson, 1977). The analyses led to the identification of distinctive 'types' of student who appeared to have different forms of motivation. One group was competitive and self-confident. Another was independent-minded with wide-ranging academic interests, while a third group was anxious and lacking in self-confidence. The final main type was described, somewhat disparagingly, as 'idle and unmotivated'.

Although some of the findings seemed to have significance for students, it was recognized that it would be difficult to present them in ways that would cause students to reflect seriously on their existing study methods. Thus the idea of using a game format was explored. Progression through higher education was imagined as a form of obstacle race. Students set out on that race with different starting conditions or 'handicaps', depending on their ability and school attainment. They also had differing personalities and motivations that would lead them to react differently to the events or obstacles they met during their course. These ideas were incorporated into *The Academic Achievement Game* (Entwistle and Wilson, 1977), a board game similar to *Monopoly*. Progress round the board was determined partly by the throw of a die and partly by instructions related to the square on which they landed and on the 'type' to which they had been allocated.

The game was used with both secondary school pupils and entering students, with some success. It helped them to anticipate some of the situations they would find in higher education, and it stimulated discussion. But its effectiveness was reduced by the limited extent to which individual 'debriefing' was possible afterwards, and students thought that the game was controlled, to an unrealistic extent, by starting conditions and by chance (Wilson, 1978). Students wanted opportunities to interact with the situations and to vary their strategies as a result of their experiences, but that was impossible within the format of the board game.

Concepts and research evidence on student learning

The early research had identified some of the student characteristics associated with academic progress, but had not looked at these in relation to pertinent features of the academic context – in particular, methods of teaching and assessment. The responsibility for success or failure was exclusively placed on the student, as if the academic staff and the institutional resources and policies had no influence on learning outcomes. The relationships between student characteristics and academic outcome were decontextualized, in common with much of the educational research of that time.

The next step forward in research involved looking at the *processes* of learning in higher education and considering how these were affected by the institutional environment. A series of studies in Sweden, Britain and Australia (Marton, Hounsell and Entwistle, 1984; Entwistle and Ramsden, 1983; Biggs, 1987) provided the concepts, categories, and the principles from which the adventure game has since been developed.

One of the first investigations into the processes of academic learning was carried out by Marton (1976). He has pioneered the systematic description of students' experiences and perceptions of the content and context of academic learning. His first study investigated students' ways of reading an academic article. The concept emerging from his analyses was *approach to learning* with its two main categories of *deep* and *surface* (Marton and Säljö, 1984). The main defining feature of each of these categories was the intention shown by students as they read the article – either to seek personal understanding or minimally to meet the task requirements. The subsequent contrasting learning processes were seen to be a product of the initial perceptions of the task in relation to the student's own intentions.

These ideas were extended by Pask (1976) who was able to show that, even when students were *required* to demonstrate personal understanding, there were still two characteristically different *learning styles* involved. He distinguished between *holists*, who sought to personalize knowledge and to interrelate ideas extravagantly, and *serialists*, who preferred a narrow focus, concentrating cautiously on details and logical connections.

Other work (Taylor, 1983; Gibbs, Morgan and Taylor, 1984) focused on the purposes students have in entering higher education and distinguished between four main educational orientations – *vocational, academic, personal* and *social*. Students' feelings about how they were progressing through their studies depended on their own 'study contract' – what they themselves wanted to gain from their courses – not just on the satisfaction of the lecturers' requirements. This research showed very clearly how students viewed the experience of studying in a broad context that included their social and personal lives, and served as a warning against narrowly intellectual and institutionally based definitions of success and failure.

A five-year research programme at Lancaster (Entwistle and Ramsden, 1983) sought to extend the work of Marton and Pask by seeking confirmation of their conceptualizations and by investigating the factors affecting the adoption of these approaches and strategies. Interview and inventory data were used to demonstrate a clear distinction between deep and surface approaches across six contrasting academic disciplines. It was, however, found necessary to introduce a further category – the *strategic approach* – in which the main intention was to obtain the highest possible grades by being alert to cues from lecturers and also by being well organized.

Other analyses showed that learning styles were partly related to underlying personality characteristics, while approaches to learning were strongly associated with contrasting forms of motivation – *intrinsic* (deep), *fear of failure* (surface) and need for *achievement* (strategic). But these approaches were influenced by the students' perceptions of the ways in which they were taught and assessed.

In interviews, students were asked what influenced their approach to learning, and a questionnaire was developed to assess their perceptions of the department in which they spent most of their time studying (Ramsden, 1984). Combining results from both types of data, it emerged that a deep approach was consistently facilitated by *good teaching* and by being given a certain degree of *freedom in learning* (both in what to learn and how to learn it). A surface approach was found to be partly attributable to *inappropriate assessment procedures* that required only detailed factual responses, and to a *heavy workload*.

These components of the *learning context* were subsequently incorporated into a heuristic model designed to draw attention to the interactions between the participants – students and teachers – and the learning contexts within the academic departments. It was also intended to draw attention to the way in which students' individual perceptions of the learning environment affected their ways of studying. This heuristic model, shown in Figure 1, influenced the early thinking about the way in which this principled adventure game was developed.

Preliminary stages in developing the computer game

Principles underlying the design

The developments in research on student learning allowed the computer simulation to make use of concepts, deriving from students' experiences, which describe *processes* of studying. This provided greater precision in outlining the probable consequences of events. It was intended to offer students an interactive simulation of some typical situations in higher education which would allow them to vary their strategies and to consider the consequences of using them. The game was designed with two main audiences in mind, secondary school pupils about to enter university or college, and students already on courses.

The intention was to develop a 'principled adventure game'. In the previous game, students were allocated different starting conditions randomly. As an integral part of the computer simulation a more realistic model of the student was required which would describe the student's ways of studying in terms of the concepts outlined in the previous section. That model would determine, to some extent, how the student was led to 'perceive' situations, and so would influence choices and strategies. The consequences of events would be decided, as far as possible, from the research findings. It was decided, as a matter of principle, that the game should not be a 'black box'. The student would be able to interrogate the game to discover the rules that had determined the consequences of actions. Periodically, the student would also be able to seek advice on improving strategies within the game, which would be presented in ways designed to highlight connections with real-life studying.

In essence, the design of the game thus envisaged a data base of information about studying, derived from research studies, together with advice tailored to the decision strategies and inferred characteristics of the individual student. In other words, it would be a simple expert system providing a form of 'intelligent' tutoring. There are considerable difficul-

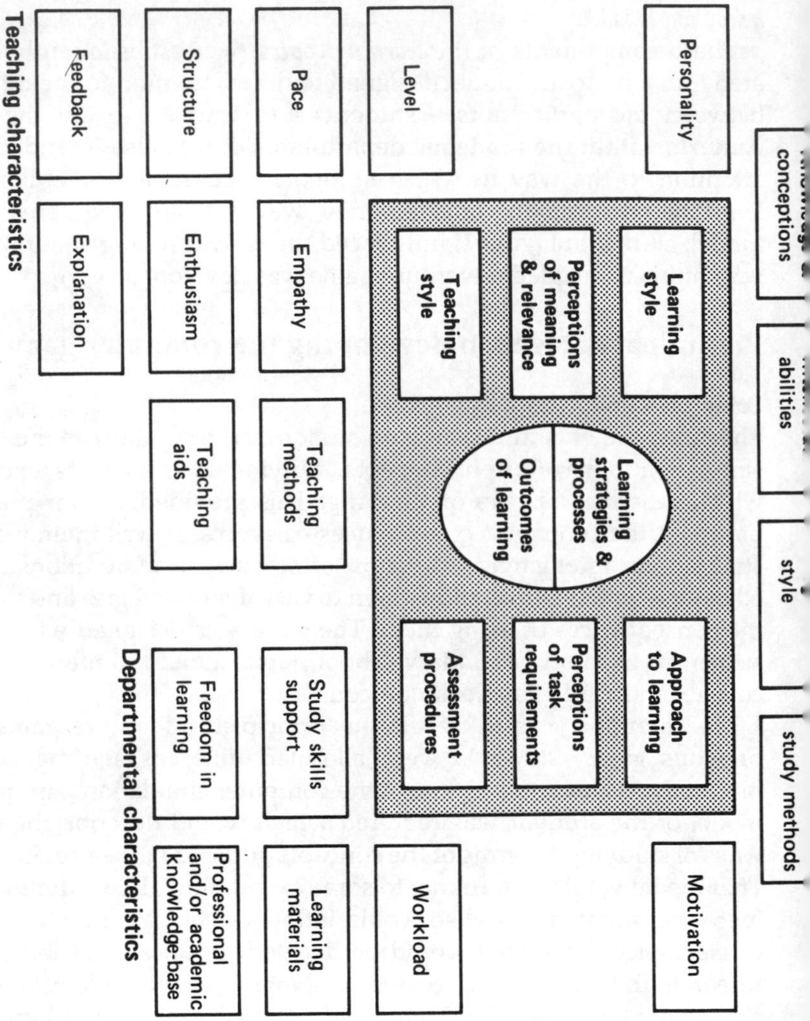

Figure 1. *An heurisitic model of the teaching learning process in higher education*

Teaching characteristics

Departmental characteristics

Personality

Level

Pace

Structure

Feedback

Explanation

Enthusiasm

Empathy

Learning style

Teaching style

Perceptions of meaning & relevance

Teaching methods

Teaching aids

Learning strategies & processes

Outcomes of learning

Approach to learning

Perceptions of task requirements

Assessment procedures

Freedom in learning

Study skills support

Learning materials

Professional and/or academic knowledge-base

Workload

Motivation

conceptions

abilities

style

study methods

ties in presenting a description of the game that is being developed, as a full appreciation of its operation could only be achieved by playing it. Here we describe first the architecture of the simulation – the various features which were incorporated into the design – and then provide two examples of what a student would see on the screen, to help to bring that description to life. Finally, the process of development will be outlined fairly briefly with the main emphasis on how the research findings were used to create realistic scenes.

The architecture of the computer simulation

To understand how the game is presented and played, it is necessary to introduce the 'architecture' of the system design first (see Figure 2). The central focus of the diagram is what has been called the *theatre*. This is where the simulated events are presented as displays on the computer screen which invite the student to make choices and so to develop a game strategy. A series of interlinked events and actions are built up into a coherent *scene*, as in any dramatic production. The student progresses through a succession of scenes chosen to represent typical academic and social situations met in higher education and developing in a natural sequence. Examples of the screen texts may be found in the next two sections. It may be helpful to preview them before reading any further.

Another major feature of the architecture is the *blackboard* that records the current state of the student model in terms of a profile of inventory scores, indicating levels on the concepts described earlier. These estimates are subsequently updated on the basis of interactions with the game events. Estimates of the current level of these variables for the student are held on the blackboard, together with information about the stage reached in the game and any additional messages intended to affect the future presentation of aspects of the game. The blackboard also records every keyboard interaction made by the student. After each interaction the blackboard is updated, and at the end of each event or scene the contents of that particular blackboard are recorded in order to produce a *history* formed from the succession of blackboard states.

As students interact with the scenes in the theatre, they choose from a set of control words that determine their movement through the scene. Some of these will be familiar from adventure games (eg 'look', 'ask', 'go to' or 'help'). Other control words will be specific to the game or to a particular scene. Two such control words, CHORUS and COMMENT, are available after any event.

The term CHORUS was chosen by analogy with the Chorus in a Greek play who comments on the developing plot. Our 'chorus' will provide a brief justification for the appearance of the existing screen display in terms of the rules, the theoretical background, the student's own estimated characteristics, or the previous actions in the game. Students will also be encouraged to type in their own COMMENT on the last event or scene, in relation either to the simulation or to real-life experiences.

At the end of each scene a MENTOR will be available. The control word

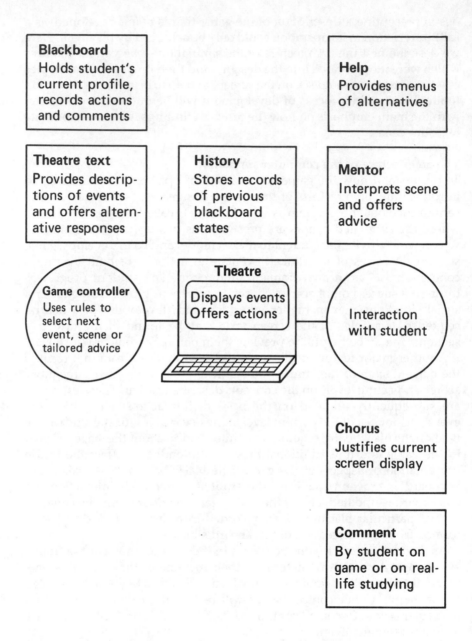

Figure 2. *The architecture of the computer simulation*

will first provide a rationale for the main events occurring in that scene and will then offer optional advice. Some of the advice will be couched in general terms, but there will also be individually tailored advice, based on the history of the student's interactions with previous events and on estimates of the student's own study characteristics held on the blackboard. MENTOR will also introduce students to the meaning of the main concepts from the research literature on student learning to allow subsequent advice to be couched in those terms.

The scenes, and the advice, are presented to the student through blocks of predefined text which are displayed on the screen as appropriate. The decision about which block of text to display is determined by rules associated with each component of the event. The rules are often written in terms of the variables that make up the student profile and in this way the game can introduce contrasting 'perceptions' of events. The rules will be interpreted and executed by a specially written program, described as a game controller, which will also make and amend entries on the blackboard and carry out pattern searches through the history of the student's previous interactions with the game.

Two illustrative scenes – events, rules, and advice

The only way to understand any simulation game fully, as we have said, is to play it. Here verbal descriptions have to be used to convey an impression of the scenes and events. The game is made up, at present, of six scenes: fresher's week and course choices; choice of options; introductory tutorial; lectures and independent study; balancing social life and work; and preparing for and taking exams.

Scene two: choice of options
The second scene can be used to illustrate how students make the choices that determine their progress through the game. The intention in this scene, choice of options, is to help students realize the need to base decisions on full information which may not always be readily available and may have to be actively sought out. The opening event places the student in the office of their Director of Studies, with the task of choosing an optional course. The Director of Studies reads out a list of four course titles from the University Prospectus she is holding and asks the student to decide which of them to take.

This is the first choice point, and the next text shown to the student depends on that choice. The control words are hidden at this stage – a device used to simulate the feeling of helplessness which many new students feel in such situations. The hidden control words can be activated if the student types in one of them in seeking to take charge of the situation. For example, any combination of words with 'prospectus' will show the student that the information there is too brief to be helpful. If the student does not make a recognizable choice or is unable to make any progress there is a pull-down menu that shows the hidden control words available for use at that time.

In this situation, of course, there is pressure on the student to make an immediate choice of options there and then. If that happens, the scene ends with a cautionary comment shown when the game controller has established that the student's past history of interactions with the game does not contain the event in which further information can be obtained. The comment seen on the screen would read as follows.

> As you are leaving, you overhear the Director of Studies muttering 'I really don't know how they can take these important decisions without bothering to find out more about . . . ' The door closes.

If the student persists in trying to obtain information, the Director of Studies will suggest that the department has more detailed course descriptions. When the student uses the 'go to' control word, various opportunities to obtain information are then provided. The scene shifts to an entrance hall in the department where there is a notice board – but this provides little additional information. The really useful guidance comes *implicitly* from meeting staff and *explicitly* from talking to second-year students. To continue the feeling of unfamiliarity, it is made fairly difficult to find people and to gain access to information.

The student model is used on several occasions in this scene to present differing perceptions of situations to students. This technique is intended to parallel the findings in the research on student learning, which emphasized that the contextual influences on learning are indirect. The contextual effects depend on the student's own perception of the situation. Here, on entering the department, for example, the student is given the opportunity to find out about the courses both from the notice board and from other students. But the descriptions have been designed to make it less likely that an 'introverted' student will speak to the other students. The game controller is instructed, at this point, to check the student's profile for the level of 'extraversion' currently shown. Then alternative texts are shown depending on that level.

> You notice out of the corner of your eye that the group of students drinking coffee in the corner is breaking up. They are still busy talking, but seem friendly.

Rule: Extravert (high).

> You notice out of the corner of your eye that the group of students drinking coffee in the corner is breaking up. They are deep in conversation and don't seem aware of your existence.

Rule: Extravert (low).

Again if the student seeks out the lecturers, they are perceived in different ways. In this case the match between learning style and teacher style is used to determine the impressions made on different students. Their reactions to a disorganized, but enthusiastic, lecturer are presented in contrasting ways. The student had tried, unsuccessfully, to see the lecturer before. This time:

> There is still no-one in, but you wait. After a while a large and cheerful man arrives and greets you effusively. He pushes you into the room and clears a pile of papers from a chair. He asks you who you are and how you are enjoying life at university. Eventually you manage to ask about his course. He launches into an enthusiastic description of his latest research. It sounds interesting, but really rather complex and confusing. You wander back towards the entrance hall, trying to work out what the course itself might be about, but feeling that the lecturer himself was friendly and enthusiastic.

Rule: Holist (high) AND Serialist (low).

The initial description is the same for both matched and mismatched conditions, but the reactions of the student with a serialist learning style are presented as being less favourable. The text block ends with

> . . . might be about. You feel that the lecturer was friendly, but disorganized and confusing.

Rule: Holist (low) AND Serialist (high)

The intention here is to mimic the contrasting perceptions of differing personal styles, but to avoid being too coercive on the student's ultimate choice of option course. These contrasting perceptions will influence the presentation of the events in the scene describing attendance at lectures.

Scene three: introductory tutorial
The intention in this scene is to help students recognize the need to prepare for tutorials, to plan ahead in obtaining books, to experience the frustration of not finding books in the library, and to provide advice on what tutors expect of students in the tutorials themselves. The scene also introduces students to the concept of 'approach to learning' through their

experiences in reading an article in prepartion for the next tutorial. The scene is set as follows:

> It is coming towards the end of your first tutorial. Students are beginning to click their files and generally indicate that it is time to go. The tutor eventually takes the hint, but gets up and writes the title of an article on the board. He says:
> I want you to read that article for next week: we'll see what you've made of it then. There should be a copy of that journal in the Reference Room. The article also appeared in a set of readings edited by . . . I think it was Davidson. We did order a copy for Short Loan so I think you will probably be able to get hold of it without too much difficulty.
> You make a dive for the door: it's definitely time for coffee.

There is no choice to be made. The student expects the scene to shift to the coffee bar. And for most students this will happen. But the game controller examines the student's profile. It checks on the levels on strategic approach and time management. If both of these are currently categorized as 'high', the student will be sent direct to the library, instead of to the coffee bar. If the student interrogates the computer through the CHORUS option about this unexpected change, the screen will show:

> You seem to be alert to the need to plan your time carefully and strategic enough to pick up the lecturer's hint, so you are expected to go to the library straight away.

Rule: Strategic (high) AND Time-Management (high)

All the other students find themselves in the coffee bar where the conversation turns to the possible difficulties in getting hold of the article. They are then offered the choice of going home to work on an essay or going to the library. If they decide to look for the article immediately, their score on 'strategic approach' will be increased at the end of the scene. If not, it will remain the same. When the students do go to the library, they locate the Reference Room easily enough, but find that the relevant journal is missing. They move on to the Short Loan Library, but if they have delayed going there, they will find that the book containing the article is out. These experiences are intended to alert newcomers to the logistic difficulties experienced in using an academic library.

Once they have obtained the article, the game controller interprets which experience of reading the article will be presented. Time-management is again involved, and so also is approach to learning. The text presents deep or surface approaches read with or without awareness of time. For example, the rule NOT (Deep Approach (high) OR Time-Management (high)) AND Surface Approach (high), if matched by the student's current profile, produces a description of a disorganized surface approach to reading.

> You look at the article, but you are not at all sure what you are supposed to get out of it. Are you supposed to 'learn' it – to try to remember all the details? Or will you be asked to join in a general discussion? You decide to try to cover both possibilities. You read the Abstract carefully and then begin to read the article slowly and carefully. You note down any fact or idea which seems important. However, you are not getting on very fast. All of a sudden you realize that you have a lecture in ten minutes. You rush through the rest of article without any chance to take any more notes. There is not time to come back to the library. You are left feeling anxious about the coming tutorial.

Students are given the opportunity to indicate immediately after this event to what extent that description of their reading seems truly applicable to them. They can indicate that they would concentrate more, or less, on meaning or details, or be more, or less, aware of time constraints. Their own estimates are then used to modify the profile on the blackboard.

When the students attend the next tutorial the game controller is asked to examine the 'history' to see how well they had prepared the article and also to check levels of 'extraversion' and 'fear of failure' in the profile. Anxious introverts are then depicted as being reluctant to join in the discussion and as finding the experience of tutorials threatening and unrewarding. Students who are self-confident extraverts are shown as dominating the proceedings to an extent that other students find unacceptable, while those who adopted a surface approach to the reading find the tutor unimpressed by a catalogue of accurate facts. If a student using a 'surface' approach is puzzled by the tutor's reaction, interrogation of CHORUS would contain:

> As you seem to have put too much effort into trying to learn details from the article, you found the tutor's broadly-based questions difficult to answer.

Rule: Surface (high) AND NOT Deep (high)

At the end of the scene, the students have the opportunity to ask the MENTOR to comment on the rationale behind the scene as a whole, and to provide advice in relation to the choices and strategies they have used in the scene. The MENTOR explains initially what the scene was intended to demonstrate to the student, and then invites the student to seek more individualized advice based on the specific choices made during that scene.

This scene was intended to suggest that:

A – tutors' comments about articles need interpreting
B – articles may not be easy to obtain in the library
C – articles have to be read for evidence and argument
D – in reading an article allocate time appropriately
E – tutors generally expect you to have your own ideas
F – tutorials involve speaking out and giving way
G – tutorials show you how to think about the discipline and allow you to check understanding of lectures.

If you would like advice about any (more) of these ideas, please type the appropriate capital letter, otherwise go on to the next scene.

The next set of advice introduces concepts and findings from research and also 'folk wisdom' about studying. Here, students typing 'C' will have the ideas of deep and surface approaches to learning introduced. The advice at this stage may also be tailored to the specific text blocks the individual student was shown and the specific choices made. Thus a student typing 'F', and currently characterized in the profile as an extravert, will be given a 'warning' about the dangers of being too dominant in small groups.

Tutorials have sensitive social dynamics. They depend on the tutor encouraging all the students to contribute, without applying the sort of pressure which creates anxiety. Many students lack confidence and are very susceptible to criticism, particularly when they are just starting a course. Each group, however, is likely to have someone who is extravert and self-confident. The danger is that such a person may dominate the discussions to the annoyance of the others, who soon get tired of his or her views. In this scene you were portrayed as behaving like that, and the coolness at coffee afterwards reflected the others' resentment of that behaviour. If you really behave like that, remember that joining in is fine but you also have a duty to the rest of the group. It will be better if you try to support the less confident members of the group. Don't try to score points: neither the tutors nor the other students will appreciate it.

Rule: Extravert (high) AND Self-Concept (high)

For the anxious student lacking in self-confidence, the advice changes half-way down the text block, after the same initial description.

> . . . the annoyance of others, and making more sensitive students very anxious and uncertain of themselves. In this scene, you were put in this position. If, in reality, you do find it difficult to join in easily, first it is important to realize that many other students feel the same. But you do need to join in. It may help to start by making a note of any idea that occurs to you, and then making a very brief remark based on your note. Your first attempt may well be hesitant and confused, but confidence grows with practice.

Rule: Fear of Failure (high) AND Self-Concept (low)

Development strategy for a principled adventure game

Having given some feel for the game itself, we can now return to the way in which the game was developed. The starting point was the heuristic model which has already been mentioned. That provided an overview of the concepts and the type of events likely to influence student learning. From the ideas and principles implicit in the model, we had to be able to create events and their consequences in a form that the computer could interpret. The scenes for the theatre were built up from a story-board which provided the shape of the game, and a story-line developed within each scene. To ensure that the game was 'principled' it was essential to construct scenes and events in ways that fufilled principles derived, as far as possible, from research findings on student learning.

From the heuristic model to the world of events
From the heuristic model and the architecture of the computer system, the next step was to develop a 'story-board' that would guide the development of a 'plot' or story-line. That plot would, in turn, guide the production of the 'scripts' or patterns of situations and choices that form the individual scenes. It was essential in developing the scenes to ensure that the events and the choices appear realistic to the student. It must be possible to act out events in the microworld of the game as a believable reality in its own right. However, as the intention of this particular game is to simulate an outside reality and to guide and advise students about everyday studying, the scenes must also encourage the student to draw parallels between the game and personal experience continuously. Within each scene the reality of the microworld should dominate, but at the end of each scene the student will be encouraged to use the MENTOR which will reinterpret the events in terms of the student's real-life intentions and strategies.

The development of the game also depended on being able to derive scenes, choices, consequences and advice from a coherent body of evidence embodied in a model. The heuristic model provided the starting point, but it was necessary to adapt it so as to provide a more gradual transition from the world of the student's everyday experience to the explanations provided in the research findings. The heuristic model

247

described important aspects of teaching and learning in higher education, but it missed out important social and experiential features that are of great importance to students. It also summarized relationships from the point of view of the *teacher*, by emphasizing aspects of the situation over which the instructor has some control, but which the *student* has to accept as 'given' – for example, the methods of teaching and the tasks set.

The transition from the real world of student experience to the abstractions used by researchers was achieved by creating two new models, existing in parallel at different levels of concreteness, and each being guided in part by the heuristic model. At the abstract level a 'concepts world' was produced which described everyday studying in terms of the researchers' concepts and categories. The second model took some of contextual influences on learning, such as assessment procedures, and added other academic and social influences to build up an 'events world' described in terms used by students themselves.

The 'concepts world' was designed to ensure that concepts were introduced into scenes in a systematic order that allowed the advice to grow in a coherent and well-ordered way. The 'events world' was devised to guide the choice of scenes and events for the story-board in a similar manner. In selecting and positioning the descriptive terms within these models, the intention was to focus attention on what was under the direct control of the student and could thus be changed as a result of either experience or advice.

Developing the story-board

The choice of scenes was guided by the model of the 'events world' which suggested those situations that would provide striking illustrations of the concepts being introduced to the students. The scenes had to provide opportunities for thinking about studying and advice on study approaches and strategies, derived, as far as possible, from research findings.

The story-board was built up, in a natural time sequence, from scenes that would sample salient features of a student's first year in higher education. The student would thus meet typical scenes such as 'freshers' (orientation) week', 'choice of optional courses', culminating in 'examinations'. The story-line should also include academic events and tasks such as 'reading for a tutorial', 'attending a lecture', and 'completing an assignment'. To take account of the importance of the interaction between social and academic experiences in higher education, a scene depicting 'balancing work and social life' would also be necessary. The use of the model of an 'events world' ensured that the scenes selected would be salient in relation to influences they might be expected to have on students' tasks and strategies and that they would also ensure the systematic introduction of advice and research concepts at appropriate times within the simulation. The current list of scenes was presented in an earlier section.

Besides a fixed sequence of main scenes, it is intended to introduce a series of variable events. Some of these events would be introduced at random, such as 'illness', but others would be triggered as consequences of earlier choices in relation to a particular event or the student's profile. For example, a student who chooses courses without due care may be faced with a substantial overload of work through an unfortunate, but avoidable, combination of courses.

As many scenes will develop in relation to the student model – the profile of scores held on the 'blackboard' – it will be necessary at an early stage in the game to obtain initial estimates of these characteristics. The first scene, 'freshers' week', has thus been designed to provide opportunities to collect background information on the student.

Constructing events
Once the story-board had been designed in outline, it was necessary to develop story-lines within the scenes and to see how these could be presented in a way that was compatible with programming requirements. The story-line within scenes was decided initially by reference to the models of events and concepts. Each scene suggested a particular group of events and an associated set of concepts. It was also decided, in outline, what advice was to be provided and what concepts were to be explained to the student in that scene. Events and concepts were allocated to the scenes within the story-board and redistributed until they occurred in a realistic sequence spread through the various scenes. To that extent the story-line was controlled by the underlying models to ensure the research information would drive this 'principled' adventure game. From then on, however, the story-line depended on imagination, tacit knowledge and personal experience to build up a believable scenario. The events could then be written in a computer-readable form with rules interpreted by the game controller to determine the text displayed.

Using the simulation

The adventure game described here would fulfil most of the criteria described by Diana Laurillard in her chapter. The student is actively involved in exploring a microworld and learns, in part, from that experience. However, the advice provided by the MENTOR also involves some direct teaching as well as tailored advice. In fact, this combination of opportunities to explore – in this case strategies and likely consequences – and provision of advice on demand, may prove to be a particularly appropriate use of computers in teaching. This project has explored the conversion of a data base of concepts and rules derived from research findings into a microworld describing everyday social reality. It has also developed non-intrusive techniques of providing individually tailored advice.

Here, our main concern has been with how a principled adventure game has been developed as a simulation of the broader context in which students learn. As indicated above, the game is intended for two main groups of users – first-year and more experienced students. The scenes, as currently written, have in mind students who are about to enter higher education. For them the game is intended to provide opportunities to anticipate, and 'play through', some of the bewilderingly rapid succession of events confronting them in the first weeks. During that period students have to make a large number of choices – academic, social and personal – without really being in a position to recognize the significance and lasting effects of some of those choices.

The game presents a selection of those events and is designed to make the consequences evident. If the game were to be reduced to a single prescription it would be – 'find out, think carefully, then decide'. If that seems obvious, it would be salutary to list the number of decisions a student typically makes in the first two weeks at university and to see how adequate the time and information is to take rational decisions.

Some scenes provide opportunities to evaluate study strategies in relation to the research evidence on what constitutes effective studying. The game enables students to use their current strategies and to explore their likely consequences. It also allows alternative strategies to be tried out. The MENTOR provides not just advice, but also a vocabulary of precise terms with which to describe aspects of studying. The game itself is intended to provoke discussions among students about the strategies used in the game, and their applicability in everyday studying. The recognition of strengths and weaknesses in their own approaches to studying should lead students to be more reflective about their purposes and strategies.

As the final scenes and the 'interpreter' are still being written, it is impossible to report how students react to the simulation. Once the game is operational, however, samples of students in their final year at school and in the first year of higher education will be asked to use it. Their interactions with, and their comments on, the game will be recorded and used to explore how best to use it, how to improve its presentation, and also how to evaluate its effects on everyday studying.

References

Biggs, J B (1987). *Student Approaches to Learning and Studying*. Hawthorn, Victoria: Australian Council for Educational Research.

Entwistle, N J and Ramsden, P (1983). *Understanding Student Learning*. London: Croom Helm,

Entwistle, N J and Wilson, J D (1977). *Degrees of Excellence: The Academic Achievement Game*. London: Hodder and Stoughton.

Gibbs, G, Morgan, A and Taylor, E (1984). The world of the learner. In: F Marton *et al.* (eds) *The Experience of Learning*. Edinburgh: Scottish Academic Press.

Marton, F (1976). What does it take to learn? In: N J Entwistle (ed), *Strategies for Research and Development in Higher Education*. Amsterdam: Swets and

Zeitlinger/Council of Europe.

Marton, F, Hounsell, D J and Entwistle, N J (eds) (1984). *The Experience of Learning*. Edinburgh: Scottish Academic Press.

Marton, F and Säljö, R (1984) Approaches to learning. In: F Marton *et al.* (eds) *The Experience of Learning*. Edinburgh: Scottish Academic Press.

Pask, G (1976). Learning styles and strategies. *British Journal of Educational Psychology*, **46**, 4–11.

Ramsden, P (1984). The context of learning. In: F Marton *et al.* (eds), *The Experience of Learning*. Edinburgh: Scottish Academic Press.

Taylor, E (1983). Orientations to study: A longitudinal interview investigation of students on two human studies degree courses at Surrey University. Unpublished PhD thesis, University of Surrey.

Wilson, J D (1978). The academic achievement game: experience with entering students. *Scottish Educational Review*, **10**, 7–18.

Part 4
Action and Reflection

Chapter 13
Achieving Change in Teaching Practices

John Bowden
University of Melbourne, Australia

The contributors to this book place great value on conceptual change learning; several are frankly contemptuous of learning that involves *no more than* a knowledge of theoretical statements, lists of properties, or set methods for solving problems. Many of the preceding chapters have addressed the challenge of organizing teaching and curricula with conceptual change learning in mind. In particular, the chapters by Eizenberg, Whelan, White and Horwitz, Svensson and Högfors, and Roth and Anderson describe successful teaching innovations based on a view of learning as a change in a person's understanding.

In one sense, however, each of these chapters could be regarded as a report of a special case. Clearly, those involved in the innovations discussed in these chapters are committed to establishing the changes they report. While there are lessons for all teachers in the outcomes they have achieved, the question remains as to how such innovations can be instituted more comprehensively throughout our education systems. Indeed, in Chapter 3 Leo West is pessimistic about the chances of substantial change of this kind taking place. He sees those who seek such improvement in teaching as passengers on a train whose direction and timetable is set; they have the opportunity to affect the train's progress only marginally. I tend to adopt a more optimistic stance and, later in this chapter, I respond to the view presented by West. However, my major intention here is to highlight two necessary aspects of any attempt to bring about substantial change in teaching practices.

Central to the strategies I propose for promoting such changes is the idea that they should be based on the same theory of learning that the book has been urging teachers to adopt. In discovering how to go about their teaching activities in new ways, teachers are learners, just as students in those teachers' own classes are. Thus, the first focus in this chapter is on how to change the way teachers see their role, using methods which mirror the principles of teaching and learning argued for in this book. But all learning, including teacher-learning, takes place in an educational

255

context. The second focus is therefore on the need to influence the context in which teachers teach, in order to make it more supportive of changes in teachers' conceptions.

Teaching as a professional activity: changing teachers' conceptions

That the content and context of learning are inseparable from the process and outcome of learning is an essential idea of our view of learning. Students are always learning *something* in a specific set of *circumstances*, but the 'somethings' and the circumstances are highly heterogeneous. The combination of many factors produces a multiply determined model of the relation between teaching and learning. An important practical consequence is that prescriptions of better and worse ways of learning are fraught with danger. Ference Marton has expressed this as follows:

We cannot make predictions in the strict sense in the field of educational and psychological research into learning except in the negative form (if $\sim A$ then $\sim B$). We can, however, still make theoretical constructions involving relations between conditions, perceptions and actions. The concrete meanings of these constructions must, however, once more be found out in each concrete case anew. The relation between research and practice cannot thus be predictive but surely it can be guiding.

(Marton, 1986)

Teaching will always remain a professional activity. Clearly there are guidelines and lessons from example which can inform professional judgement, but spontaneous human decision-making will remain an irreplaceable feature of the teaching process. Biggs has suggested that moving from educational theory to practice occurs on two levels:

The first is more deliberate . . . planning, setting up operational procedures in the classroom, 'negotiating' with the class and so on. These are long term decisions and evolve gradually, both formally and informally.

The second level is more spontaneous. Usually we are talking of quick decisions that need to be made in the heat of the moment, often with respect to just one student or another staff member: these are routine decisions that have to be made every day, and for which there is usually insufficient time to plan a proper strategy.

(Biggs and Telfer, 1987, p 530)

Espoused theory v. theory-in-use

Difficulties arise when the practical rules used to guide such spontaneous decision-making do not correspond with the 'espoused theory' on which more deliberate planning has been based. We see such a discrepancy in many circumstances whenever individuals fail to 'practise what they preach'. It is common at all levels of education.

Argyris and Schon (1978) originally developed the distinction between espoused theory (values and strategies we proclaim in public) and theory-in-use (values and strategies which inform our actions and of which we are largely unaware, and over which we have little control). It has been used in a variety of ways since then to explain discrepancies between professional beliefs and actions. Biggs and Telfer (1987), for example, make a distinction between 'the explicit theory underlying teaching and the practice that takes place anyway on the basis of tradition, wisdom, habit and the intuition of the individual teacher'. They see that contrast as 'the distinction between teacher education and teacher training'.

Fleming and Rutherford (1984) use the espoused theory/theory-in-use discrimination to explain the generally negative reaction by academics to a set of 'Recommendations for Learning' arising from a recent British National Study into the Future of Higher Education (the 'Leverhulme Study'). They suggest that many academics are informed by a particular theory-in-use which means their actions are both secretive and competitive; they seek control and power over colleagues and students. The Leverhulme recommendations supported, among other things, student-centred courses with peer review of teaching, re-examination of assessment practices, development of more autonomy for students in their learning, and reduction in the focus on exposition by teachers. Fleming and Rutherford argue that these recommendations correspond to a set of values that are

. . . incompatible with (those) that typically inform the actions of academics. Although the general recommendations may command assent at the espoused theory level, the specific recommendations which propose action will conflict with the prevalent . . . theory-in-use.

(Fleming and Rutherford, 1984)

Teachers' espoused theory of learning

What kinds of learning do teachers value? This is a question that I have raised at in-service workshops for a wide range of university and college teachers in Australia over a number of years, and more recently in Sweden. In nearly every case, teachers make a distinction between, on the one hand, the mere memorizing of information or the development of skills and, on the other, more desirable, higher level goals which include (but are not dominated by) a knowledge of facts, procedures and skills. The contrast is similar to the distinction which has been made over and over again in previous chapters.

Let me cite the outcome of one such exercise with a group of Australian university teachers: it is exemplary. When asked what qualities they would like their students to possess on graduation, the teachers included such attainments as problem-solving ability in their profession, lateral thinking, insight, integrity, perspective, self-motivation, ability to 'self-learn', and an understanding of the structure of knowledge in related disciplines. Teachers often include in their lists minimal competencies such as literacy and numeracy skills, general knowledge and knowledge of core facts. Invariably, however, the latter are seen as being inadequate in themselves; their attainment is viewed as an expected outcome in the development of the higher-level aims.

It is interesting that employers and politicians often use similar language to describe the desirable outcomes of learning. For example, a recent policy discussion paper on higher education, published by the Australian Government Department of Employment, Education and Training (1987), argued that:

The major function of education is . . . to increase individuals' capacity to learn, to provide them with a framework with which to analyze problems and to increase their capacity to deal with new information.

Biggs has suggested that a similar pattern exists in the schools:

Most State departments refer to independence, autonomy, creativity, as well as to mastery of particular content, including basic literacy and numeracy skills.
(*Biggs and Telfer, 1987, p 536*)

The highest level aims cited by teachers, educators and politicians are of course very general and difficult to implement. They are by no means identical to the content-related understanding espoused by contributors to this book. Nevertheless, it is clear that teachers and others concerned with all levels of education are concerned that students achieve more than minimal competencies.

Yet many teachers lament the fact that their students clearly do not approach their learning with higher-level aims in mind. Students are criticized for their tendency to memorize information for examination purposes and to promptly forget it afterwards. Later testing often demonstrates that, despite students' having successfully negotiated the assessment system, little understanding has been gained (see Chapter 1). Why are the theoretical intentions of the teachers not reflected in student practice?

My explanation, which has been formed both by theoretical considerations and practical experience, is very close to that stated in Chapter 1: the problem lies in a mismatch between espoused theory and the way students are actually taught and assessed. Research has shown us that it is possible to teach students and to test their achievements in ways which, unintentionally one hopes, may encourage them to learn with the purpose merely of reproducing information; and that conditions such as these commonly exist at all levels of education. The theory-in-use in many of our universities, colleges and schools differs markedly from the theory which most teachers of those classes publicly espouse. How can we help teachers to change their teaching practices so that they relate more closely to espoused theory?

Conceptions of teaching

What is required is for teachers themselves to undergo a learning process – to change their conceptions of teaching. Teaching should be concerned with finding out how students are conceptualizing the material under study and then helping students modify their unsophisticated conceptions. Methods of teaching involving provision of excessive amounts of unstructured information and assessment that rewards the regurgitation of such 'knowledge' are not consistent with this desired conception of teaching. Strategies that help student confront the inadequacies of their ways of thinking and that lead to conceptual change are required; some of these will be discussed in detail by Marton and Ramsden in Chapter 14.

How can we help teachers to think about teaching as a process of changing students' conceptions? There is no point in merely informing teachers of general principles they should adopt, principles that would be largely content-free and meant to apply to all contexts. Decisions about teaching methods concern context and content. To make general statements about teaching strategies requires assumptions about the content of learning, the existing conceptions students have of the subject matter and the skills of the teacher. In fact, none of these can be assumed. No particular approach could be expected to be equally effective for a teacher of primary school mathematics in a deprived, inner-city school, for a teacher of a foreign language at junior secondary level and for an anatomy lecturer teaching medical undergraduates in a university? These represent an extreme range, but the principle still holds when differences are narrower. It will always be the case that teachers will exercise judgement and make choices at every stage in their interaction with their students. Any particular pattern of decision-making and consequent action cannot be prescribed. Each teaching episode is unique and requires active diagnosis and problem-solving by the teacher. We need, therefore, to create an opportunity for teachers to develop an understanding of what those processes involve and for them to discover actively the ways in which they might apply them to their own disciplines.

It is likely that there are many ways of doing this. The workshop that I have developed for tertiary teachers, described below, is a concrete example of one way. It is described only briefly here but has been written up in detail elsewhere (Bowden, 1988). Readers will discover that the workshop is based on the principles of learning argued for in this book.

A workshop to help change teachers' conceptions of teaching

The workshop requires about three hours of teacher activity. In that time the following aspects are dealt with.

(1) Introduction: overview of workshop.
(2) Activity 1: participants asked to write down a list of statements representing

259

qualities they wish their graduates to have developed – followed by pooling of ideas and discussion.

(3) Presentation – with questions to and from participants – on the following topics:

>phenomenography;
>approaches to learning and learning outcomes;
>influence of learning context on approaches to learning;
>intervention programmes in recent decades designed to improve learning;
>research findings on student approaches to learning in Australian universities.

(4) Activity 2: participants (in groups of three to six by discipline) asked to consider one of their own courses and to write down four or five statements representing key understandings they want students to develop during the course – followed by discussion.

(5) Presentation of ideas about how teachers can apply this approach to their own teaching. Assessment methods are shown to be of crucial importance. Some examples of good and poor types of question are presented. The notion of alternative student conceptions is introduced.

(6) Activity 3: participants (in same groups as in Activity 2) asked to consider one of the understandings listed in Activity 2 and to represent different conceptions students have of it – followed by discussion.

(7) Discussion of the implications of the above for day-to-day teaching.

(8) Roles of university administration, teachers and student groups in institutionalizing quest for improvement in the quality of learning.

The fundamental principle of the workshop is that participants are required actively to apply their espoused theory to the practice of teaching in their own particular subjects. They must reflect on the goals they have for students, which they normally express in the fairly general form described earlier in this chapter; they are asked to be specific about the intended outcomes of one of their own courses and to describe some of the alternative conceptions students have of one of these. They are then invited to discuss what they would do to help those students who are known to have an unsophisticated or inadequate conception to change to a more acceptable one, what to do when they discover a distribution of student conceptions about a particular phenomenon and, finally, how to go about determining just what the students' conceptions are at various stages in a course.

Is the workshop successful? Well, in most respects, it is. The response of teachers to the task of listing qualities they would like their graduates to attain was described earlier in this chapter; the results are consistent and satisfactory. Teachers do usually want their students to develop understanding of their discipline and to be able to apply that theoretical understanding to the real world. But when they engage in the other workshop activities, teachers soon begin to realize that their normal teaching practices are often incompatible with the desired outcomes. These discrepancies are exposed in the second task when participants are asked to list the key understandings they want students to acquire in one of their first-year tertiary courses. Usually, the lists read like part of a table of contents from a textbook rather than statements of understanding. Two examples from workshops run in Australian and Swedish universities demonstrate this point:

Electricity:

> what is a field?
> concept of current, voltage;
> Kirchoff's laws;
> how fast does an electron move in a wire?

Mathematics:

> algorithmic understanding – how to do it;
> interpretational understanding – how to connect an abstract concept with one or several concrete situations;
> mathematical structural understanding – awareness of the strict nature of mathematical reasoning; explanation = proof;
> functional understanding – ability to use mathematics in different applications and experience how it functions.

It is clear that teachers have generally tried to express the central issues in their courses but have struggled when they are asked to go beyond a description of content areas (cf Chapter 8). Often they try to insert the word understanding, or similar words, but still do no more than describe *topics* to be covered.

When the workshop was conducted for the first time, I was disappointed after activity 1. I felt that teachers did not understand the message that was being given – that there is a need to think of course goals not in terms of simply what topics are 'covered', but rather in terms of the sort of conceptions students should have of the phenomena related to those topics.

I soon found that the difficulty teachers had in this task was common to all participant groups no matter where the workshop was held – in general or technological universities, in Sweden or in Australia. One explanation for this may be that in the past, teachers have probably had to write down the objectives of their courses in a context in which descriptive statements of topic areas are expected; in most syllabus statements in tertiary education, this is the way the curriculum is defined. When confronted with this task in the workshop, participants have relied on their previous experience in what appears to be a similar activity – without focusing on the different emphasis which the workshop task was really demanding.

This explanation is reinforced by the fact that participants carried out the next task (activity 3), one they would have had no experience with before and for which they would have had no ritual response, in a way which demonstrated that understanding had been achieved. They had all experienced a discussion of the outcome of the previous activity and further examples had been provided by the workshop leader. Furthermore, the influence of assessment had been discussed prior to this third activity which required participants to write down a statement of one understanding students on their course should develop, along with several alternative conceptions of that particular phenomenon commonly held by students. Participants were advised to create a typical question that would elicit student understanding and to express the various conceptions as answers to that question. The following example illustrates how some participants responded in this activity.

Electricity: You are an electron in the middle of a copper wire. At a certain time, I will connect a battery across your wire. How will you react before and after connection?

> My neighbour bumps me immediately and then I bump the neighbour on the other side.
> I sit still before connection but gradually move together with the others after connection.
> I gradually accelerate.
> I take off with the speed of light.
> Before connection, I am dancing around randomly. I do not feel the field from the battery immediately, but when it gets here (at the speed of light) my dance is biased a bit in the direction of the field.

The value of this exercise is that teachers come to grips with the essence of teaching as a process in which they need to understand the ways in which their students conceive of particular phenomena related to important concepts being taught. They need to know this in order to be able to structure student experience in ways that will lead them to change those conceptions to the one that is preferred. The outcomes are similar in form to those derived from research as reported in several chapters of this book (eg Lybeck *et al.* and Svensson and Högfors).

Understanding students' conceptions: A joint responsibility
Research activities. The approach described above makes use of research findings from investigations into ways of testing students' understanding (see, for example, Chapter 3 and Ramsden, Masters, Martin and Bowden, 1987). There is a need for such research to continue – to develop a better understanding of students' conceptions of an ever-widening range of phenomena. The workshop experience shows clearly that the fruits of such research provide an important stimulus to teachers trying to understand the theory and its application to their own teaching. The closer the examples are to their own teaching, the better. In addition, quite apart from serving as a model, such examples inform teachers of ways of thinking specifically about their own subjects; this is exemplified by the work of Lybeck *et al.* Teachers can learn from the research outcomes as well as from the methodology and its implications for teaching.

Teacher education and educational development. Groups of teachers can make use of the workshop experience to develop their understanding of student conceptions, teaching strategies and skills. This is an area where teacher educators and educational development personnel can play an important role. The general approach exemplified in the workshop is applicable to both initial teacher education and in-service programmes.

Past teacher experience. The workshop demonstrates that through their past experience teachers possess important data, provided they learn how to utilize them. A few years ago a two-day symposium, in which phenomeno-graphic research was related to practical attempts being made to improve student learning, was organized in Melbourne. I wrote at the time:

In a sense phenomenographic research mirrors what good teachers do. It tries to understand what the students are doing in their learning. It attempts to discover what different approaches students are taking and to understand these in terms of the outcomes of their learning activities. Good teachers do that as a preliminary to further action to help their students come to understand the concept concerned and, of course, many do it instinctively. That is the appeal of Marton's work, of most phenomenographic research into learning; teachers can identify with both the methodology and the findings.

This identification with the phenomenographic method raises an interesting point. It often happens that when teachers do try to apply the method to their own students' learning, it is used incorrectly . . . Does this mean that, unless teachers steep themselves in the phenomenographic methodology, they cannot help their students? Clearly not. For one thing, they are themselves so proficient in the discipline, they may well engage in the recommended processes anyway, provided they appreciate the distinctions being made by phenomenographers about approaches to learning. This is what I was referring to earlier as instinctive behaviour. Not every teacher will have that capacity but teachers may not need to undertake formal research in each and every case. Phenomenography introduces a way of thinking about learning that may be unfamiliar to teachers but which is congruent with the aims and activities of good teachers.

(*Bowden, 1986*)

My experience with the workshop has confirmed the central theme quoted above. Many teachers, previously unfamiliar with phenomeno-graphy itself or the view of learning on which it is based, are able within a few hours to grasp the basic ideas and apply them to their own teaching and the learning of their own students. This is related to their teaching experience. Over the years they have interacted with students and, in a sense, collected data about student conceptions. They will be less accurate, perhaps less comprehensive, than those obtained through research, but if teachers are given the opportunity to develop an understanding of how to convert the data they have collected over time into a rough representation of likely student conceptions of a particular phenomenon, they will be able to use that as a basis for teaching. They will probably be catering for the majority of students if they assume that the range of conceptions, such as those developed in the workshops described earlier, represent the ways their students are likely to understand the phenomenon. Provided they develop strategies to test students' understanding, they will be able to modify their model in the light of experience.

The institutional context of change

Educational development involves educational theory, research and practice; it also concerns people, institutions and communities. Teachers who want to bring about change in their teaching practices have to operate within that context. A researcher or faculty development officer who wishes to see improvements in teaching take place in, say, a university, must not only address the educational questions but must also take account of the institutional context in which the change is to occur.

Clearly, this requires more than interaction with the individual teacher. Those who desire change must concern themselves with ways of influencing the context in which teachers find themselves. To achieve changes in conceptions of teaching we need to change the environment in which teachers teach. Some aspects of that environment include the value system in the institution or system, the reward structure for teachers, and the normal educational practices in the institution which may be based merely on habit or precedent. Those who want to bring about change in school curricula cannot afford to work only with teachers. The influences of the structure of the school system, its bureaucracy and procedures, need to be addressed.

For the probability of comprehensive change to be high, a whole series of activities, decisions and variations in thinking must take place. Research into student learning produces guidelines about the appropriate conditions for learning of particular kinds. This assumes that certain values are held about what is 'good learning' and about what is an appropriate methodology. Teachers need to be convinced that both these values and the research conclusions are acceptable. But even then, many teachers may not respond unless there is some way that the educational institution or system *rewards* them for devoting time to changing their teaching in this way. It may be necessary to convince those with power in the institution to support the activities desired. Often, even when institutions do show such support, teachers need to be convinced that time spent on the new activities will be rewarded in practice. There is always a doubt that the institution may be paying only lip-service to the need for change. Even in the most favourable situation, students will need help to ignore past practices (of teachers and institutions) and embrace the new order.

Books such as this one and workshops such as the one I have described in this chapter address the early links in this chain. However, in an unsupportive or actively hostile environment where committed teachers are discouraged from implementing changes they now believe in, comprehensive change, particularly among the great majority of teachers, is less likely to occur. To make the sorts of changes discussed in this book requires effort. Does the employer support that effort? Are in-service activities provided and supported? Are teachers encouraged to participate? Does participation result in enhancement of the teacher's reputation? What tangible career rewards will result from efforts to improve teaching?

Just as the context in which students learn affects their approaches to learning, so the context in which teachers teach affects their approaches to teaching. The relation between teachers' career goals and what they perceive will enhance their career prospects is important. In some tertiary institutions, the reward system for academic staff may not favour excellence in teaching at all. Emphasis in promotion procedures on other functions such as research or administrative responsibility will militate against much effort being expended on teaching at all, let alone extra effort on improving the quality of teaching. Those who seek changes will need to influence such policies if teachers' attitudes – which, like students' responses to assessment, are rational responses to the environment – are to be altered.

If an individual teacher makes an effort to develop better curricula and assessment, the educational system may not be able to cope with the changes the teacher wants to introduce. Does the school assessment system allow for testing of conceptual change or is the system rigidly encased in an alien conception of teaching and learning? Is there pressure from peers to conform because they fear the impact of the proposed changes on their own activities? Is the education system (or institution) so complex that those in it see the task of changing any of its fundamental characteristics as too daunting?

Despite all these impediments, changes in teaching and learning do take place. But they require sustained effort over a lengthy period of time. For example, The University of Melbourne student learning project is firmly based on the principles outlined here. However, it began *ten years ago* as a programme aimed at improving student learning skills, and moved through various stages to its present form which is based on cooperative research among teachers in a number of departments with the intention of improving teaching practices in specific subjects. The project's success has been influenced by direct educational development activities in the University, and institutional support for the underlying philosophy of the proposed changes through statements by the Academic Board, which in turn was influenced in its position by reports from committees on which the education development faculty served.

Some of the changes have occurred in line with national and world-wide trends; some based on research findings. However, all have been affected by, and some would never have taken place without, deliberate effort by individual educators in the University. Writing of papers, of submissions for funding, serving on key committees, assisting such committees to write reports to the Academic Board, discussing teaching and learning issues with key decision-makers as well as working directly with teachers in the University all played their part in the developments that have taken place. Without those deliberate interventions, the activities with teachers would have been to no avail.

In a similar way, in research and development that we (Masters and Hill, in press; Ramsden, Bowden and Martin, 1988) are currently doing at Year 12 level (the final year of secondary school in Australia), we are working

265

not only in cooperation with school teachers and principals but are also seeking interaction with state education authorities responsible for curricula and assessment in the schools. Work at several levels, with teachers, in the schools where they teach, with the examination and other education authorities, and with the tertiary institutions to which many students seek admission, is essential for success.

This is why I was not really surprised to see the outcomes of the PEEL project described by Leo West in Chapter 3. The teachers enthusiastically engaged in innovative activity over a period of years but that effort has dwindled. Some of us would probably want to cast doubts on the theory of learning underlying that particular intervention, but the central point I want to make is that those teachers and their students are a small part of a vast enterprise. Secondary school curricula and assessment, especially at the senior school level, are under considerable centralized control in the state of Victoria. Parents have been well aware that at the end of Year 12, their children would have to face external, state-wide examinations in each subject. The pressure has been on conformity and guaranteed success. These pressures make it extremely difficult for a teacher to introduce innovative approaches. What is needed is for the education system to sanction such innovations. To do this, of course, the centralized systems need to change and this will not occur without the education authorities learning about and being convinced by the need for change. They are already being approached by parent groups, teacher organizations, employer associations and the like. Those who want educational change must operate alongside such groups and, incidentally, they must collaborate with those groups too.

Let me repeat my major theme. Unless the range of individuals and groups affected by or able to influence any proposed change are included, then isolated efforts to improve teaching and learning will remain just that. Strong individuals may be able to maintain local change even in the long term, but the system is unlikely to be affected unless a comprehensive effort is made. While West is pessimistic about the prospects of that happening, I am optimistic. I believe that if the proposed changes are as good as their advocates believe, then by deliberate and coordinated effort they do have the possibility of influencing all those parts of the system which are important.

This means, of course, that those who seek change must see their role in the long term. None of the changes mentioned can be achieved overnight. They then face a further responsibility, along with the teachers. That obligation is to convince students that the system they have experienced for so long, a system that may have rewarded superficial approaches to learning, is no longer in place. Students will not be convinced merely by being told that the system has changed. They will need to experience a new context in which minimalist approaches to learning are clearly not valued and one in which efforts to understand subject matter and relate it to real-life problems are rewarded. Given the state of the education systems in many countries, colleges and schools (and the teachers within them) face a daunting task in gaining credibility among students for the changes they may wish to implement.

References

Argyris, C and Schon, D (1978). *Organizational Learning: A Theory-of-action Perspective*. Reading, Massachusetts: Addison-Wesley.

Australian Government Department of Employment Education and Training (1987). *Policy Discussion Paper on Higher Education*. Canberra: Australian Government Printing Service.

Biggs, J B and Telfer, R (1987). *The Process of Learning* (2nd edition). Sydney: Prentice-Hall.

Fleming, W and Rutherford, D (1984). Recommendations for learning: rhetoric and reaction. *Studies in Higher Education*, **9**, 17-26.

Bowden, J A (1986). Educational development and phenomenography. In: J A Bowden (ed), *Student Learning: Research into Practice*. Melbourne: CSHE, University of Melbourne.

Bowden, J A (1988, in preparation). Changing academics' conceptions of teaching: An institutional perspective. *Higher Education Research and Development*.

Marton, F (1986). Some reflections on the improvement of learning. In: J A Bowden (ed), *Student Learning: Research into Practice*. Melbourne: CSHE, University of Melbourne.

Masters, G N and Hill, P (in press). Reforming the assessment of student achievement in the senior secondary school. *Australian Journal of Education*.

Ramsden, P, Bowden, J A and Martin, E (1988). Students' learning and perceptions of teaching: School effectiveness reconsidered. Paper presented at the Annual Meeting of the American Educational Research Association, New Orleans, April 1988.

Ramsden, P, Masters, G N, Martin, E and Bowden, J A (1987). Assessing the elements of competence: A relational approach. Paper presented at the Annual Conference of the Higher Education Research and Development Society of Australasia, Perth, August 1987.

Chapter 14
What Does it Take to Improve Learning?

Ference Marton and Paul Ramsden
University of Gothenburg, Sweden and University of Melbourne, Australia

This book has been concerned with the way educational research can be more closely linked to teaching through the study of how and what students learn. Research in education is often regarded as an abstract and rather remote venture; teaching is typically seen as practical and active. An underlying theme of the book is that these simple conceptions should be replaced by the authentically educational view that headed the first chapter. Action and reflection in education ought to be seen as parts of the same process. In this chapter we try to draw together recommendations for practice through reflecting on the implications of our view of learning and teaching.

Basic principles

Perhaps for readers who have travelled this far in the book our view of improving learning seems no more than common sense. What are we saying that is so different?

In the history of education, two major schools of thought concerning ways of improving learning are discernible. One points towards methods of teaching a variety of subject matter. The idea is that we can develop general principles for teaching whatever it is we want to teach. We can then apply these general principles to any content. If the principles are correct, their application is supposed to lead to better learning.

The other imagined path towards the same goal is the development of general thinking and learning skills. It is assumed that these skills can be applied by the person who has learned them to any subject matter – that they are transferable. Again, if the skills are the right ones, their application supposedly results in improved learning.

The 'new perspectives' of the book's title allude to the fact that neither of these alternatives for improving learning has been adopted in its various chapters. Before presenting the framework that serves to unify the contributions, we would like briefly to illustrate the two traditional alternatives in order to sharpen the outlines of our own approach.

General teaching principles and general learning skills

Roth and Anderson open their chapter with a reference to debate about the relative merits of using textbooks and what they call 'the activity approach'. This is a classic way of framing questions about pedagogy: what are the comparative effects on learning of different teaching methods? The aim is to discover general principles of 'good teaching'. There are many other examples of this approach. The comparative merits of lectures v. group discussions, expository teaching v. discovery learning, going from the abstract to the concrete v. going from the concrete to the abstract – and many other contrasts – have been examined in study after study.

At the 1986 meeting of the American Educational Research Association, Philip H. Winne presented some findings from an analysis of the conclusions of 64 articles in the previous year's edition of a respected educational research journal (*Journal of Educational Psychology*) (Winne, 1986). Winne's analysis is revealing. The first three studies summarized in his paper deal with principles for designing teaching materials. The conclusion from the first is that if a text describes several categories of information in terms of their similarities and differences, the text should be preceded by an introduction naming the categories and mentioning the dimensions in terms of which the comparisons are made. Such an arrangement, it is asserted, will result in 86% recall of the names of categories and 29% recall of the ideas in the text. The second study argues that long texts should be preceded by 'advance organizers' that present the information to follow in a more general form. If learners write out a paraphrased version of the organizer before reading the text, they will recall about 16 ideas from a 1000-word text and about 24 ideas from a chapter-length text. The third study concludes that if questions that demand analysis are inserted after each paragraph 42% of the ideas will be recalled.

We do not want to be unjust to these studies. We would simply like readers to note that they embody the assertion that educational research often draws conclusions about teaching methods regardless of content and context. The studies also measure learning in terms of average level of recall.

The second alternative approach to improving learning is the notion of equipping students with general and highly potent skills. This idea has been a recurrent theme in education at least since Aristotle's time. General learning skills are something of a philosopher's stone. A contemporary manifestation of the idea is the conviction that students can be trained to be 'metacognitive' about their learning: that they can learn strategies of monitoring and managing learning which are *independent of* content and context.

Segal, Chipman and Glaser (1986) have collected reports on various programmes aimed at improving thinking and learning skills. In one chapter of Segal *et al.*'s book, Dansereau (1986) describes the development of a course designed to improve college students' skills in comprehension, memory, planning, scheduling, concentration management and monitoring. These 'primary strategies' were taught through techniques such as paraphrasing texts and creating networks of concepts. Dansereau also describes the teaching of a knowledge scheme for learning scientific theories. Students were trained to learn theories in six stages: description, inventor, consequences, evidence, other theories, and extra information. The effects of the training were evaluated by having students read a text and measuring retention using multiple-choice, essay, and short-answer tests. In the same volume, Weinstein and Underwood (1986) report an experimental three-credit-hour learning strategy course, also for college students, with somewhat similar aims. The course seems to have been inspired by Weinstein's earlier work (Weinstein, 1975) on enhancing retention by training students to use 'rehearsal and elaboration skills': the use of devices such as mnemonic images and summarizing. Weinstein evaluated the effectiveness of her 1975 programme using seven kinds of retention test. Both Dansereau's and Weinstein's learning skills programmes were judged successful in terms of enhancing retention.

A very large number of studies in which teaching methods and learning skills have been examined have adopted the two central principles that these inquiries demonstrate. First, conclusions are drawn about methods and skills regardless of content and context. Thus the learning skills described in Dansereau's and Weinstein's work are meant to be generally applicable to any academic reading assignment. The use of questions interpolated into a text will supposedly result in better learning, no matter what the text is about and no matter what the purposes of its reader. The second principle is that learning is measured in terms of average level of recall. Even when ideas and concepts are being learned, whether they have been learned is considered in terms of whether the words representing them have been retained.

These studies seem to us to imply a certain model – a particular conception, if you like – of teaching and learning. In this model, learning is essentially about gathering information and retaining it, using certain content-free skills; teaching is about transmitting that information and the techniques that will enable it to be remembered efficiently.

This model of teaching and learning is associated with a complementary view of educational research. Research is seen as an attempt to answer general questions concerning cause-and-effect relations; ideally it should provide answers that will enable teachers to determine students' behaviour accurately. In the educational drama for which this traditional model is the script, the purposive elements in learning – the students' perceptions and decisions – and the world as seen through the eyes of the learner play very minor roles.

Learning as changing conceptions of subject matter within a learning context

The examples given above were specially selected to make a point. But they represent a dominant paradigm in research into teaching and learning. That paradigm is, of course, diametrically opposed to our own. Deriving context- and content-free principles for teaching and learning and measuring learning in terms of recall is not at all the way learning has been dealt with in this book. This is not the *kind* of learning (or research) the book has considered. A few themes and quotations will remind us what learning means to the authors here.

Laurillard (Chapter 11) stresses the importance of the learners' perspective on learning. She contrasts learning the statements of Newtonian mechanics with learning about what happens when you throw a ball in the air. 'Students need experiences . . . that allow them to *see* that their conception is inappropriate, which is far more powerful than *telling* them it is wrong.' White and Horwitz (Chapter 4) use the same example. By requiring students to operate in a computer simulation of a world with gravity (microworld 3), they intend to help them understand just what *does* happen when you throw a ball in the air. Svensson and Högfors (Chapter 8) differentiate knowing a theory from knowing about a theory. In a similar vein Roth and Anderson (Chapter 6) compare 'changing ideas about the real world' with the 'process of acquiring and memorizing facts'. West (Chapter 3) speaks of learning as 'constructing one's own understanding of reality; making one's own sense of other peoples' understanding of the world' rather than 'repeating teachers' knowledge or textbook knowledge'.

In the context of medical problem-solving, Whelan (Chapter 10) stresses 'looking for entities that can act as intermediate links between the cause of disease and its effects'. Eizenberg, dealing with teaching and learning in anatomy (Chapter 9), highlights the importance of 'understanding anatomical principles and their clinically important applications, at the expense of detailed minutiae'. Entwistle, Odor and Anderson refer to the distinction between 'the intention . . . either to seek personal understanding or minimally to meet task requirements'. Perry describes the different 'constellations through which the students (make) sense of their worlds' (Chapter 7). Säljö (Chapter 2) talks about learning as 'the acquisition of conceptions of reality' related to particular 'provinces of meaning'. Lybeck, Marton, Strömdahl and Tullberg point to 'a view of learning as a change from one way of understanding a phenomenon to another, and qualitatively different way, of understanding the same phenomenon'.

Just so. The most fundamental principle in this book is that learning should be seen as a qualitative change in a person's way of seeing, experiencing, understanding, conceptualizing something in the real world – rather than as a quantitative change in the amount of knowledge someone possesses. It is logically impossible for learning defined in this way to be content- and context-free. Learning techniques and instructional strategies are inextricably linked to subject matter and the students' perceptions.

This kind of learning obviously differs from being able to remember something one has read. But is also different from 'knowing' facts and principles, and from being able to carry out a particular procedure. It is a change in one's understanding. There is no doubt that there are other forms of learning: we maintain that the kind of learning discussed in this volume is the most fundamental. The question of what kind of under-standing of a phenomenon a student arrives at is, in our view, superordi-nate to issues of procedural and factual knowledge.

We are well aware that some people will argue that if a student obtains new knowledge and acquires new procedures related to a phenomenon, then his or her understanding of that phenomenon will – more or less automatically – change. It is an attractive theory for several reasons. But on the whole it appears to be false. One of the major achievements of the research on conceptual change in science quoted in many of the book's chapters (see especially Chapter 3) has been to refute this apparently reasonable suggestion. As Svensson and Högfors and White and Horwitz point out, learning the definitions of Newton's laws does *not* imply a Newtonian view of seeing bodies in motion. Or again, as Roth and Anderson so convincingly show, a student who has learned the correct description of 'photosynthesis' does *not* necessarily see the difference between how plants and animals obtain food.

From this principle of learning as a change in conceptions flow the themes and injunctions that should by now be familiar: a view of content and process in learning as parts of the same whole, an emphasis on *students'* conceptions and perceptions, and learning about student thinking as the key that will unlock the door to better teaching and course design. If we want to change students' understanding, we have to deal with their present understanding in a methodical way. Not only can this kind of learning not be dealt with solely in general terms; it also cannot be value-free. We have to know what view of a particular phenomenon we would like a learner to develop.

Aspects of a relational view of learning
Content and process. The idea of content and process ('what' and 'how') as interlinked parts of learning is central to our view, but it is one that some people – especially those taking a psychological perspective – have found very puzzling. Perhaps an example drawing on a repeated instance in the book will help to clarify matters. One of the questions asked in Svensson and Högfors' investigation concerned the forces acting on a car being driven along a highway. The answers revealed two distinct conceptualiza-tions of bodies moving at a constant speed. According to the first of these, the forces acting on the car are in balance. According to the second, the sum of the forces acting in the direction of movement has to be greater than the sum of the forces acting in the opposite direction. Even if you have never studied physics, you will know by now that only the first conception is Newtonian and 'correct'.

Forgetting the issue of which answer is right for a moment, however, we can see that these two conceptions represent two different ways of structuring the phenomenon (Johansson *et al.* 1985). The first conception focuses on velocity. Because the velocity is constant the forces have to be in balance. The second conception focuses on the fact that the car is moving: the difference between rest and movement has to be accounted for by some extra force in the direction of the movement. A change in the learner's *structuring* of the phenomenon (from a focus on movement to a focus on velocity) is accompanied by a change in *meaning* (from 'motive disequilibrium' to equilibrium).

Now this is what we imply when we say that learning of the kind discussed here has both a 'how' (structural) and a 'what' (referential) aspect (Marton, 1988; see also Chapter 9). The former corresponds to the act of structuring the phenomenon; the latter corresponds to the meaning that the phenomenon structured in this way has for the learner. Structure and meaning are dialectically intertwined. In our understanding, while one can separate process and content analytically, the two aspects simply cannot exist without one another. There is obviously no learning without a content – you have to learn *something*. And there cannot be any learning without an act of learning – something has to be learned in a certain way.

General and specific. Can it really be true that we can only deal with students' understanding of specific subject matter when we consider ways of improving learning? You may feel tempted to say that we are over-stating our case. It will be apparent from the chapters in this book that there is a sense in which we can derive generalizations about improving learning. Entwistle, Odor and Anderson (Chapter 12) certainly do not emphasize any particular content; they contrast different approaches to learning in quite general terms. Similarly, the different levels of thinking described by Perry (Chapter 7) are of a general character and are not tied to any particular content.

But the general character of these categories is not the same as in, for example, Dansereau's and Weinstein's studies. In those investigations the categories refer to components of content-independent study strategies (such as planning, scheduling, concentration management, monitoring and the use of mnemonic devices). These are specific activities that students are supposed to be capable of carrying out in a variety of situations.

Approaches to learning as discussed by Entwistle *et al.*, on the other hand, refer to *how* subject content is dealt with. Approaches are not specific activities at all. Rather, they are general *relations* between learners and particular content (which may lead to study activities related to that content). Again, this could be a difficult conception to understand. Some examples from other chapters may help to elucidate it.

The main aim of Eizenberg's alternative method of presenting anatomy concepts (Chapter 9) is to develop a deep and holistic (instead of a surface and atomistic) approach to learning anatomy. The idea is that by teaching anatomy in a certain way one can encourage students to deal with it in a certain way. As we pointed out above, the process (or act) of learning and the content of learning are not two separable components but two inter-woven aspects of the same whole. An approach to learning is simply one of the ways in which the process aspect appears. This is particularly obvious in Whelan's study. The distinction he makes between an ordering and a structuring approach clearly refers to two qualitatively different ways of handling medical problem-solving tasks.

Similarly, the reading strategies described by Roth and Anderson are of the same nature as approaches to learning or problem-solving. They are characterized entirely as a more general aspect of how students relate to the specific content. Perry's general categories also derive from students dealing with particular content domains: 'The students . . . were not taking a course in cognitive development . . . They came to "realize" through the necessities of the intellectual disciplines as you taught them' (Chapter 7).

Levels, means and ends. It is clear that we can talk meaningfully about learning at different levels of generality within our perspective. In between the most and the least general levels are intermediate ones such as those identified in Laurillard's and White and Horwitz's contributions. These concern the nature of science and its laws: how laws evolve and why they are useful, and the contrast between science as an inductive process of gathering masses of unrelated data and a deductive process aimed at understanding and making sense of a few main ideas that explain the evidence.

Students can learn about things at different levels of generality at the same time. In fact we believe this is the only way they can learn. We should not try to separate the levels: learners cannot learn about what is general except through what is specific. But we should not ignore the levels either. They have to be the subject of our explicit and systematic attention.

If the levels are considered separately, a curious phenomenon may arise. The means of learning may become the ends of learning. What is supposed to be instrumental in realizing the learning of subject matter becomes the end itself. This sometimes happens when attempts are made to 'improve study skills' separately from subject content. Technical, content-independent strategies are adopted and understood but students do not use them as a means of changing their conceptions in a subject area (Ramsden *et al.*, 1986; Martin and Ramsden, 1987). Even if there were no other arguments against separating skills and content, these findings indicate that we should be very cautious about trying to develop content-independent skills and strategies.

The thesis we want to advocate is that learning and thinking skills are not separate entities that have a life of their own. They are ways of dealing with and reasoning about various aspects of subject matter and their character should be defined by the imperatives of that subject matter. Glaser (1984) and Biggs (1986) have expressed similar views from the standpoint of cognitive psychology. We should teach specific knowledge domains in such a way that a student's general capability is developed at the same time; we should not teach 'metacognitive skills' but should encourage students to reflect on learning in specific content domains.

Changed conceptions of teaching

Although, as we shall see in a moment, many teachers may conceptualize teaching in a way that makes it hard for their students to achieve the aims these same teachers desire, the kind of learning that they value is *not* mainly the kind characterized in many of the research studies.

As Bowden observed in the previous chapter, teachers are attentive to the differences between having learned quantities of information and procedures, on the one hand, and the expert qualities they want their students to possess. Usually, teachers are not interested in general learning skills that students can apply to any subject matter; for obvious reasons, they do not believe in the existence of 'teacher-proof' methods of presenting content; and they are not primarily concerned with their students' ability simply to recall information. Teachers want their students to be able to think about and do things in a subject area, whether the subject is elementary mathematics or graduate-level medicine. We think this discrepancy between teachers' concerns and one of the dominant paradigms in research on teaching and learning is one reason why teachers often say the results of educational research are 'irrelevant'.

In Chapter 1 the key to the problem of why students so often memorize information and so often fail to change their conceptions of phenomena was said to lie in the way students are taught and assessed. Generalizations about negative side-effects of assessment and teaching methods can certainly be validly made. Conditions that permit 'learning' which is aimed solely at satisfying institutional requirements through minimalist approaches to studying exist at all levels of education. The really difficult obstacle is to devise teaching and assessment that actively demands conceptual change learning. Research and experience has persuaded us that it *is* possible to teach students and to test their achievements in ways that encourage the sort of learning teachers desire. What kinds of changes to teaching are needed if these aims are to be achieved?

In Chapters 1 and 2 a special, somewhat perplexing, relationship between teaching and learning was identified. It was asserted that good *teaching* was fundamentally concerned with *learning* – learning about how students conceptualize subject matter, how they perceive the institutional context in which that subject matter is presented and evaluated, and how these ways of thinking on the students' part differ from one's own. Some implications of this view were worked out in the following chapters.

We believe that this way of looking at teaching is different from many others; so different that it may involve some teachers in changing their conceptions of teaching. It will be obvious, therefore, that there are important implications for faculty development and teacher education. *Just as the key to improving learning is students' conceptions of subject-related phenomena, so the key to improving teaching is teachers' conceptions of subject-related teaching phenomena.* The institutional context in which instructors teach (and learn to teach) and the ideas they already have about teaching should be two focuses of attempts to improve teaching and learning. John

Bowden has shown us in Chapter 13 some ways in which these changes might come about through putting into practice the principles the book has advocated.

Our own experiences have convinced us that there is often a paradoxical relation between teachers' views of learning and their conceptions of teaching. In our work as teachers, researchers and professional advisers we have noticed many aspects of teachers' ways of thinking about teaching and learning that are opposed to the conceptions we advocate here. In accordance with our principles, teacher educators and faculty development officers should carefully delineate the differences between the desired conceptions and the current ones. We shall briefly list some differences prior to considering in more detail strategies for improving learning that are associated with the conceptions we value.

Desirable conceptions of teaching

(1) Teachers frequently espouse a theory of *learning* as changing students' conceptions, but in practice define their chief task in *teaching* as transmitting information or procedures. They are often unclear about how transferring quantities of information can result in conceptual change (as we have said above, there is no evidence that it does). The change required on the teachers' part is towards a view of teaching as changing conceptions.

(2) Teachers often hold a view that Svensson and Högfors (Chapter 8) call an 'administrative' conception of curricula. The goals of courses are seen in terms of mastering their component parts; what it means to know these parts is considered unproblematical. A more desirable conception is a critical and relativistic view of the relation between aims and the tasks students are expected to perform, and between the general goals and the specific objectives.

(3) Teaching is often seen (if we may borrow a medical analogy) as a kind of *treatment*. The students' 'disease' is unproblematic. A more desirable conception is of teaching as *diagnosis prior to treatment*. Learning about what students think is an integral part of teaching.

(4) Assessment is often defined primarily in terms of the products of a student's performance. A more desirable conception is in terms of the *processes* which students display and the diagnostic information about the student which these processes, together with their resulting products, provide.

(5) How students will respond to teaching and assessment is regularly taken for granted; and it is often assumed, particularly in higher education, that students will all perceive the demands in the same way. The change required on the teachers' part is towards a self-critical awareness of the differing reactions of students to their teaching; this is another aspect of learning about what learners think and an indispensable element of good teaching.

(6) Teachers typically see educational theory and research as separate from the 'real' world of classroom strategies. The desirable concep-

tion is of educational research and teaching as complementary ways of thinking and acting.

Teaching strategies for conceptual change learning

What exactly will a teacher who has changed her conception of teaching do differently? The various chapters of the book provide several recommendations for promoting learning which involve changes in students' conceptions. It is appropriate to gather together these suggestions here.

1. Make the learners' conceptions explicit to them

The crucial message of the book is that teachers should focus on students' conceptualizations. Deliberately trying to change the learners' conceptions does not necessarily mean making the conceptions explicit to the learners, but it *is* an approach frequently used and advised, and it is the first of the approaches to teaching we recommend here.

Svensson and Högfors, West, Roth and Anderson, and White and Horwitz, all argue for making students aware of the different conceptions they hold. The aim is for them to become conscious of the fact that there *are* different conceptions of the phenomenon in question, and see what the conceptions are. In this way, a foundation is laid for comparing the relevance and relative merits of different conceptions. Comparison between conceptualizations (the student's v. the textbook's v. the teacher's, etc) is one of the main ways of dealing with conceptions explicitly.

2. Focus on a few critical issues and show how they relate

Roth and Anderson's successful conceptual change teachers focused on the central issues that were most problematic for younger students, rather than trying to 'cover' everything in the science textbook. Eizenberg and Whelan came to similar conclusions with medical students. They discovered the extreme importance of making explicit links between pieces of knowledge and ideas and challenging students to understand the structure. Paradoxically, providing a structure built on a solid foundation of a few main issues, at the expense of covering detail, led to students remembering more details in the end. In effect, this emphasis on core issues and their relations provides an opportunity for students to become aware of their different conceptions; so this strategy is closely related to the first.

3. Highlight the inconsistencies within and the consequences of learners' conceptions

This strategy involves building on the conceptions' internal dynamics – on the contradictions inherent in students' ways of interpreting phenomena. Laurillard compares this exploration of contradictions with the Popperian view of scientific method. Hypotheses erected from students' conceptions are subjected to crucial experiments. In these, new facts surface which are irreconcilable with the misconception held and which require the scientifically valid conception if they are to be explained satisfactorily.

The idea of creating cognitive conflicts, put forward by Roth and Anderson, and West, has the same basis. In the computer simulations described by White and Horwitz, learners are confronted with their own misconceptions whose consequences become apparent in the frictionless Newtonian universe. White (1984) has pointed to an example of a common misconception (that an object always moves in the direction in which it is kicked) which, when applied to an already moving object, fails to take account of inertia. In microworld 2, acting in accordance with this conception would lead to the moving dot's crashing into the wall.

There is another important aspect of this strategy. Only through exploring the differences and similarities between their own ideas about historical explanation, projectile motion, light, or any other phenomenon can students come to realize that the world that books and teachers are trying to explain to them is the *same world*, the 'real world' they inhabit. If, instead, they view academic knowledge as part of a separate domain, their conceptions will remain unchanged. This is another instance of the importance of considering learning at different levels of generality.

4. Create situations where learners centre attention on relevant aspects
In the above approaches we try to create a need for learners to restructure the way they think about a phenomenon. The fourth method demands that we, as instructional agents, actively participate in bringing about a shift of focus to one aspect of the phenomenon instead of another. The relevant aspect of the situation can be made visible by introducing variations in it.

Microworld 1 in White and Horwitz's chapter is an illustration. When Svensson and Högfors asked students about the forces acting on a car moving at a constant speed, they found that a focus on the movement of the car was associated with the pre-Newtonian conception that movement was due to forces in the direction of movement being greater than those in the opposite direction. A shift in focus away from movement to velocity is needed to help students 'see' the Newtonian conception. What varies in microworld 1 is velocity (when the student applies impulses to a moving object). This emphasizes the relevant aspect of the situation (velocity) and makes it more likely that students will concentrate on it. This transient stress on the act of structuring the phenomenon helps students to understand the meaning of equilibrium.

5. Present the learner with new ways of seeing
This approach involves presenting students with a new conceptualization. We find an example in Lybeck *et al.*'s chapter. Lybeck and his colleagues identified two crucial components of students' understanding of the concept of 'amount of substance' and its unit ('mole') in chemistry. One was the distinction between the quantity to be measured and the unit used to measure it. The other was the relation between a 'continuous perspective' (how we think about what is available to our senses, eg volume and mass) and a 'discontinuous perspective' (how we think about the funda-

mental structure of material). Successful chemistry teaching should distinguish between two things that are often undifferentiated in students' thinking – the measure and what is measured. It should also focus on the relation between two things that are normally seen as entirely separate – the experiencable qualities of matter and its microstructure.

Eizenberg's chapter provides another example of introducing students to things they have not seen before. The regional and systematic perspectives on anatomy, which are traditional forms of presenting the subject, are combined in the new approach to teaching the subject he has developed at Melbourne. Eizenberg's curriculum emphasizes the links between different regions of the body and the interaction between the different systems within the regions. The structure of the body (its anatomy) accounts for the functions it has to perform and the functions lend meaning to the structure. Such a presentation enables Eizenberg to evolve the idea of the body as a super-rational design. Students then find it easier to understand how the parts relate to each other and to avoid focusing merely on discrete details.

6. Integrate substantive and syntactic structures
An important lesson of the book is that teaching strategies which aim to link the 'knowing how' of a subject (eg why scientists do experiments and how they explain things) and the 'knowing what' of a subject (eg Newton's laws) are to be favoured. To present the two aspects as part of one whole permits students to learn in a way that is isomorphic with the way an expert learns.

Laurillard provides an illustration of how this holistic view might inform the design of computer-based instruction. Integrating content and method increases the chances that students will realize that they too can 'act like scientists', and that scientific conceptions will be seen as explanations of reality rather than statements that belong to a special educational world in which 'right answers' have to be remembered. A corollary of this approach is that the *treatment* and *selection* of curricular material should proceed in tandem. As Svensson and Högfors show in their discussion of teaching mechanics, the form of presentation should match the content to be presented.

7. Test understanding of phenomena; use the results for diagnostic assessment and curriculum design
Wherever possible, teachers should aim to test students' understanding of phenomena related to desired conceptions rather than their knowledge of the concepts themselves. They should do this both when asking questions in class and in more formal assessments.

The effects of failing to take this approach were graphically illustrated in Roth and Anderson's chapter: learning science became a mainly passive process of remembering facts and 'big words' quite separate from everyday experience. Instead of demanding and praising 'right' answers all the time – a strategy that actively encourages students to use inappropriate strategies to find those answers – it is necessary to pause to examine incorrect answers. This involves both *listening* to what students are thinking and responding to what is heard. The teacher should focus on the process by which students arrive at an answer to the problems he sets them and practise framing further questions which remorselessly expose that process.

There is a complementary need to design questions in assessments that cannot be answered by repeating previously learned knowledge, but that oblige students to apply their ideas about phenomena to new situations. Successfully designing assessments of this kind is an exceptionally demanding task, but it is essential if the occurrence of educational means turning into ends, referred to above, is to be avoided. We should also take time to contrast our students' conceptions with our expert conceptions of phenomena. What are the precise points of similarity and difference? What are the consequences of each separate point for teaching?

8. Use reflective teaching strategies

The last suggestion is at the highest level of generality. It refers particularly to teachers' attitudes to their work. To follow this recommendation, a teacher should take steps to gather specific feedback from his or her students on their perceptions of his or her requirements. How do they see the purpose of assignments and what processes are they following in order to complete them? What kinds of demands will a certain task place on students, and will their perception be the same as the teacher's? Biggs and Telfer (1987, p 164) have called this reflective process 'metateaching'.

Content as figure: method as ground

We have described some variations in conceptions of teaching and have outlined strategies that teachers might use if they want to encourage in their students the kind of learning so repeatedly advocated in this book. Our recommendations for improving teaching are defined in terms of what should happen to the students' thinking rather than in terms of the teaching arrangement (the eight refers to what should happen to students' thinking about the context of learning).

Naturally, in any study of teaching methods there is always a content: there cannot be any teaching without something to be taught. But the method is what is usually focused on. The teaching method or other form of presentation is the object of study, like a figure placed on a background of subject content. In the studies described in this book, the content is the figure displayed on the background of the teaching or presentation method. In the study comparing reading an experimental text with two commercial texts, described by Roth and Anderson, for example, the main focus is not on learning from textbooks but on the way in which photosynthesis is dealt with in the texts. In White and Horwitz's chapter, the most important thing is not that the experimental group is learning by using computer simulations, but that conceptualizations of Newtonian mechanics are embodied in the simulations.

Changing conceptions v. learning the answers
Readers of this book will know that we would not expect the changes we have outlined to occur simply by informing teachers of the general principles they should apply. What we have said about student learning applies just as much to teacher learning. If we aim at conceptual change learning, *telling* teachers the 'right' answers is next-to-useless. Informing people about desirable conceptions will not change their conceptions. Telling teachers about desirable strategies will not develop their professional judgement. The principles must always be critically interpreted and their specific application to real circumstances understood. A concrete example of one kind of faculty development or in-service teacher education which has been successfully used to encourage teachers to think differently about teaching and learning has been presented in Chapter 13.

Research and practice

I don't think the teacher in the classroom is ever really taken seriously enough. I think their knowledge and experience is invaluable. A lot of research is not relevant to what goes on in classrooms – it hasn't got any connection to the teeming world of education that researchers are supposedly trying to influence.
(*A British primary school teacher, quoted in May and Rudduck, 1983*)

We think there are probably three reasons why this teacher says what she does. First, she has a non-relativistic conception (see Chapter 7) of educational research as an activity that provides the 'right' solutions to teaching problems. Research can very rarely do this: usually it can only act as a guide to professional action. Secondly, much educational research itself derives from a conception that is basically at odds with teachers' views of learning, as we have seen above. And thirdly, a lot of research asks questions that logically cannot be answered. Is it a 'good thing' to use 'advance organizers' in texts? Should we insert questions in a text at the end of each paragraph? Is computer-assisted learning better than teacher-directed learning? Is peer teaching more effective? Do students learn more in informal classes?

We hope that readers will now be able to appreciate the naivety of these research questions if they could not do so before reading this book. There is no unambiguous definition of 'inserted questions' or 'computer-assisted learning' or 'activity approach'. Their effect is contingent on the actual content being taught and the way the content is dealt with by the students. But *possible* relations are still the only things we can draw conclusions about from the majority of studies of the type described in the book; we can only show that a certain teaching strategy might possibly result in a certain kind of outcome. Where does that leave the teacher?

The great English teacher educator, Lawrence Stenhouse, spent much of his professional life in pursuit of an elusive goal: a closer and more productive relationship between classroom teaching and the practice of educational research. One of the ways in which he tried to forge a firmer link between the two areas was his introduction of the activity of educational research as part of teacher education.

By carrying out 'systematic enquiry made public' (Stenhouse, 1985), teachers could sharpen their professional curiosity, excitement and insight. At the same time, the closed world of the professional educational research community would be opened up to teachers; a democratization of research would occur. It was hoped that this would lead to a radical change in teachers' views of educational research. It was hoped it would help them to learn from what it had to say to them. Instead of being subordinate consumers of the research products of an elitist tradition, they would become producers themselves – and better teachers as a result. The attitudes Stenhouse and his colleague Rudduck sought to alter were summarized by the teacher, quoted above, speaking at the beginning of her teacher-as-researcher project.

We share many of the hopes and ideals of Stenhouse and Rudduck. We too believe (cf Rudduck, 1985) that teaching suffers from the domination of routine practice and maintain that research is the powerful and natural bridge between theory and practice in education. It will also be clear that we espouse a commitment to a closer relation between practice and research, that we believe in increasing professionalism through a shift in teachers' conceptions, and that an implication of what has been said is that there is a need for changes in teacher education.

The answers proposed in this book to the problem of improving learning have been based on research and they aim at practice. They certainly have 'a connection with the teeming world' of real educational settings, but they are also much more than this. They are *about* what teachers work with every day. The particular view of learning underlying the contributions provides a theoretical basis for 'teacher-research' and has unique implications for the research–practice relation. The conception of education we regard as desirable considers both research *and* practice as active *and* reflective enterprises.

Didactics of subject areas and cooperation between teachers and researchers

From our perspective on learning and teaching, research and teaching are related but distinct. The heart of the relation is that educational research and teaching both entail *learning* about students.

As we have pointed out above, many educational generalizations are about possible relations. However, descriptions of how learners think about particular content domains have the unique quality of being able to reveal, in some instances, a highly structured system of capabilities. These studies enable us to make general statements about necessary (but not sufficient) relations. Thus they have a special relevance to teaching. An example of such a study is Dagmar Neuman's investigation of arithmetic skills in young children (Neuman, 1987). Neuman was able to show that older children's mathematical difficulties stemmed from their failure to develop a grasp of relations between the numbers 1 and 10, and that this grasp of elementary number concepts was in turn dependent on the development of their understanding of part–whole relations from their simple, pre-school notions of counting words. The development of arithmetic skills was strictly hierarchical: each level presupposed the previous one. Charting these levels enabled the teacher to plan appropriate teaching interventions to minimize the difficulties.

An implication of our view of education is that a more professional approach to teaching requires the development of a body of knowledge concerning how various kinds of subject content are learned and taught. We believe that the study of 'subject didactics' – the analysis and mapping of the different ways learners experience and conceptualize various content domains – should form a major part of teacher education and the research that teacher educators carry out. 'Subject didactics' is neither the sum nor the intersection of teaching methods, educational psychology and subject matter. It is a distinctive discipline, a kind of science of education, in its own right. It is concerned with how specific content is taught and learned. Teachers' own research should also be in this area: such research will then be directly related to their practical concerns and will help them to change their conceptions of teaching and learning (Ramsden, 1987). It will be both active and reflective.

How can teachers and researchers learn from each other? There are strong arguments for collaborative research between educational researchers and teachers. Collaboration typically generates commitment. And if you are committed to finding out, you are more likely to change as a result of what you find out. If teachers are involved in planning and perhaps doing research, there is a greater probability of changes to teaching and learning practices and conceptions of teaching and learning. If researchers are working closely with practitioners, they are likely to feel committed to researching problems that are genuinely educational, and to develop new insights into effective teaching methods.

Another, related reason for a cooperative approach is that it fosters professional development. The professional authority of the teacher should rest on a body of didactic knowledge. That knowledge is not a series of techniques; it is a series of concepts and supporting evidence that invites reinterpretation in the context of particular classes and students. The quality of this reinterpretation and application is best guaranteed by rigorous professional standards internalized by teachers themselves. Our view of learning implies a pluralistic concern to provide practitioners with tools they can use to improve their students' learning, rather than an absolutistic conception of 'right' and 'wrong' teaching and learning methods. Our view accepts that almost every act of teaching is an act of practitioner–research. There is a real sense in which teachers must, in their everyday activities, strive to test hypotheses about why children are failing to learn and make critical judgements based on the results of their tests.

The nature of the cooperative research that will fulfil these aims is not obvious, however. For some recent writers, the solution lies in an abandonment of the distinction between teachers and researchers and in the adoption of 'action research' as the only valid form of collaboration. We would deprecate that view and favour, as we are sure the father of teacher-research, Lawrence Stenhouse, did, a more eclectic approach. There are good practical reasons for this. It seems naive to assume that the professional skills of researchers can be developed by every teacher. It seems unrealistic to argue that the time-consuming activity of discovering different conceptions of phenomena can be carried out by busy teachers. It is disingenuous to maintain that all conscientious studies of learning phenomena (such as those represented in the previous chapters) must be carried out by teachers if they are to be useful to teachers. The very fact that the researcher does not have to make judgements about how to act in a practical situation may permit a more searching and comprehensive analysis to be made. There is also an important place for research in education, as in other fields, that does not have an instant practical payoff. No-one can predict the relevant questions of tomorrow.

This book is an example of the variety in approach we are enjoining. There is a revolutionary potential in the idea of step-by-step uncovering of the hidden world of thoughts and taken-for-granted skills in various fields of knowledge. Cooperation between professional educators and subject experts is logically inescapable if this work is to be done. But if we try to force all the research into an action mould, we will probably end up with a series of studies without a clear theoretical focus that hardly begins to explain problems in learning subject content. That would not seem to serve the cause of professionalism in education, any more than arguing that all medical research should be undertaken by General Practitioners would serve the cause of professionalism in medicine.

Professional cooperation can come in many forms. Learning about students' ideas should happen in different ways: by critically reading research findings, by participating in in-service activities of the type described in the last chapter, by cooperating in research projects, by carrying out action research, and by listening more actively in class to what students are saying. The roles of teachers and researchers in education are therefore best seen as complementary. This does not mean that teachers cannot sometimes be researchers, and vice versa, or that reflection-in-action is to be discouraged. But we cannot expect all research into teaching and learning to be undertaken by 'teacher-research' or reflective practice. In short, a closer relationship between teachers and researchers can best be achieved not by denying the differences between teaching and educational research, but by harnessing the two endeavours to the same purpose. We submit that the conception of research and education we have ventured to describe can forge the link.

Conclusions

The book has argued that to help students learn better, we must describe the various ways they conceptualize the domains of knowledge dealt with in educational settings. But descriptions, however perspicacious and precise, can only take us part of the way. In everyday educational contexts we aim actively to develop learners' capabilities – not just to describe and understand them. Teaching implies that we expect our predictions to be accurate. A certain form of teaching is expected to lead to a certain form of learning.

We have seen in the previous chapters how teachers and researchers have successfully used educational research to improve the quality of learning. Contrary to some sceptics' views, it is perfectly possible for teachers and curriculum designers to learn from students and to apply the findings of research to good effect. To that extent, accurate predictions are possible. But the predictions are neither general nor conclusive. In truth we cannot ever be *sure* that what we do will help our students to learn. We shall never discover the right ways to teach, but we may hope to discern better ones. We hope this book may have contributed to that understanding.

References

Biggs, J B (1986). Enhancing learning skills: The role of metacognition. In: J A Bowden (ed), *Student Learning: Research into Practice*. Melbourne: CSHE, University of Melbourne.

Biggs, J B and Telfer, R (1987). *The Process of Learning*. (Second edition). Sydney: Prentice-Hall.

Dansereau, D F (1986). Learning strategy research. In: I W Segal *et al.* (eds), *Thinking and Learning Skills: I. Relating Instruction to Research*. Hillsdale, New Jersey: Lawrence Erlbaum.

Glaser, R (1984). Education and thinking: The role of knowledge. *American Psychologist*, **39**, 93-104.

Johansson, B, Marton, F and Svensson, L (1985). An approach to describing learning as change between qualitatively different conceptions. In L H T West and A L Pines (eds), *Cognitive Structure and Conceptual Change*. New York: Academic Press.

Martin, E and Ramsden, P (1987). Learning skills or skill in learning? In: J T E Richardson, M W Eysenck and D Warren Piper (eds), *Student Learning: Research in Education and Cognitive Psychology*. Milton Keynes: SRHE and Open University Press.

Marton, F (1988). Describing and improving learning. In: R R Schmeck (ed), *Learning Strategies and Learning Styles*. New York: Plenum.

May, N and Rudduck, J (1983). *Sex Stereotyping and the Early Years of Schooling*. Norwich: School of Education, University of East Anglia.

Neuman, D (1987). *The Origin of Arithmetic Skills: A Phenomenographic Approach*. Gothenburg: Acta Universitatis Gothoburgensis.

Ramsden, P (1987). Improving teaching and learning in higher education: The case for a relational perspective. *Studies in Higher Education*, **12**, 275–86.

Ramsden, P, Beswick, D G and Bowden, J A (1986). Effects of learning skills interventions on first year university students' learning. *Human Learning*, **5**, 151–64.

Rudduck, J (1985). Teacher research and research-based teacher education. *Journal of Education for Teaching*, **11**, 281–9.

Segal, I W, Chipman, S F and Glaser, R (eds) (1986). *Thinking and Learning Skills: I. Relating Instruction to Research*. Hillsdale, New Jersey: Lawrence Erlbaum.

Stenhouse, L A (1985) (eds J Rudduck and D Hopkins) *Research as a Basis for Teaching*. London: Heinemann.

Weinstein, C E (1975). Learning of elaboration strategies. Unpublished doctoral dissertation, University of Texas.

Weinstein, C E and Underwood, V L (1986). Learning strategies: The how of learning. In: I W Segal *et al.* (eds), *Thinking and Learning Skills: I. Relating Instruction to Research*. Hillsdale, New Jersey: Lawrence Erlbaum.

White, B (1984). Designing computer activities to help physics students understand Newton's laws of motion. *Cognition and Instruction*, **1**, 69–108.

Winne, P H (1986). What last year's research says about teaching: Findings from volume 77 of the Journal of Educational Psychology. Paper presented at the Annual Meeting of the American Educational Research Association, San Francisco, April 1986.

Index